Treatment Programmes for High Risk Offenders

AF739476

High risk offenders can have a disproportionate impact on their communities because, despite all manner of sentencing options, they continue to commit a wide range of crimes, both minor and serious. It is tempting to throw the book at them, sometimes even to throw away the key. However, anything that helps offenders to change their propensity for re-offending can really make a difference.

Over the last 30 years, scientific research has guided the provision of treatment, rehabilitation and reintegration services that lead to reductions in re-offending. Much of what we know, however, comes from work with medium-risk offenders. Although this work is important and valuable, there is a lower level of complexity to working with medium-risk offenders than most high-risk offenders require.

This book recognises the need to research and develop different approaches to rehabilitating high-risk offenders. Each of the contributions takes a different approach, with a different group of offenders, in a different setting. Cumulatively, the chapters provide encouragement for those working with high risk offenders, along with a wide range of ideas about how to develop better services.

This book was originally published as a special issue of *Psychology, Crime & Law.*

Devon L.L. Polaschek is a Professor in the School of Psychology at Victoria University of Wellington, New Zealand. Her research interests include theory, intervention, and intervention evaluation with serious violent and sexual offenders, psychopathy, desistance and parole, and experimental approaches to offender assessment. She works closely in a number of roles with New Zealand's Department of Corrections, making her research distinctly practice-focused, with a particular emphasis on the effective treatment of high-risk psychopathic violent prisoners.

Treatment Programmes for High Risk Offenders

Edited by
Devon L.L. Polaschek

Routledge
Taylor & Francis Group
LONDON AND NEW YORK

First published 2016 by Routledge

2 Park Square, Milton Park, Abingdon, Oxon OX14 4RN
711 Third Avenue, New York, NY 10017, USA

Routledge is an imprint of the Taylor & Francis Group, an informa business

First issued in paperback 2017

Copyright © 2016 Taylor & Francis

All rights reserved. No part of this book may be reprinted or reproduced or utilised in any form or by any electronic, mechanical, or other means, now known or hereafter invented, including photocopying and recording, or in any information storage or retrieval system, without permission in writing from the publishers.

Notice:
Product or corporate names may be trademarks or registered trademarks, and are used only for identification and explanation without intent to infringe.

British Library Cataloguing in Publication Data
A catalogue record for this book is available from the British Library

ISBN 13: 978-1-138-92803-9 (hbk)
ISBN 13: 978-1-138-09491-8 (pbk)

Typeset in Times New Roman
by RefineCatch Limited, Bungay, Suffolk

Publisher's Note
The publisher accepts responsibility for any inconsistencies that may have arisen during the conversion of this book from journal articles to book chapters, namely the possible inclusion of journal terminology.

Disclaimer
Every effort has been made to contact copyright holders for their permission to reprint material in this book. The publishers would be grateful to hear from any copyright holder who is not here acknowledged and will undertake to rectify any errors or omissions in future editions of this book.

Contents

Citation Information

The chapters in this book were originally published in *Psychology, Crime & Law*, volume 19, issues 5–6 (June–July 2013). When citing this material, please use the original page numbering for each article, as follows:

Chapter 1
How to train your dragon: an introduction to the special issue on treatment programmes for high-risk offenders
Devon L.L. Polaschek
Psychology, Crime & Law, volume 19, issues 5–6 (June–July 2013) pp. 409–414

Chapter 2
The Chromis programme: from conception to evaluation
J. Tew and R. Atkinson
Psychology, Crime & Law, volume 19, issues 5–6 (June–July 2013) pp. 415–431

Chapter 3
Delivering effective therapeutic interventions for men with severe personality disorder within a high secure prison
Jacqui Saradjian, Naomi Murphy and Des McVey
Psychology, Crime & Law, volume 19, issues 5–6 (June–July 2013) pp. 433–447

Chapter 4
Resettle: a significant new step in an emerging pathway that manages risk and addresses need in high-risk personality disordered offenders on their release into the community
V. Baker, D. Johnson and S. Oluonye
Psychology, Crime & Law, volume 19, issues 5–6 (June–July 2013) pp. 449–460

Chapter 5
The Violence Reduction Programme: a treatment programme for violence-prone forensic clients
Stephen C.P. Wong and Audrey Gordon
Psychology, Crime & Law, volume 19, issues 5–6 (June–July 2013) pp. 461–475

Chapter 6
A description and research review of the Clearwater Sex Offender Treatment Programme
Mark E. Olver and Stephen C.P. Wong
Psychology, Crime & Law, volume 19, issues 5–6 (June–July 2013) pp. 477–492

Chapter 7
Challenging the 'urban myth' of psychopathy untreatability: the High-Risk Personality Programme
Nick J. Wilson and Armon Tamatea
Psychology, Crime & Law, volume 19, issues 5–6 (June–July 2013) pp. 493–510

Chapter 8
New Zealand's special treatment units: the development and implementation of intensive treatment for high-risk male prisoners
Devon L.L. Polaschek and T. Glen Kilgour
Psychology, Crime & Law, volume 19, issues 5–6 (June–July 2013) pp. 511–526

Chapter 9
Treating high-risk rapists in a New Zealand intensive prison programme
Nick J. Wilson, Glen Kilgour and Devon L.L. Polaschek
Psychology, Crime & Law, volume 19, issues 5–6 (June–July 2013) pp. 527–547

For any permission-related enquiries please visit:
http://www.tandfonline.com/page/help/permissions

How to train your dragon

Devon L.L. Polaschek

School of Psychology, Victoria University of Wellington, Wellington, New Zealand

The plot of the popular movie *How to Train Your Dragon* includes several features that are paralleled in the efforts of programme designers and treatment providers who work with the highest risk offenders in criminal justice systems. This introduction to the special feature on programmes for high-risk offenders notes that there are important differences in how treatments are provided for offenders with varying levels of risk, need, and responsivity. It asks if what is known about effective offender intervention – much of it derived from moderately risky offenders – applies to those who are thought to be at high risk of new criminal activity. It observes that the relative lack of intervention theory for these offenders provides an important justification for a feature that focuses primarily on describing a range of these interventions and their theoretical underpinnings. The papers that follow are then introduced.

The 2010 DreamWorks Animation film – *How to Train Your Dragon* – portrays the discoveries of a young man who lives in a time and place where dragons are feared and detested because of assumptions about their unmitigated dangerous nature. In this community, the only proper response to the appearance of a dragon is to capture and kill it, thus protecting the community. However, the young man finds out differently. Against this punitive cultural substrate, he inadvertently comes eye to eye with a dragon he previously wounded but failed to kill, and he recognises in its eyes the same fear he feels towards the dragon. Consequently, he sets about rehabilitating the dragon to help it fly again, and in the process, he learns how to communicate and interact safely with other dangerous dragon species, using tailored approaches to progressing his relationship with each one. The community around him struggles to accept that the dragons are not mindlessly malevolent killing machines, and it is only after the movie's climax that the village accepts dragons back into its midst and sets about learning how to live alongside them.

High-risk offenders are not dragons. But it is hard to miss the similarities between the experiences of the boy in this story and the endeavours of those whose work is featured in this issue. The issue reports on a small number of initiatives to rehabilitate and reintegrate some of the most dangerous people in our custodial systems. There is no 'quick fix' to doing so as there was in the movie. High-risk offenders are not merely misunderstood as dragons were. But like dragons, they certainly can be dangerous; the diverse endeavours reported here represent the 'training' efforts of groups of people who recognise both of these facts. Beyond the dragon comparison, these efforts show that these offenders have many characteristics and needs, and at least some of these look remarkably similar to those of ordinary people. The result has been the development of a diverse range of approaches to remediating dangerousness, to beginning the process of rebuilding lives and, in a number of cases, to reintegrating high-risk offenders back into their communities, albeit against a backdrop of fear and lack of acceptance, and with limited resources to ensure safety and success.

The provision of rehabilitation and treatment programmes that are effective in reducing reoffending has a relatively short history, and despite its brevity, the key characteristics of such programmes are highly accessible through the summaries of the 'what works' literature (Aos, Miller, & Drake, 2006), and the Risk-Need-Responsivity model (RNR; Andrews & Bonta, 2010). Confidence has grown about how to conduct good assessment and intervention with offenders, but growth has been uneven. In particular, there is still limited evidence on how to work with the highest risk offenders. Research supporting the risk principle (Andrews & Bonta, 2010) imposes no upper limit on the level of criminal risk that yields benefits from treatment. But much of our research on offenders and what works in their rehabilitation is based on medium-risk offenders (Campbell, French, & Gendreau, 2007; P. Gendreau, personal communication, 16 September 2007); and other sources (e.g., research on treatment attrition, see Olver, Stockdale, & Wormith, 2011; and beliefs about psychopaths' treatability, see Skeem, Polaschek, Patrick, & Lilienfeld, 2011) suggest that the highest risk offenders may be relatively less treatable than those identified as being at medium risk.[1]

A recent appraisal of the RNR model concluded that important and useful as it is, the model is best understood as a high-level rehabilitation theory and should not be expected also to serve the function of a mid-level treatment theory (Polaschek, 2011a). Mid-level intervention theories meet the RNR principles but are the richer, more-detailed conceptual guides that feed specific intervention design and delivery (e.g., guiding programmes for offenders with specific characteristics and in particular settings). There remains a dearth of documented examples of these second-tier intervention resources outside the domain of specialised sex offender treatment.

Polaschek (2011b) proposed that one important dimension on which programme theories should and do differ is in how they respond to the risk and responsivity needs of the target client group. Polaschek surveyed a range of current programme theories and suggested they could be categorised into three levels. Basic-level programmes are low-intensity, highly manualised, require limited therapist skill and suit offenders who have few treatment targets and can utilise psycho-education for personal change. Mid-level multi-factorial programmes target more challenging clients with a wider range of treatment needs but also some areas of relative strength. Specific information about individual clients informs the treatment. Therapists are more skilled, and the programme has at least *some* ability to respond dynamically to client needs and attends more to processes that facilitate in-programme change (e.g., rehearsal with feedback). Finally, high-level comprehensive forensic therapy programmes are designed for clients with diverse, highly entrenched and complex needs, who are resistant to treatment engagement, learn slowly, and struggle to make and maintain changes. Interventions – whether individual or group-based or both – are formulation driven and respond to new information about the client as it emerges. Multiple, highly skilled facilitators may be involved, and the programme is embedded in a residential environment that supports the treatment and the offenders who are taking part (Polaschek, 2011b).

In keeping with (a) the need to develop knowledge about whether and how high-risk offenders can be rehabilitated and (b) the dearth of examples of high-level intervention theories and their associated programmes noted by Polaschek (2011b), this special issue draws together a range of papers on rehabilitative approaches to high-risk offenders. The papers are somewhat unconventional in format, in that the focus is primarily on the programme itself, not on the offenders who attend it, and each paper describes the programme theory along with delivery characteristics. Client descriptive data are also included to give an indication of who is served by the programme. Data on client changes and outcomes are presented where they are available. A substantial empirical evidence base supports some programmes, but most are in the early stages of development, and limited information is available.

The issue opens with three programmes that are associated with the British government's Dangerous and Severe Personality Disorder (DSPD) initiative. According to the diagnostic criteria, DSPD offenders have high PCL-psychopathy and other personality disorders, high risk of reoffending and a functional link between personality disorder and offending. The first of two prison-based programmes included in the DSPD pilot, Chromis (HMP Frankland), was developed over five years in association with 20 days of consultation with an international expert panel. Its aim was to create a state-of-the-art cognitive-behavioural programme that would reduce violence in high-risk PCL-psychopaths in a custodial environment. Tew and Atkinson report on the evolution of that programme, noting its innovative design features, and how it has responded to the changing needs of the referral population.

Saradjian reports on the second of the two DSPD prison initiatives: the Fens Unit (HMP Whitemoor). Housed in an adapted prison wing, the Fens represents a contrasting approach to working with prisoners meeting DSPD criteria. The accredited treatment model at the Fens is described as cognitive-interpersonal – it has a primary focus on emotional intimacy, in contrast to Chromis' relatively greater emphasis on more pragmatic and behavioural elements, so it will be interesting to see over time how the two programmes compare on outcomes. Offenders also stay the longest in the Fens unit; about five years compared to about 2.5 to 3 years for offenders in Chromis.

The third UK programme, Resettle, is notable for being the only intervention in the issue that has an almost entirely community focus. It is a response to the problem of how to adequately provide for the needs of high-risk prisoners with finite sentences who do not undertake custodial rehabilitation before they return to their communities. Baker, Johnson, and Oluonye note that because of the programme's community basis, on-going risk management inevitably becomes a significant part of the daily work with this clientele. Nevertheless, the programme's primary objectives are to provide formal treatment to clients and work with them on their reintegration. Also notable is that Resettle is recognising the need to evaluate treatment effectiveness with such high-risk offenders not simply in terms of who 'fails' and who does not because by some definitions (e.g., parole breaches and minor reconvictions) most high-risk offenders will fail. Instead, they are counting the number of returns to prison as a sign of programme effectiveness. In addition, the programme responds to prison recalls by conducting 'in reach', following offenders back into prison, helping them back onto their feet and working to see them return to the programme. This continuous care approach may serve as a model for other services in jurisdictions with these aspirations, such as New Zealand.

The DSPD programmes represent relatively resource-intensive responses to the needs of high to very high-risk offenders. By contrast, the two Canadian custodial programmes that follow, while still high intensity, are briefer, and their stated target group is medium- to high-risk offenders. Both programmes have been running for longer than the DSPD initiatives, and both use versions of Wong and colleagues' Violence Risk Scale tools (Wong & Olver, 2010) to identify treatment needs and evaluate client change. Wong and Gordon first describe the Violence Reduction Programme (VRP). Like Chromis and the Fens programme, the VRP targets reductions in violent behaviour, using a range of treatment theories, techniques and modules. It represents the most recent instantiation of violence rehabilitation programming based at the Regional Psychiatric Centre in Saskatoon, Saskatchewan, over the last 15 years or so. The effectiveness of this treatment approach has been established through several outcome studies, including research examining the effects on criminal gang members and PCL-psychopaths. The VRP is also distinctive for having been adapted recently for use in some UK services; few of these high-intensity programmes appear to be duplicated outside of the services that develop them.

Olver and Wong describe the second Canadian programme: the Clearwater programme for high-risk sex offenders. More than 20 years old, the programme has accumulated an impressive body of associated empirical research: on treatment outcomes, treatment change, attrition and outcomes for psychopaths. Overall, the Clearwater programme is relatively short, at six to eight months duration. But in contrast to the difficulties the sex offender programmes, with low base rates of reconviction, often have in demonstrating outcome effects, the Clearwater programme's outcomes are quite striking. Clearwater's rolling cohort format also makes it somewhat distinctive as does the preponderance in the client group of men who sexually assault adults, and the high proportion of Canadian aboriginal offenders.

Although most of these high-risk programmes are inevitably working with a high proportion of PCL-psychopathic clientele, New Zealand's High-Risk Personality Programme (HRPP) represents the only initiative other than Chromis to explicitly target that client group. Wilson and Tamatea report that the HRPP was an experimental intervention, delivered in 2007 to a single cohort of 12 men on a mixed-purpose prison wing. Like Chromis, the HRPP sought not to change psychopathic traits per se but to reduce violence in people with high levels of these traits. Unlike most of the interventions in the issue, the programme was delivered in a closed-group format, the treatment setting did not allow for participants to interact with each other outside of formal treatment sessions and the unit custodial staff were not formally part of the therapeutic environment (i.e., there was no formal therapeutic community environment). The HRPP model was influenced by both the DSPD initiative and the Canadian programmes mentioned above, and interesting, although personality pathology was not a direct focus, there was an improvement in self-reported personality functioning scores over the course of the programme.

Finally, the remaining two New Zealand programmes – along with the HRPP – are unique in serving a majority non-European adult offender population. Polaschek and Kilgour trace back to the 1980s the roots of the treatment programmes based in the High Risk Special Treatment Units (HRSTUs), though three of the four current units are less than five years old. Wilson, Polaschek and Kilgour report on an initiative for high-risk rapists (the ASOTP) that is delivered in these same units. The two programmes are significantly shorter than the custodial DSPD interventions, significantly less resourced and less flexible in their ability to be tailored dynamically to individual clients. They are quite highly manualised and are run as closed cohort programmes: all members of the cohort are exposed together to the programme content. Recently, the programmes have begun to make progress with establishing a therapeutic community environment in the dedicated units in which they are delivered. Few ASOTP graduates have yet been released from prison, but the results of an outcome evaluation of the main high-risk violent offender treatment programme are expected soon.

In some arenas of offender rehabilitation, the RNR model has been translated into a very limited range of programme types, creating a false impression of the potential for diversity under its umbrella (Polaschek, 2011a). The interventions described in this issue clearly dispel this concern. They depict quite a diverse and creative array of approaches to the most difficult clientele, men who have often been in the 'too hard basket'. Comparing and contrasting them also speaks to several topical issues in intervention development, including (a) how interventions work to foster desistance and (b) the extent to which they focus on internal offender changes vs. altering the environment around offenders.

Just as with dragon training, the treatment of high-risk offenders is not yet a well-established endeavour. Most of the interventions reported in this issue are 'demonstration programmes'; they have not been disseminated for wider use, and few have convincing research data on their effects. And during the commissioning of this issue, several other high-risk offender programmes closed; sometimes initiatives are short-lived, limiting the overall growth of this area. But encouragingly, several programmes in this issue are also quite old, speaking to the importance of local circumstances in keeping such initiatives alive through the inevitable ups and downs. Very different levels of resourcing are evident across the programmes, and further down the track, it will be important to see whether these investments are translated into relatively different outcomes. However, the main immediate purpose of this issue is to stimulate the development and documentation of other approaches to working with these challenging clients. The range of offerings here optimistically suggests that despite the naysayers, and the array of very real practical and political difficulties, there may be a number of ways to successfully train a dragon.

Note

1. Of course, there are no hard-and-fast definitions of what constitutes 'medium-risk' and 'high-risk'. One useful indicator is the rate of re-conviction or re-imprisonment of a risk-matched untreated comparison group.

References

Andrews, D. A., & Bonta, J. (2010). *The psychology of criminal conduct* (5th ed.). Newark, NJ: Matthew Bender.

Aos, S., Miller, M., & Drake, E. (2006). *Evidence-based adult corrections programs: What works and what does not*. Olympia, WA: Washington State Institute for Public Policy.

Campbell, M. A., French, S., & Gendreau, P. (2007). Assessing the utility of risk assessment tools and personality measures in the prediction of violent recidivism for adult offenders. Ottawa, ON: Department of Public Safety and Emergency Preparedness Canada.

Olver, M. E., Stockdale, K. C., & Wormith, J. S. (2011). A meta-analysis of predictors of offender treatment attrition and its relationship to recidivism. *Journal Consulting and Clinical Psychology*, *79*, 6–21.

Polaschek, D. L. L. (2011a). An appraisal of the Risk-Need-Responsivity Model of Offender Rehabilitation and its application in correctional treatment. *Legal and Criminological Psychology*, *17*, 1–17. doi:10.1111/j.2044-8333.2011.02038.x

Polaschek, D. L. L. (2011b). Many sizes fit all: A preliminary framework for conceptualizing the development and provision of cognitive-behavioral rehabilitation programs for offenders. *Aggression and Violent Behavior*, *16*, 20–35. doi:10.1016/j.avb.2010.10.002

Skeem, J. L., Polaschek, D. L. L., Patrick, C. J., & Lilienfeld, S. O. (2011). Psychopathic personality: Bridging the gap between scientific evidence and public policy. *Psychological Science in the Public Interest*, *12*, 95–162. doi:10.1177/1529100611426706

Wong, S. C. P., & Olver, M. E. (2010). Two treatment- and change-oriented risk assessment tools: The Violence RIsk Scale and Violence RIsk Scale-Sexual Offender Version. In R. K. Otto & K. S. Douglas (Eds.), *Handbook of violence risk assessment* (pp. 121–146). New York: Routledge.

The Chromis programme: from conception to evaluation

J. Tew[a,b] and R. Atkinson[a]

[a]*National Offender Management Service, Ministry of Justice, London, UK;* [b]*Centre for Forensic and Criminological Psychology, The University of Birmingham, Birmingham, England, UK*

Offenders with high levels of psychopathic traits present particular challenges to the criminal justice system. These offenders are at high risk of re-offending and have a range of complex issues impacting on their response to treatment. This paper outlines the development, structure and implementation of the Chromis programme: a programme designed specifically to reduce the risk of violence in offenders with high levels of psychopathic traits. It outlines the context in which the programme currently runs and the challenges faced in evaluating its impact. Initial findings and plans for evaluation are discussed.

Psychopathy, as defined by Hare (2003), is recognised as a significant issue for the criminal justice system. Those with high levels of psychopathic traits have increased risk of re-offending (Dolan & Doyle, 2000; Salekin, Rogers, & Sewell, 1996; Walters, 2003; Yang, Wong, & Coid, 2010), reduced compliance with institutional rules and regimes (Dolan & Davies, 2006; Leistico, Salekin, DeCoster, & Rogers, 2008) and poorer responses to treatment (D'Silva, Duggan, & McCarthy, 2004; Hemphill & Hart, 2002; Thornton & Blud, 2007). More recently there has been a shift in focus from identifying the existence of such associations to trying to establish why these associations occur. Cooke (2010) considers how different traits linked to psychopathy have impacted differently on the associations highlighted above. For example, individuals who have a need for status may have this fulfilled by respect from criminal peers and protect this need for status through aggression towards those who threaten their position. Also, a lack of empathy, guilt and fear may act as a disinhibitor for violent behaviour for those who possess these traits.

There has been some debate on the effectiveness of treatment on those with high levels of psychopathic traits, a debate which has significantly impacted on clinical practice (Barbaree, 2005; Rice, Harris, & Cormier, 1992; Seto & Barbaree, 1999). Meta-analysis (Garrido, Esteban, & Molero, 1996; Salekin, 2002) and literature reviews (D'Silva et al., 2004; Hemphill & Hart, 2002; Thornton & Blud, 2007) looking at psychopathy and treatment seem to have come to similar conclusions; namely that higher scorers on the Psychopathy Checklist Revised (PCL-R; Hare, 2003) tend not to do as well in treatment as lower PCL-R scorers, that the response of individuals to treatment is quite diverse, but that, on the whole, offenders with high levels of psychopathic traits do seem able to benefit from treatment. These conclusions have shifted thinking from the earlier view that treatment actually increases risk of re-offending in psychopaths (Rice et al., 1992) to a position where the right treatment approach needs to be found in order to work effectively with people with high levels of psychopathic traits. The diverse response of high PCL-R scorers to treatment is again a reflection of the complexity of the different traits that make up this disorder. For example, those with a need for stimulation may become easily bored and disinterested in treatment; those with a grandiose sense of self-worth and a lack of guilt may not see any reason to change or engage in treatment; and, those with poor behaviour controls and high levels of impulsivity may fail to adhere to the boundaries of treatment. Wong and Hare (2009) summarise this issue by observing it is not that treatment makes psychopaths worse but that the *wrong* treatment makes them worse. Given the relevance of psychopathy to the criminal justice system it is from this more optimistic position that researchers and practitioners within the National Offender Management Service (NOMS) for England and Wales sought to develop a programme specifically for this heterogeneous group.

This paper will outline and critically reflect on the development and implementation of the Chromis programme with the aim of informing future practice and the literature regarding treatment with high-risk offenders with high levels of psychopathy traits. The paper will outline the structure of Chromis alongside preliminary findings of outcome. Plans for programme evaluation and further development will also be discussed.

Developing the Chromis programme

The Chromis programme spent over five years in development. This began in 1999 when a programme development team in the Interventions and Substance Misuse Group (ISMG) within the NOMS convened a panel to find ways of addressing the needs of high-risk violent individuals with high levels of psychopathic traits. Panel members included world leaders in the field of psychopathy and treatment such as Ron Blackburn, James Blair, Linda Blud, David Cooke, Adelle Forth, Derek Perkins, Robert Hare, Steven Hart, David Thornton and Stephen Wong.

The panel met on four occasions, with each meeting lasting about five days. Discussions covered the community management of psychopathic offenders, engagement and retention, treatment targets, structure of units and the wider therapeutic environment, subgroups of psychopathic offenders, incentives for programme participation, PCL-R cut-offs for the UK, staff competence and training, the management of treatment interfering behaviour, and programme framework and design.

NOMS initiated a range of research projects to support the development of the programme and learn more about the needs of this population of offenders. These projects included focus groups and interviews with high-risk and psychopathic individuals to explore what motivates them and what they thought made treatment engaging and credible. NOMS also spoke to therapeutic and custodial staff about approaches that staff considered to work well with psychopathic offenders.

It was agreed that Chromis should draw on the 'what works' literature (McGuire, 1995) and be guided by the principles of effective practice in reducing offending in general offenders. Best practice in treatment planning for offenders is guided by the principles of risk, need and responsivity, developed by Andrews and Bonta (2010), and it was thought that treatment for psychopathic offenders should be no exception. From the evidence available it was believed that offenders with high levels of psychopathic traits were capable of change, but that current treatment programmes were not designed to meet the range of risk, need and responsivity issues associated with this group. For example, given the associations between psychopathy and risk of violence (e.g. Cooke, 1994; Wong, 1996), those with high levels of psychopathic traits would likely require a higher intensity and higher dose intervention to reduce their risk of violence than was currently available. There was also a considerable body of research relating to how the interpersonal, affective and behavioural traits associated with psychopathy impacted on engagement and levels of benefit gained in treatment (e.g. Blud, Thornton, & Ramsey-Heimmermann, 2003; Clark, 2000; Hobson, Shine, & Roberts, 2000), which contributed to how treatment could best be designed to meet the responsivity and treatment needs of psychopathic offenders.

Relying totally on the risk, need and responsivity principles has not been without criticism, and Ward and Brown (2004) suggest a 'Good Lives' approach in which offenders are helped to identify what is important to them and to find pro-social ways of living fulfilling lives. Again this approach can be applied to planning work for offenders with high levels of psychopathic traits.

Around the same time as Chromis was being developed, the dangerous and severe personality disorder (DSPD) initiative also began to take form. The DSPD programme delivers services specifically for people who present a high risk of committing serious violent or sexual offences as a result of a severe personality disorder (see http://www.personalitydisorder.org.uk/criminal-justice/about-dspd-programme/ for more information).

Given the clear overlap in their target groups, the Chromis development team became involved in supporting, advising and liaising with the central DSPD team. Following consultation it was agreed that the DSPD programme would fund Chromis's pilot implementation into a prison unit, and the Westgate unit in HM Prison Frankland was selected. Westgate offers a range of interventions to this complex group of offenders of which Chromis is only a part. That said, the whole treatment approach of Westgate is underpinned by the same core principles and model of change.

Chromis was accredited by the Correctional Services Accreditation Panel (CSAP; Lipton, Thornton, McGuire, Porporino, & Hollin, 2000; Maguire, Grubin, Lösel, & Raynor, 2010) and started to be delivered in Westgate units' regime in 2005. The CSAP is an Advisory Non-Departmental Public Body, which was established to advise the Home Secretary on programmes aimed at reducing offending. The CSAP's rigorous accreditation criteria are based on the 'what works' literature (McGuire, 1995).

What is Chromis?

Chromis is a treatment programme aimed at reducing violence in offenders whose level or combination of psychopathic traits disrupts their ability to engage in treatment and change. It does not aim to change personality traits but to work with these to reduce individuals' risk of violent offending. As with other accredited interventions, Chromis combines the identification, reduction and management of risk, with developing new fulfilling ways of living pro-socially. However, it aims to be particularly responsive to the diverse range of complex needs associated with psychopathy, while maintaining a commitment to treatment integrity.

Chromis is based on a set of core principles that underpin the assessment, treatment and progression strategy of the programme from beginning to end. These principles are also embedded into the wider therapeutic environment of the Westgate unit in order to provide opportunities for the generalisation of skills and continuity of approaches with other interventions on the unit. For example, offenders can make choices about whether to attend activities, consequences of choices are made clear to individuals, offenders are encouraged to achieve what is important to them through more pro-social means and other treatment components supplement the aims of Chromis, while following the same treatment principles, for example, drug use or emotional management. Additionally, all treatments are transparent (see 'The Chromis principles' section), and facilitators work collaboratively with participants to individualise sessions and tasks to make them personally relevant to each individual's learning style and specific treatment needs. Programme's principles also underpin the selection and training of staff delivering and supporting Chromis. For example, staff are taught to be 'role models' and uphold and model the ethos of choice, transparency, mutual respect and self-responsibility in all of their interactions with both participants and colleagues.

The Chromis' principles

The principles of Chromis have emerged from the research literature on effecting change with psychopathic and other treatment-resistant offenders. The literature reviewed was extensive, covering models of change, target factors to address, treatment methods, sequencing intensity and duration, engagement and motivation, treatment integrity, continuity of services and programme evaluation. In-depth interviews with offenders and staff also helped inform these principles. It is not possible to summarise the scope of this review here but it is recorded in the programme's theory manual (Offending Behaviour Programmes Unit, 2005). The principles aim to enable offenders to engage in treatment and to see a personal benefit in behavioural change and the reduction of violence. The key principles focus on the importance of acknowledging the complexity of each individual and ensuring that all work appeals to any vested (pro-social) self-interest, while also reinforcing self-responsibility by providing choices and control within the treatment milieu. This ethos is reinforced through a transparency about the rationale for each aspect of treatment, and by ensuring that sessions are engaging, interesting, positive and future-focused. The following sections summarise the core principles of Chromis:

Complex needs and personal relevance

From our research and experience, psychopathic offenders often see themselves as having complex and special needs and many of them find aspects of treatment patronising, boring or irrelevant. Chromis individualises treatment and establishes with the participant what he really cares about, his priorities and his strengths, as well as aspects of his life that need to be improved, and areas of risk that need to be addressed.

Control and choice

For individuals high in psychopathic traits, change might be particularly challenging, and they may see no reason for it. Central to Chromis is the belief that we cannot expect people to change unless they acknowledge a need to, and have some sense of what change might look and feel like. To support this principle, a method called the Strategy of Choices (Harris, Attrill, & Bush, 2005) is used throughout the programme and in the wider unit. The strategy sounds something like 'We can't make you change, and we don't intend to try. But if you are willing to learn we can teach you how to change'. The respect for an offender's right and ability to direct his own life pervades the Strategy of Choices. Of course, offering a choice means that we have to accept that offenders are free to choose not to obey rules. In effect, the strategy says, 'we will accept your choice, whatever you choose'. However, in accordance with the 'transparency principle', the Strategy of Choices requires facilitators to be clear about the consequences of each choice. Only when an offender makes a choice in the full knowledge of both the consequences and sequelae of each choice can they be said to be making an objective decision. The Strategy of Choices seeks to enhance an offender's skills in objective decision-making.

Fundamentally, the Strategy of Choices is a risk reduction strategy. Choosing not to participate, or to behave disruptively or disrespectfully, will have a different set of consequences for an individual. These may include greater emphasis on external risk management, which will generally result in a reduced range of choices and less personal control. In this way the programme is transparent about each offender's right to choose his own path, but also about society's right to choose to protect itself from violence. It is only at the end of treatment, when they have had a chance to try the new skills out in their life on the unit, that offenders will be in a position to make an informed choice about change.

Future focused

Chromis is 'approach focused', in that the emphasis of all sessions and components is on how the individual would like his life to be. Many treatment programmes focus on the individual's past offending behaviour; Chromis seeks to understand this behaviour, but views the identification of historical personalised risk scenarios to be most relevant in the development of treatment goals. For example, an individual who identifies the need to 'be respected' as a personal motivator, and uses violence to obtain such respect, would be encouraged to explore how he can work towards gaining respect through other means in his life. This need for respect would be looked at in greater depth as he progresses through each component, and specific strategies built on to help him achieve this.

Novelty and stimulation

Chromis aims to help participants develop their tolerance of boredom, frustration and unstructured time by developing new skills for managing their time and coping more pro-socially with boredom. The material and style of delivery has been adapted to accommodate a proneness to boredom and need for stimulation. The programme uses novel and stimulating material in sessions, avoids repetition and employs a wide range of techniques and methods including elements of competition. Sessions last no longer than an hour, with some variation of session length purposely built in. Sessions include work outside of the formal group room, and include the collaborative development of generalisation tasks that can be carried out anywhere in the unit.

Collaboration and transparency

The programme aims to be highly transparent in order to engage psychopathic offenders and avoid their mistrust. This approach aims to reduce game playing and manipulation by offenders high in psychopathic traits. There is also a strong emphasis on collaboration in order to promote feelings of control. For example, session materials can be adapted and even created by individual participants so that they meet their own preferred learning styles. Facilitators explain the rationales for each session and in some components collaboratively set agendas for the session to ensure that the participants have input into their own treatment. As the programme has developed, NOMS has held focus groups with participants to seek feedback about the treatment, and many ideas have been incorporated directly as a result of participants' suggestions.

Status and credibility

The programme openly acknowledges that each participant is the expert in his own life. Problems of dominance can interfere with treatment delivery. To counter this, facilitators avoid presenting as experts or teachers, but instead reinforce that their role is to facilitate the participant in pro-socially maximising his own potential. The language used to describe each participant is professional and respectful, and not unlike that which would be adopted with a colleague. Complex contemporary examples – such as current news topics or successful businesses – are used that demonstrate the status and credibility of the programme content and skills being discussed.

The structure of Chromis

Chromis comprises five separate components, each with specific treatment targets aimed at addressing the risk and needs of violent psychopathic men (see Figure 1). The length of time a participant will be in treatment depends on his individual needs and progress, but is likely to be 2½–3 years in total, including assessment and preparation for progression. The time between components will also be dictated by the individual's needs and response to treatment.

Chromis begins with an introductory session in which staff introduce the participant to the Strategy of Choices (Harris et al., 2005). This sets the tone for transparent and respectful therapeutic relationships, introduces a mechanism for maintaining focus and boundaries within treatment and begins the process of reinforcing choice and control.

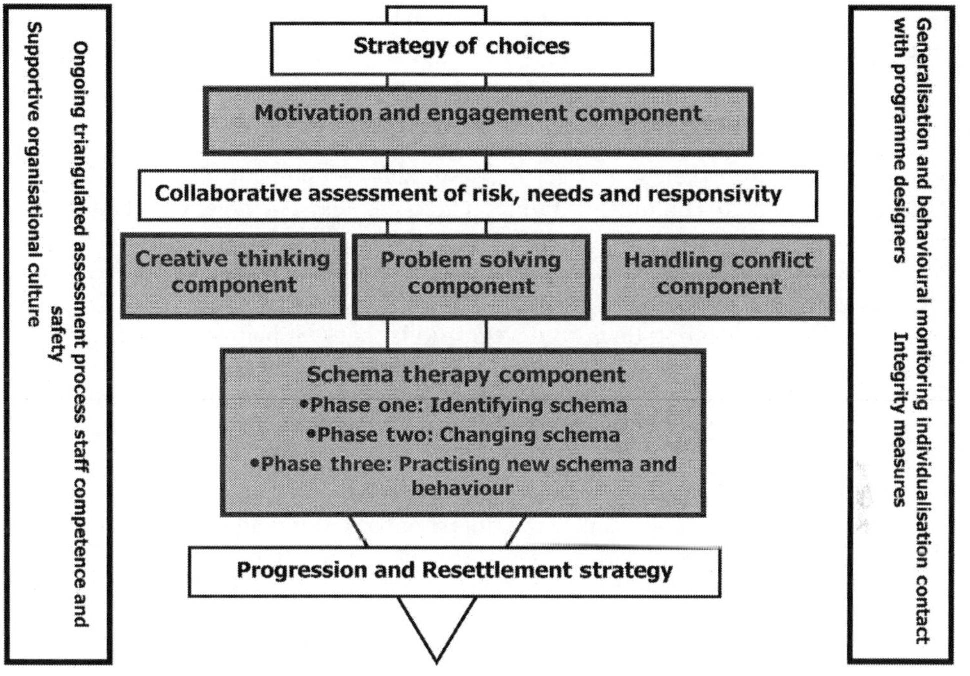

Figure 1. An overview of the elements of Chromis.
Note: Grey-shaded areas are the Chromis components.

Motivation and Engagement component

The Motivation and Engagement component is structured, yet flexible, and creates a way of working with the participant that fits with his responsivity needs (Andrews & Bonta, 2010). The Motivation and Engagement component consists of 12 individual sessions and focuses upon tasks that have been designed specifically to engage participants in treatment and other unit activities. It aims to motivate participants to choose to constructively engage in treatment, and see a personal relevance and value in doing so, and later, to choose real change rather than just compliance.

The component focuses on understanding what offenders really care about and want, and how they usually try and achieve this. It uses the Good Lives Model (Ward & Brown, 2004) as a tool for pulling out underlying themes for each participant. This is supported by a facilitative treatment style and demonstration of interest in the participant by facilitators.

The component also introduces the use of objectivity as a skill. Participants are taught what 'objectivity' means, and learn how 'cognitive distortions' can get in the way of understanding one's experiences and impede effective change. Teaching this skill enhances constructive, open and respectful engagement in the programme and increases the chances of participants and staff understanding each participant's experiences.

At the end of the Motivation and Engagement component, participants then complete an assessment battery of psychometric tests. These tests contribute to an individualised treatment and responsivity plan for participation in the programme.

Cognitive skills components

As shown in Figure 1 there are three cognitive skills components: Creative Thinking, Problem Solving and Handling Conflict. These are again flexible, to accommodate individual responsivity and treatment needs, and can be delivered using a range of individual and group sessions paced for the individuals concerned. Components are designed to meet the needs of psychopathic participants by being challenging and stimulating, while enabling them to develop skills that will help them fulfil their life goals without the use of threats or violence. Skills are introduced and practised with an emphasis on personal relevance, value to participants and generalisation to everyday life. The following briefly outlines each of the three components:

(1) The Creative Thinking component comprises around 20 sessions. It gives participants the opportunity to understand, develop and generalise a range of creative thinking skills for understanding and resolving problems, achieving their goals, making the most of opportunities and reducing some of the boredom and monotony in their lives.
(2) The Problem Solving component comprises around 17 sessions and provides participants with a range of skills in critical reasoning and for defining and resolving problems.
(3) The Handling Conflict component lasts around 21 sessions. It focuses on enabling participants to pro-socially understand, avoid and resolve conflict situations and develop negotiation skills. It includes the use of a Lifemap (a timeline charting significant events in the person's life) to help participants reflect on key experiences in their lives, how they interpreted these experiences, and how such experiences influenced their views of themselves, others and the world. This work then continues into the next component.

Schema therapy component

The Chromis Schema Therapy (CST) component is a high-intensity intervention based on cognitive behavioural therapy for personality disorders (Davidson, 2007). It aims to reduce violence and other harmful (including self-harming) behaviours by using a formulation-based approach to explore and address the development and maintenance of unhelpful schema, beliefs and consequent behaviours. The CST component is delivered in three phases: formulation, then change, and finally, generalisation, practice and maintenance. These distinct phases support participants to manage their own progress, gradually reducing the need for support and guidance from staff. It is delivered in a rolling format, enabling each participant to progress through the component at his own pace.

The component also provides staff with information about what risks have to be managed and how this can be achieved, which is particularly important for the final progression and resettlement phases. The CST component builds on the skills learned in earlier components to provide an opportunity to 'try on' new thinking and behaviour in a safe and supportive environment, using cognitive techniques and behavioural experiments. Behavioural experiments are planned experiential activities that are undertaken by participants in or between sessions. They are developed from the individuals' formulations, and their main purpose is to obtain new information which may help to test the validity of beliefs, to construct or test new more helpful beliefs and to help to further develop the formulation (Bennett-Levy et al., 2004).

The first phase of CST aims to identify how personal core beliefs or schema developed and how they are maintained by, and result in, unhelpful behaviours. This work is completed on an individual basis through the use of mind maps and thought records (Davidson, 2007). The information from phase one is used to inform phases two and three. The second phase of CST uses behavioural experiments to explore the existing schema and help develop new, more adaptive schema. It is delivered in a group setting, with up to five participants per group. This practice has worked well, with participants supporting and encouraging each other to identify and review each other's experiments. Phase three of CST builds on new skills and prepares the person for progression. It aims to consolidate skills and learning, enabling them to become their 'own therapist'. It includes the ongoing testing of new schema with the support of staff.

Finally, there is a Progression and Resettlement strategy that provides Chromis participants with individualised pathways for progression. Particular emphasis is placed on identifying and responding to any emerging resettlement needs and consolidating the relapse prevention plan. The focus is on supporting the individual in generalising skills to reduce and manage their risk, and identifying where external risk management is required. It includes mechanisms for documenting and communicating progress and risk within and across agency and services.

Implementing Chromis and some lessons learned

The implementation of Chromis began at the Westgate unit in 2005 and is an ongoing project although the pilot phase has now ended. In the six years of delivery to date, much has been learned about embedding a complex intervention into a regime for offenders with complex and challenging needs. These needs have been more complex than originally anticipated, in terms of criminal histories as well as psychological and behavioural difficulties. For example, from the outset, Chromis aimed to target high-risk violent men with high levels of psychopathic traits. This remains the target population. However, over time, Chromis has been required to meet the needs of men whose criminal history might be much more complex or versatile. Many of the men are not 'simply' violent; they may have a sexual element to their use of violence, or kidnap and arson might be part of their offending behaviour. In addition, while high levels of psychopathy would be expected in this population, the programme has had to adapt to high levels of co-morbidity with other personality disorders (e.g. borderline and narcissistic personality disorders), or mental health issues (e.g. anxiety and depression), which need to be addressed in or before treatment. Another significant factor requiring consideration was the intellectual and educational needs of this population. In developing the programme it was anticipated that many participants would be relatively high-functioning individuals and sessions and exercises were designed accordingly. In practice, many participants have required adaptations to be made to materials in order to respond to their personal learning styles and educational needs. As a consequence of each of these emerging factors, treatment content and therapeutic style have evolved and subsequently been incorporated into the programme in order to better meet these additional responsivity issues.

One way in which responsivity has been enhanced is through greater consideration being given to assessing both suitability and readiness for treatment. This has been achieved by the use of a developmental formulation to aid treatment decisions and pathways. For example, given that Chromis is based on a model of violence, before referral to the programme it must be ensured that the individuals' primary risk is of future violence, and where necessary a hierarchy of treatment needs and risks is established so that all treatment (including Chromis) is sequenced appropriately. Similarly, consideration needs to be given to any active mental health problems, and it is now policy that any depressive or anxiety disorders are addressed prior to participation in Chromis. This policy ensures that participants are well supported and able to engage in treatment to the best of their ability. For example, one participant suffered from severe social anxiety, and it was deemed inappropriate to place him in a group setting until this anxiety had been managed and treated. Once addressed, he was able to work more effectively with others and this in turn gave him confidence to address the other difficulties in his life linked to his risk of offending. For others suffering from depression, engagement in exercises such as behavioural experiments could be too challenging and therefore de-motivating and so steps must be taken to address depressive symptoms prior to participation.

To address educational and intellectual difficulties, care is taken to understand how the individual has participated in previous treatment or educational programmes and what his preferred learning style is. Responsivity to all of the above factors is achieved through both the formulation approach and also through participation in the Motivation and Engagement component outlined earlier. This component is central to understanding how best to work with an individual and information gleaned there will be used to inform, and where necessary, adapt aspects of future Chromis components. This might simply be by changing the pace of a session or a component, choosing to run particular sessions on an individual rather than group basis, or changing the actual content of a session or its assignment. In all cases these adaptations will be discussed and achieved in collaboration with the individual. Adaptations provide valuable information about how to engage the individual in the future, and also tip on how best to engage future participants who might have similar needs. This open and collaborative approach minimises the need to exclude individuals who might have already struggled to access treatment during their prison sentence, and programme staff work hard to engage and support individuals whatever their responsivity needs.

In addition an understanding about what makes a member of staff effective when working with these men has evolved, as has understanding of the kind of operational support required to successfully deliver such an intervention. The process of evaluating the Chromis staff selection and development process is currently underway with an aim of identifying what makes staff effective. Anecdotally, and perhaps unsurprisingly, experience has shown that staff who are able and willing to reflect openly on their practice, both individually and in group supervision, are key. The ability of staff to self-monitor, and signal when they need a break from treatment, is crucial, as is an organisational ethos and structure that makes this acceptable and practical. For example, during their first Chromis training course, staff of all disciplines develop personal checklists which help them to identify their personal signs of burnout or boundary breaches (e.g. spending too long with one particular participant on the unit; minimising or overestimating his risk; thinking about a participant when off duty, etc.). These checklists are done in the spirit of transparency and shared with their colleagues, and also raised routinely in supervision. There is no stigma to asking for time out of treatment delivery, and managers respond to this immediately and without judgement. Staff are welcome to return to treatment when they feel ready, subject to a collaborative health review by their supervisors and managers. Regular supervision (particularly externally provided group supervision) has been invaluable in maintaining staff health and programme integrity. The importance of supervision has been highlighted in the literature. For example, Lloyd-Owen (1997) suggested that regular group supervision facilitated by an experienced external consultant is central to staff well-being and effectiveness. This supervision should take place in addition to individual supervision, and the external consultant should take an impartial view, and not be involved in the dynamics of the organisation. Lloyd-Owen also argued that individual supervision alone would not address dynamics in the staff group, and supervisors from within the service are inevitably constrained by their ability to make observations regarding the organisation of which they are a part. It is also difficult for them to comment on the practice of their colleagues, and particularly on the work of those more senior to them. These considerations have certainly been borne out in the experience of implementing Chromis, and so regular internal and external supervision is mandatory.

Another significant lesson has come from the ongoing, open communication between programme developers and programme deliverers. Staff delivering the programme are encouraged, even beyond the pilot stage, to note and make suggestions about aspects of the programme that do not work or need to change. Programme developers have also held regular discussion groups with participants to ask for their views on the programme. Such feedback is welcomed and in most cases acted on. For example, the developers were surprised when participants and staff told them that they would like more sessions to be added to the Schema Therapy component, as they wanted more time to consolidate new thinking and behaviour. It is often the case that this population, for various reasons, are impatient for treatment to be completed. This feedback was carefully considered, accepted and the suggested changes subsequently implemented. Clinical support from the programme developers is also helpful in terms of providing objective perspectives on a participant's suitability for the programme and progress (or otherwise). This also ensures that programme developers are in touch with the demands placed on treatment staff.

As a consequence of this learning, Chromis has been required to be flexible in its evolution, whilst retaining a high standard of integrity. Integrity has been maintained through regular change control meetings in collaboration with the treatment site, annual clinical audits and also successful resubmission to the CSAP in 2009. As mentioned, regular contact between the programme developers, staff and participants has enabled programme materials, treatment manuals, staff training and clinical practice to be adapted to respond quickly and appropriately to the emerging needs of this population and the staff working with them. Taken together this learning is supported by Andrews and Dowden (2005) who include these areas in their indicators of programme integrity for a meta-analytical review.

At the time of writing (September 2011), 84 men have been involved in Chromis to some degree. This group has a mean age of 41 (range 24–70; SD = 9.4), mean PCL-R score of 29.6 (range 14.7–40; SD = 4.7), with a mean factor one score of 11.2 (range 3.4–16; SD = 3.1) and a mean factor two score of 13.9 (range 6–18; SD = 2.6). Only eight offenders with total PCL-R scores below 25 (average score 20) were admitted onto the programme, due to these individuals being assessed as having difficulties engaging as a result of their psychopathic personality traits. Eleven men have completed Chromis with eight moving on from Westgate and two of these eight having been released into the community (M. Wilson, Chromis progression lead, personal correspondence 22 June 2011).

Evaluating Chromis

Following the development, accreditation and implementation of the Chromis programme thoughts then turned to evaluating its outcome. It is important to establish the extent to which Chromis is achieving its aim of reducing violence in those whose level or combination of psychopathic traits disrupts their ability to engage in treatment and change. The more deeply this task is considered the more complex it seems to be with the client group, setting and the programme itself all presenting challenges to a robust demonstration of treatment success. Considered here are the two initial approaches: process evaluation and impact evaluation.

Process evaluation

ISMG within NOMS undertook a process evaluation of Chromis in 2009 (Interventions and Substance Misuse Group [ISMG], 2009). The study addressed two key questions: is Chromis being delivered to the right people, and is it being delivered in the right way? A systematic review of the 43 men who had participated in Chromis at that point was conducted. This review concluded that the right people were accessing Chromis, considering risk, need and responsivity issues. All participants met the DSPD criteria, had sufficient time to complete the programme, presented with treatment needs that the programme targets and evidenced a level or combination of psychopathic traits that would be likely to disrupt treatment engagement and capacity for change.

The characteristics of Chromis participants and the quality of programme delivery are continually assessed through video monitoring and monthly population monitoring. The review also found, through session monitoring and programme audit, that the quality of delivery was consistently high and continuously improving. This was promising news for the implementation of an innovative programme for a complex group of prisoners.

Impact evaluation

Clearly the next important question is whether or not Chromis is having the desired impact on participants (i.e. reducing their risk of violence). To effectively evaluate a programme, methodologies such as randomised control trials or quasi-experimental designs would offer the most robust findings (Harper & Chitty, 2005). For practical reasons such designs are rare in programme evaluations. The nature of the Chromis programme does not allow for such studies at the present time due to factors such as limited sample size, the complex nature of participants and the integration of the programme into the Westgate treatment regime.

A multiple case study design, following protocols that take steps to address validity issues, and which relate back to the theory base for the programme, currently offers the most effective way to answer questions around what changes are observed in Chromis participants over time (Yin, 2009). This work is ongoing, looking at changes in areas considered significant for key stakeholders in five case studies of individuals who have completed Chromis and progressed to lower security establishments or the community. One key element of this project, namely considering changes in anger and aggression in the individuals, has been completed (Tew, Dixon, Harkins, & Bennett, 2012). This study found that looking across case studies individuals experienced a reduction in self-reported anger as measured by the Novaco Anger Scales and Provocation Inventory (NAS-PI; Novaco, 1994) pre- and post-treatment. In general individuals had a reduction in actual acts of physical and verbal aggression as they progressed through treatment. Cooke's (1997) equation was used to compare actual and expected rates of aggression across varying time periods. This showed that individuals had lower than expected rates of physical aggression while on Westgate and post-Westgate relative to their behaviour before moving to the unit and starting treatment. Generally individuals had higher than expected rates of verbal aggression while in treatment, and post-Westgate, considering their pre-treatment behaviour. Reasons for this are considered and include the disruptive effects of being in treatment, a reaction to their apparent reduction in physical aggression or differences in the way behaviour is identified, recorded and monitored before, during and after their stay in the DSPD unit. It may also indicate that further work is needed post-Chromis to help individuals appropriately manage and express the anger they still experience. While there are limitations to this project and the ongoing further work is essential it is encouraging that improvements in areas related to a key target of Chromis – reducing violence – have been found in individuals who have moved on from the unit.

A number of unpublished studies by staff at the Westgate unit also provide some preliminary evidence of positive changes in Chromis participants. In a small study ($n = 14$), Morris (2010), considering effect sizes according to Cohen (1988), found positive changes in psychometric assessments of attitudes, thinking styles and emotional regulation administered before and after the Chromis cognitive skills components addressing these areas. He also found that the clinical team judged 95% of participants were making progress in treatment (Morris, 2010). Liell (2009) found improved positive engagement in education for Chromis cognitive skills component completers ($n = 11$), which could be considered a protective factor against violence for some. ISMG within NOMS (2009) found that offenders reported that the feedback they get from facilitators was accurate, and treatment was relevant to them. While this might be expected from offenders with high levels of psychopathic traits, this finding was supported by staff who observed participants becoming less resistant, more engaged, forming more positive and trusting relationships with staff, being more focused, and working together more within group sessions as they progressed through the Chromis components (Interventions and Substance Misuse Group [ISMG], 2009). While these studies have limitations, for example small sample sizes and a lack of control groups, these findings offer promising indications of the impact of Chromis.

Preliminary investigations of the Chromis database also offer some promising results. The data indicate a completion rate of around 95% for each Chromis component. Data from the progression team (M. Wilson, personal correspondence, November 2010) show that only nine men (out of 64 starters at that time, 14%) had been permanently deselected from Chromis. These are encouraging attrition figures considering the difficulties anticipated with offenders who were challenging, dismissive, very hard to keep focused, volatile, inconsistent in the information they provided and of varying levels of intelligence.

The problem of psychopathic offenders potentially learning to 'talk the talk but not walk the walk' is clearly an issue when considering the impact of a programme like Chromis. This is the concern that offenders may learn the language of therapy but not make meaningful changes in their behaviour. The triangulated assessment approach (Flick, 1992) aims to detect if this is the case, and open discussions with participants aim to address this issue where it does occur. Anecdotally there is encouraging information from the treatment team involved in Chromis that offenders are good at applying behavioural experiments, which form part of the Schema Therapy component. This indicates they are learning and able to put new skills into practice when they choose. This observation has since been confirmed by non-treatment staff at Westgate who have spontaneously commented on notable and pro-social behavioural changes in men involved in the CST component. For example, gym staff commented on one individual's significantly improved self-management on the football pitch.

Future plans

The refinement of Chromis as a treatment approach is ongoing. As our understanding of this population further develops through evaluation and clinical practice, changes to the programme design, content and delivery are required. A number of observations lead us to consider ensuring better access and responsivity for offenders with learning difficulties, either through developing an adapted version of the programme or through enhancing the information in the current manuals to make material more accessible to this group. Another development may be to deliver the programme with female offenders who meet DSPD criteria; the first component of Chromis (Motivation and Engagement) is currently being delivered effectively with this population. Further work is needed to better understand the impact of Chromis, the role of the Westgate regime in supporting it and the economic costs associated with delivery before it can be considered for delivery in other environments outside of the DSPD estate.

The evaluation strategy for Chromis includes a commitment to creating a robust evidence base for the programme through thorough and accurate data gathering on all aspects of delivery to inform studies to place the outcomes of Chromis participants in the context of the outcomes for similar offenders in different regimes. A multiple case study project is currently underway and findings will continue to be published. Research is also being planned to investigate those who have dropped out or been deselected from Chromis to see if anything can be learnt to help reduce attrition. Also, work is planned to evaluate the effectiveness of the staff assessment centre.

While having a long-term positive impact on participants' offending behaviour is a central aim of Chromis, there is also an economic argument to be had. If we are able to show that Chromis is 'worth it' in cost-benefit terms then it will have independent value for the service in its task of managing this group of difficult and disruptive prisoners. An economic evaluation will consider what these offenders typically cost the service (e.g. time in segregation, adjudications, police and ambulance call-outs to prisons, staff sickness, hospital visits for themselves and those around them) and compare this with what it costs to manage them within the Westgate regime which contains and is informed by Chromis principles.

Summary and conclusions

The design and implementation of an evidence-based intervention for violent offenders with high levels of psychopathic traits has been a challenging but informative journey. It would be fair to say that Chromis remains an experimental programme: a form of action research (McCutcheon & Jung, 1990). The approach is one of continual evaluation and improvement. The Chromis experience over the last six years has already led to some useful learning: staff need to be psychologically robust, fully briefed about working with this population and well trained and supported to deliver evidence-based treatment. Contact between programme developers, participants and staff delivering the intervention regarding treatment and staff training is key to maintaining integrity and enhancing responsivity. Evidence should be gathered regarding participants' skills generalisation to ensure they can 'walk the walk and not just talk the talk'. Genuine interest, transparency and respect modelled by staff are key factors in maintaining engagement and facilitating a therapeutic rapport. Finally, a healthy cynicism combined with therapeutic optimism helps to prevent staff working with such populations becoming conditioned into mistrustfulness and pessimism about change. Trying to understand the reasons for violent and seemingly self-destructive behaviour helps to facilitate psychological curiosity and awareness in staff about the offenders.

While the investigations to date do not allow for firm conclusions about the impact of Chromis, the indications thus far are that the efforts of developers, facilitators and participants have been worthwhile. It appears that men in Westgate are engaged in the programme and continue to attend treatment for longer than we might typically expect given the complexity of this population. Those involved in Chromis show some improvements in their attitudes and behaviours, particularly relating to anger and aggression on Westgate and after transferring on as indicated by psychometrics and actual behaviour. Continuing evaluation will help to understand Chromis' effectiveness with participants, and its effect on staff, with a view to further developing the programme and considering its potential delivery in other settings.

Acknowledgements

Special thanks go to the staff at the Westgate unit within HMP Frankland for their continued hard work in implementing the programme and input into its development. Also to Rosie Travers and David Cooke for their valuable feedback in the preparation of this article.

References

Andrews, D. A., & Bonta, J. (2010). *The psychology of criminal conduct* (5th ed.). Cincinnati, OH: Anderson.

Andrews, D. A., & Dowden, C. (2005). Managing correctional treatment for reduced recidivism: A meta-analytic review of programme integrity. *Legal and Criminological Psychology*, *10*, 173–187. doi:10.1348/135532505X36723

Barbaree, H. E. (2005). Psychopathy, treatment behavior, and recidivism: An extended follow-up of Seto and Barbaree. *Journal of Interpersonal Violence*, *20*, 1115–1131. doi:10.1177/0886260505278262

Bennett-Levy, J., Butler, G., Fennell, M., Hackman, A., Mueller, M., & Westbrook, D. (2004). *Oxford guide to behavioural experiments in cognitive therapy*. New York, NY: Oxford University Press.

Blud, L. M., Thornton, D., & Ramsey-Heimmermann, D. (2003). *Psychopathy and response to cognitive skills programmes: Analysis of OBPU research data*. Unpublished report for Her Majesty's Prison Service.

Clark, D. (2000). The use of the Hare *Psychopathy Checklist Revised* to predict offending and institutional misconduct in the English prison system. *Prison Research & Development Bulletin*, *9*, 10–14.

Cohen, J. (1988). *Statistical power analysis for the behavioural sciences* (2nd ed.). Hillsdale, NJ: Lawrence Erlbaum Associates.

Cooke, D. J. (1994). *Psychological disturbance in the Scottish prison system: Prevalence, precipitants and policy*. Edinburgh: Scottish Home and Health Department.

Cooke, D. J. (1997). The Barlinnie special unit: The rise and fall of a therapeutic experiment. In E. Cullen, L. Jones, & R. Woodward (Eds.), *Therapeutic communities for offenders* (pp. 121–157). Chichester: Wiley.

Cooke, D. J. (2010). Personality disorder and violence: Understanding violence risk: An introduction to the special section personality disorder and violence. *Journal of Personality Disorders*, *24*, 539–550. doi:10.1521/pedi.2010.24.5.539

Davidson, K. M. (2007). *Cognitive therapy for personality disorders: A guide for clinicians* (2nd ed). Hove: Routledge.

Dolan, M., & Davies, G. (2006). Psychopathy and institutional outcome in patients with schizophrenia in forensic settings in the UK. *Schizophrenia Research*, *81*, 277–281. doi:10.1016/j.schres.2005.07.002

Dolan, M., & Doyle, M. (2000). Violence risk prediction. *The British Journal of Psychiatry*, *177*, 303–311. doi:10.1192/bjp.177.4.303

D'Silva, K., Duggan, C., & McCarthy, L. (2004). Does treatment really make psychopaths worse? A review of the evidence. *Journal of Personality Disorders*, *18*, 163–177. doi:10.1521/pedi.18.2.163.32775

Flick, U. (1992). Triangulation revisited: Strategy of validation or alternative? *Journal for the Theory of Social Behaviour*, *22*, 175–197. doi:10.1111/j.1468-5914.1992.tb00215.x

Garrido, V., Esteban, C., & Molero, C. (1996). The effectiveness in the treatment of psychopathy: A meta-analysis. *Issues in Legal & Criminological Psychology*, *24*, 57–59.

Hare, R. D. (2003). *Hare psychopathy checklist-revised (PCL-R)* (2nd ed.). Toronto: Multi-Health Systems.

Harper, G., & Chitty, C. (Eds.) (2005). *The impact of corrections on re-offending: A review of 'what works'* (2nd ed.). Home Office Research Study 291. London: Home Office.

Harris, D., Attrill, G., & Bush, J. (2005). Using choice as an aid to engagement and risk management with violent psychopathic offenders. *Issues in Forensic Psychology*, *5*, 144–151.

Hemphill, J. F., & Hart, S. D. (2002). Motivating the unmotivated: Psychopathy, treatment, and change. In M. McMurran (Ed.), *Motivating offenders to change: A guide to enhancing engagement in therapy* (pp. 194–219). New York, NY: Wiley.

Hobson, J., Shine, J., & Roberts, R. (2000). How do psychopaths behave in a prison therapeutic community? *Psychology, Crime & Law*, *6*, 139–154. doi:10.1080/10683160008410838

Interventions and Substance Misuse Group (2009). *Chromis review: A review of implementation of Chromis for submission to CSAP March 2009*. Unpublished paper. London: NOMS.

Leistico, A. R., Salekin, R. T., DeCoster, D., & Rogers, R. (2008). A large-scale meta-analysis relating the hare measures of psychopathy to antisocial conduct. *Law and Human Behavior*, *32*, 28–45. doi:10.1007/s10979-007-9096-6

Liell, G. (2009). *Chromis: Cohort of cognitive skills completers – Activities and adjudications.* Unpublished manuscript.

Lipton, D. S., Thornton, D. M., McGuire, J., Porporino, F. J., & Hollin, C. R. (2000). Program accreditation and correctional treatment. *Substance Use & Misuse, 35*, 1705–1734. doi:10.3109/10826080009148238

Lloyd-Owen, D. (1997). From action to thought: Supervising mental health workers with forensic patients. In B. Martindale, M. Morner, M. E. C. Rodriguez, & J. P. Vidit (Eds.), *Supervision and its vicissitudes* (pp. 87–153). London: Karnac.

Maguire, M., Grubin, D., Lösel, F., & Raynor, P. (2010). What works and the Correctional Services Accreditation Panel: An insider perspective. *Criminology and Criminal Justice, 10*, 37–58. doi:10.1177/1748895809352651

McCutcheon, G., & Jung, B. (1990). Alternative perspectives on action research. *Theory Into Practice, 29*, 144–151. doi:10.1080/00405849009543447

McGuire, J. (Ed.) (1995). *What works: Reducing reoffending: Guidelines from research and practice.* Chichester: Wiley.

Morris, J. (2010). *Costs in context: A report on the function of the Westgate DSPD unit.* Unpublished manuscript. Westgate unit, HMP Frankland.

Novaco, R. W. (1994). Anger as a risk factor for violence among the mentally disordered. In J. Monahan & H. Steadman (Eds.), *Violence and mental disorder: Developments in risk assessment* (pp. 21–59). Chicago, IL: University of Chicago Press.

Offending Behaviour Programmes Unit. (2005). *Chromis theory manual.* Unpublished report. London: HM Prison Service.

Rice, M. E., Harris, G. T., & Cormier, C. A. (1992). An evaluation of a maximum security therapeutic community for psychopaths and other mentally disordered offenders. *Law and Human Behavior, 16*, 399–412. doi:10.1007/BF02352266

Salekin, R. T. (2002). Psychopathy and therapeutic pessimism: Clinical lore or clinical reality? *Clinical Psychology Review, 22*, 79–112. doi:10.1016/S0272-7358(01)00083-6

Salekin, R. T., Rogers, R., & Sewell, K. W. (1996). A review and meta-analysis of the psychopathy checklist and psychopathy checklist-revised: Predictive validity of dangerousness. *Clinical Psychology: Science and Practice, 3*, 203–215. doi:10.1111/j.1468-2850.1996.tb00071.x

Seto, M. C., & Barbaree, H. E. (1999). Psychopathy, treatment behavior, and sex offender recidivism. *Journal of Interpersonal Violence, 14*, 1235–1248. doi:10.1177/088626099014012001

Tew, J., Dixon, L., Harkins, L., & Bennett, A. (2012). Investigating changes in anger and aggression in offenders with high levels of psychopathic traits attending the Chromis violence reduction programme. *Criminal Behaviour and Mental Health.* doi:10.1002/cbm.1832

Thornton, D., & Blud, L. (2007). The influence of psychopathic traits on response to treatment. In H. Hervé & J. C. Yuille (Eds.), *The psychopath: Theory, research and practice* (pp. 141–170). Mahwah, NJ: Lawrence Erlbaum.

Walters, G. D. (2003). Predicting institutional adjustment and recidivism with the psychopathy checklist factor scores: A meta-analysis. *Law and Human Behavior, 27*, 541–558. doi:10.1023/A:1025490207678

Ward, T., & Brown, M. (2004). The good lives model and conceptual issues in offender rehabilitation. *Psychology, Crime & Law, 10*, 243–257. doi:10.1080/10683160410001662744

Wong, S. C. P. (1996). Recidivism and the criminal career of psychopaths: A longitudinal study. In D. J. Cooke, A. E. Forth, J. P. Newman, & R. D. Hare (Eds.), *Issues in criminological and legal psychology, 24, International perspectives on psychopathy* (pp. 147–152). Leicester: British Psychological Society.

Wong, S. C. P., & Hare, R. D. (2009). *Guidelines for a psychopathy treatment programme.* Toronto: Multi-Health Systems. Retrieved from http://www.personalitydisorder.org.uk/criminal-justice/about-dspd-programme/

Yang, M., Wong, S. C. P., & Coid, J. (2010). The efficacy of violence prediction: A meta-analytic comparison of nine risk assessment tools. *Psychological Bulletin, 136*, 740–767. doi:10.1037/a0020473

Yin, R. K. (2009). *Case study research: Design and methods* (4th ed.). Thousand Oaks, CA: Sage.

Delivering effective therapeutic interventions for men with severe personality disorder within a high secure prison

Jacqui Saradjian, Naomi Murphy and Des McVey

Cambridge & Peterborough Foundation Trust, Cambridge, UK

The Fens Unit is a government-initiated facility for male prisoners reaching criteria for Dangerous and Severe Personality Disorder (DSPD). Prisoners are assessed using a standardised process; those meeting criteria engage in a five-year treatment programme using a cognitive interpersonal model. Personality disorder is seen as a combination of coping strategies, developed in response to experience, which results in dysfunctions of thinking, feeling, behaviour and interpersonal relationships. These dysfunctions are linked to offending. Therefore, in order to reduce risk, multiphasic interventions – individual and group therapies – specifically target each dysfunction area, focusing on the developmental experiences that generated them. Each man's individual risk factors become treatment targets that are addressed in every aspect of the programme. All staff on the unit, clinical and operational, attempt to improve the quality of interpersonal relationships the prisoner has access to in order to create remedial experiences that are necessary to attain the capacity to develop socially adaptive cognitive, emotional and behavioural responses. This paper describes the treatment provided to these prisoners and the outcomes for the first cohort to have completed treatment ($n = 18$). Results indicate that there is a reduction in violent behaviour, a higher than expected attendance at therapy, a decrease in actuarial risk measures and the majority of men are successfully managed in lower security after programme completion.

Introduction

The Fens Unit, based in HMP Whitemoor was one of the four high-secure units, two prison based and two hospital based, developed as a result of the 1999 government manifesto pledge to address the treatment needs of men who had a diagnosis of 'severe personality disorder'. The risk posed by these men was considered to be linked to their personality psychopathology and hitherto there were previously few, if any, services available in either the prison or the health service. A smaller service was established to meet the treatment needs of women who presented with similar characteristics. These units became known as the Dangerous and Severe Personality Disorder (DSPD) units and the aims were:

(1) to ensure high quality, detailed, risk assessments thus protecting the public from some of the most dangerous people in society;
(2) to provide high-quality services for the individuals themselves to improve their health outcomes;
(3) to reduce the risk that these individuals pose and enable them to work towards successful integration into the community or to be able to be detained at the lowest level of security without harming others.
(Planning and Delivery Guide, MOJ/DH, 2002, 2007)

A joint Ministry of Justice and Department of Health team set the criteria for admission and assessment tools to be used. However, each unit developed different treatment programmes, which were regularly scrutinised by an international expert advisory panel. The staff teams differed depending on the interventions being delivered which consequently impacted on the running costs for each unit; each hospital placement costing approximately three times that of a prison placement. Interestingly, however, research undertaken as to the characteristics of the men in these units revealed that the men in the prison units were likely to have committed more serious offences than those in the hospital units, and that the prisoners in the Fens Unit (HMP Whitemoor) tended to have more complex personality psychopathology and also greater levels of mental health problems than the patients in the hospital units (Burns et al., 2011).

Due to the complexity of the prisoners' psychopathology, it was agreed that the duration of treatment at all units would be five years, with a review of the man's ability to use the therapy available after three years. Two cohorts of prisoners have now completed treatment at the Fens Unit in HMP Whitemoor: 31 prisoners in all. Due to the severity of these men's offences, they are unlikely to be released for several years thus reoffending rates in the community will not be available for several years. However, repeated administration of risk tools, coupled with incident data, indicates an overall trend of significant risk reduction. This article will describe the unit and the treatment delivered. It will also use the outcome measures from the first cohort of 18 men as post-treatment data has not yet been completed for the second cohort.

The facilities of the Fens Unit

The Fens Unit was the only male DSPD unit not to be based in a purpose-built facility. It is an adapted prison wing. This initially appeared a disadvantage, since accommodation for both prisoners and staff is inferior to that within the purpose built units and there are no custom designed therapy rooms or activities facilities. However, in many ways there were advantages; the prisoners are always mindful that they are in a prison with all the strictures that this entails; they know and understand prison and therefore, 'the known' gives them a secure base to move into the 'unknown' area of making different kinds of relationships and doing intensive therapy. Additionally, the clinical staff both work and are based alongside operational staff, thus reducing the propensity for splitting between clinical and operational teams, and also enabling clinical staff to have greater awareness of all aspects of the prisoners' behaviour and relationships. There are three spurs, each having the capacity to hold approximately 24 prisoners. The association rooms on each of the spurs are used as group rooms for therapy during the working day and cells on the top landing overlooking the other two floors of each spur have been converted into individual treatment rooms (three per spur) and staff offices. Prisoners can access the prison library, chapel facilities, gym, healthcare and segregation unit in the same way as prisoners on other wings. There is, however, a specific workshop that is set aside for the use of the prisoners on the unit. This mainly provides educational work.

The unit has the capacity for 70 prisoners; 65 prisoners in assessment and treatment equally distributed across three spurs plus an additional five prisoner progression places. There is a small crisis suite of three safer custody cells and an additional gated cell. It is common for people in therapy undergoing real change to go into a state of crisis. People with personality disorder often express crisis by self-harm, bullying, violence, decompensation into psychosis and/or withdrawal from therapy. Treatment must be able to accommodate fluctuating motivation and periods of crisis when people are at their most emotionally vulnerable. At such times, people are in their greatest need of treatment, but some services may discharge such patients. If people are rejected from treatment at this point then psychological damage to the client could occur and result in increased risk to self or others. Clients can choose to leave therapy but treatment ensures that they are given every opportunity to work through periods of crisis. The crisis suite is used when prisoners are in such a crisis so that they can access additional support in a smaller unit. This is seen as an active opportunity to have reparative experiences and learn new strategies to manage overwhelming emotions. The gated cell is a facility used only if a prisoner is actively suicidal. This is a safer custody cell with a locked, perspex-covered gate through which the prisoner can be continually observed.

Staffing

Primarily prison officers staff the unit. The clinical team consists of psychologists, psychotherapists, nurse therapists and a part-time psychiatrist who are all based on the unit. Psychologists or psychotherapists deliver individual therapy and all clinical staff and some prison officers jointly facilitate groups. All staff, clinical and operational, are given individual and group supervision. There is a regular rolling programme of training and additional specific courses arranged in response to the needs of the unit.

General characteristics of prisoners referred to the Fens Unit

Men referred to this service have often been ‘a management problem’ in normal prison locations. Many have been violent in prison towards staff and/or other prisoners; many have spent years in and out of segregation and some have been in Close Supervision Centres (CSCs): small units aimed at containing prisoners who have been very violent in prison. Some have repeatedly damaged property by smashing or burning out cells. Some men engage in prolific self-harm or are regularly suicidal, thus engineering location moves to gated-cells and healthcare through these behaviours. Some present with psychotic and delusional symptoms when they are under extreme stress. All suffer significant emotional and psychological distress that hitherto they have attempted to manage by offending or using substances to self-medicate the distress associated with their personality disorder. Prisoners with severe personality disorder are also prone to what is known in the prison service as 'conditioning behaviour'. This means that they try to engage seductively with staff to encourage them to break boundaries. This leads these men to in turn be vulnerable to being exploited by staff. Many have previously been involved in inappropriate relationships with officers, teachers, nurses or psychologists. Some have had several such relationships.

The assessment process

Assessment aims to see whether a prisoner meets criteria for treatment. These criteria were determined centrally as were the assessment tools. Prisoners offered treatment places are considered to

(1) be at high risk of reoffending: measured by Risk Matrix 2000 (Thornton, 2003), Static 99 (Harris, Phenix, Hanson, & Thornton, 2003), Violence Risk Scale (VRS; Wong & Gordon, 1999–2003), Historical-Clinical-Risk Management-20 (HCR-20; Webster, Douglas, Eaves, & Hart, 1997) and Structured Assessment of Risk and Need (SARN; Thornton, 2002);
(2) have a severe personality disorder: measured by International Personality Disorder Examination (IPDE; Loranger, 1999) and Psychopathy Checklist-Revised (PCL-R; Hare, 2003);
(3) have a link between their personality pathology and the offences committed (assessed by the combination of detailed offence analysis and clinical developmental history).

Prisoners are primarily referred by psychologists, offender managers or personal officers from other prisons; some prisoners, however, refer themselves. The men that are referred tend to be those that have been problematic within the prison service and/or who have not been able to benefit from standard prison programmes. Referred prisoners are interviewed prior to admission for assessment to establish and increase motivation to attend the unit. On the Fens Unit, six to eight prisoners are admitted at a time, for assessment. These six to eight prisoners form the assessment group. Assessment consists of psychologists and the psychiatrist reviewing all collateral documents available on each prisoner and completing individual interviews with prisoners alongside daily officer-led group work. The purpose of the group work is to closely observe and record the prisoner's interpersonal behaviour and for the prisoners to learn to work in a group and to establish group identity. This group work appears to increase motivation and prepare men for the process of therapy. The process takes 16–20 weeks. Those who reach the criteria as described above, remain working together as a group throughout treatment. Those that do not reach criteria, or who refuse a treatment place, are returned to the referring prison with a detailed assessment report.

The treatment model

Whilst the assessment tools were 'prescribed', each of the four units was requested to devise a treatment programme independently. The Fens Unit treatment programme was influenced by the work of Salekin (2002), who reviewed 42 papers on the treatment of 'psychopaths'. This concluded that the most effective were eclectic approaches, such as group and individual therapy using both psychoanalytic and cognitive behavioural therapies, which were both intensive and long term. Thus the framework chosen by the Fens Unit was cognitive interpersonal (Blackburn, 1995), which supports this combination of approaches. Each of the units had to present and rigorously justify the chosen programme to a panel of 12 internationally known experts, clinicians and researchers in the field of personality disorder. The Fens Unit programme was agreed without any modifications required.

Rationale for the content of the programme

The theoretical model underpinning the Fens programme is based on a holistic model of human functioning where it is believed that the personality characteristics a person develops are a result of the interaction between genetic predisposition and experience. Experience impacts on both brain development and subsequent behaviours (Cozolino, 2002; Seigel, 2001). Brain development has been found to remain 'plastic' across the life span and there are indications that reparative therapeutic relationships based on the strategies needed for secure attachment relationships can bring about change (Cozolino, 2002). Thus, the treatment model on the unit aims to develop those kinds of reparative relationships both in formal therapeutic interventions and the development of a therapeutic milieu.

To reach criteria for treatment, a functional link must be established between a man's offending behaviour and his personality pathology. This means that unless the core personality pathology is addressed, at times of stress, it is highly likely such men will resort to previous maladaptive behaviours that led to offending. Thus the treatment model aims to address the aetiological factors that led to the development of the personality disorder in addition to working therapeutically with the dysfunctions of thinking, feeling, behaviour and interpersonal relationships; a constellation of coping strategies that a person develops as a response to formative experiences (see Saradjian, Murphy, & McVey, 2010).

Formulation

Following initial intake assessment is a formulation phase in which each person's life history is described and, using psychological theory, hypotheses made as to the development of his personality disorder(s) and the function of the offending behaviours for that individual. Those factors that increase risk for that individual become treatment targets and these treatment targets are subject to intervention throughout the programme. Each of these factors are worked on in both formal interventions (described below) and on a daily basis by officers on the landings and in workshops who observe and address the prisoners' behaviours. These daily observations are communicated at debriefing so there is constant monitoring of the prisoners' behaviours, cognitions, interpersonal processes and capacity for emotional regulation (see Evans & Watson, 2010).

Process of the treatment model: strategies to increase therapeutic potency

The aim is for staff to develop boundaried relationships with prisoners through which they can experience reparative interventions that will impact on all aspects of their functioning. To do so, staff employ the strategies known to develop good attachment relationships: collaborative, contingent communication; verbal sharing focusing on the internal experience of both people; repair of the relationship ruptures; connection of the past, present and future to create the autobiographical form of self-awareness; and emotional communication, to share joy and soothe distress (Seigal, 2001).

The focus of treatment is on establishing emotional intimacy and working to overcome obstacles to intimacy in the relationships with these prisoners. Magnavita (2000) argues that intimacy is the *currency* of corrective therapeutic experiences. Emotionally intimate relationships enable both people to experience warmth, tenderness and a heightened awareness of themselves (Meares, 2003) and to stay emotionally connected to that other party who thinks, feels and behaves differently. Three primary interactive strategies have been found essential in developing emotional intimacy: optimising affect, working with the logical perspective of clients and using explicit communication. These strategies have been found to optimise the potency of both individual and group therapies, enabling therapists to work effectively with even those clients who were labelled 'untreatable' (see Murphy & McVey, 2010). Prison officers on the unit also use these strategies, thus creating a *therapeutic milieu* that supports the formal therapeutic interventions (see Fox, 2010). Thus treatment within the unit aims at creating the quality of interpersonal relationships and remedial experiences that are necessary for people to attain the capacity to develop socially adaptive cognitive, emotional and behavioural responses. The aim is for all staff to develop appropriate relationships with prisoners through which prisoners can experience reparative interventions that will change all aspects of their functioning. Thus, interactions with staff upon the landing are considered as necessary for change as the more formal psychological interventions, and prisoners are able to access support via access to prison officers. Attention is also given to the prisoners' employment to ensure that their work is not maintaining their psychopathology. For example, obsessive-compulsive prisoners are not provided with employment as cleaners since this prevents them from acquiring new ways to manage their interpersonal relationships and emotions that they avoid by cleaning.

Content of treatment

The programme involves the following components (see Figure 1):

Individual therapy starts immediately when the prisoner enters treatment and continues throughout the five years of treatment. The focus is on the development of an emotionally intimate attachment relationship in which the aetiological factors of the personality disorder can be explored and addressed, working therapeutically at the level of affect. This allows the prisoner to experience empathy at the level of affective attunement (feeling with the person) rather than solely at the level of verbal cognitions. All aspects of the person's life are worked on – past, present and future – and all areas related to offending are thoroughly explored in depth and at both an emotional and a cognitive level.

Personality disorder awareness and human relationships groups are each primarily 25 sessions of psycho-education facilitated by therapists and prison officers to help prisoners understand their disorders including psychopathy and components of human relationships.

0 - 6 Months	6 - 12 months	12 - 18 months	18 - 24 months	24 - 30 months	30 - 36 months	36 - 42 months	42 - 48 months	48 - 54 months	54 - 60 months
3 sessions/week		4 sessions/week				5 sessions/week			
INDIVIDUAL THERAPY (focuses on the developmental roots of the personality disorder)									
COGNITIVE INTERPERSONAL GROUP THERAPY (addresses dysfunctional relationships)									
		SCHEMA FOCUSED THERAPY GROUP (addresses thinking errors)							
Group-based: PD Awareness (0 - 3 months) Human Relationships (4 – 6 months)				AFFECT FOCUSED THERAPY GROUP (addresses emotional dysregulation)		AFFECT REGULATION SKILLS TRAINING (individual)		ADDICTIVE BEHAVIOURS THERAPY GROUP	
								INTERPERSONAL RELATIONSHIPS THERAPY GROUP	
						OFFENCE FOCUSED THERAPY GROUP (summarises work on offending)			

Figure 1. Overview of Fens Unit cognitive interpersonal treatment programme.

Cognitive interpersonal group therapy is an unstructured psychotherapy group beginning soon after the start of treatment and continuing to the end of the programme. The group's focus is on the interpersonal relationships between all involved in the group, including the facilitators, making explicit the connection between the behaviours, cognitions and emotions within those relationships and the connection between relationships and offending. This group also aims to develop a sense of connection between group members, encourages prisoners to develop the capacity to challenge one another and enables them to be challenged about their distorted beliefs about themselves and others as well as finding ways to resolve conflict with others in a healthy manner. Finally, this group focuses on developing the prisoner's ability to take emotional responsibility for his maladaptive behaviours in both the past and the present and making positive changes to reduce such strategies.

Schema-focused therapy group lasts for approximately three years. Schemata are underlying beliefs developed through experience, which have a powerful (mostly unconscious) influence on behaviour. The group works with prisoners to identify the maladaptive schemata that govern their behaviour and the modes they employ when a schema is triggered. The focus is especially on the schema connected to their offending. Prisoners are enabled to identify how they maintain these schemata and to actively challenge each schema to change beliefs, associated emotions and ultimately behaviour.

Affect-focused therapy group runs for approximately 18 months and aims to facilitate the prisoner to recognise and regulate emotion in a healthy way, to recognise when he is diverting one emotion into another and to understand the role of emotional dysregulation in offending. It also aims to help prisoners experience and demonstrate empathy and compassion at the level of affect. Prisoners are encouraged to challenge their over-reliance upon one affective state and avoidance of other emotions. Emphasis is placed as much on those that use repression and dissociative strategies to deal with emotional arousal as on those whose high levels of emotional arousal are tangible. After the group work, there are 10 individualised affect regulation skills training sessions to consolidate the group work. These skills sessions are based on dialectical behaviour skills training (Linehan, 1993).

Offence-focused therapy group lasts for approximately two and half years and treats both violent and sexual offenders in the same group. This is because such offences are often inextricably linked and offenders have also often been convicted of both forms of offences. It also allows for the challenging of the construct of 'offence hierarchy' whereby prisoners can minimise the impact or shame of their offending by considering offending on a social hierarchy scale. This group is scheduled into the latter half of the programme, as people cannot have sincere compassions for their victim/victims unless they first develop compassion for themselves as victims. The group aims to draw together the work that has been done to date on each man's offending behaviour and explores offending patterns. Group work in particular facilitates healthy acceptance and management of the shame and guilt associated with their offending. It also enables them to become more aware of their own and each other's patterns of parallel offending processes (i.e., thoughts, emotions, interpersonal styles and behaviours that represent their offending without being illegal; Daffern, Jones, & Shine, 2011). Individuals' triggers to offending, needs met by offending and how the person learnt that offending could meet those needs are formulated and the group addresses the role of violent and sexual fantasy in offending. Individualised offending formulations are produced and a relapse prevention plan developed incorporating (1) acceptable ways of meeting needs that the person finds desirable and obtainable and (2) coping mechanisms that work fast and effectively.

Addictive behaviour-focused therapy group lasts for approximately 12 months and focuses on the use of dysfunctional strategies that prisoners use to manage affect that have become addictive. Addictive behaviours are seen as a maladaptive attempt to find a solution to a problem when a more healthy solution was unavailable. This group addresses all forms of addictive behaviours (not only substance abuse) and how craving a 'perceived need' masks the 'real need'. These behaviours may have a direct effect on their physiological system via prescribed or illicit drugs, alcohol, nicotine or an indirect effect through behaviours such as violence, self-harm, sexual behaviours, gambling, eating (in excess or starving) and thrill seeking behaviours. Prisoners are enabled to recognise the role these addictive behaviours have played and find alternative and more socially adaptive strategies for meeting their needs, which feed into individualised relapse prevention plans.

Interpersonal relationships therapy group also lasts for approximately 12 months and focuses on the sexual beliefs and attitudes held and how these impact on behaviour and relationships. The beneficial role of appropriate sexual fantasy and components of a healthy sexual relationship are also the focus of intense work. The programme aims to develop more healthy sexuality by managing patterns of sexual arousal, increasing healthy sexual interest and focusing on relapse prevention for those men who have sexually offended.

Overall, individual relapse prevention plans are devised with each prisoner. Plans are based on those factors identified in their individual clinical formulation that will increase and decrease their likelihood of offending behaviour.

The first cohort that completed treatment

Demographic data

There were 18 men in the first cohort that completed treatment. Nine of these men came to the unit directly from segregation units. All bar one of the men were Caucasian. The mean age of the men at the start of treatment was 39 (range 25–49 years). Fourteen of the men had previously been subject to therapeutic interventions, either prison service programmes or therapy within a high secure hospital. All had either dropped out of treatment or showed no treatment gain. The other four men had previously refused all intervention.

Offences and sentences

Most of the men began offending at a young age (mean age 16, range 10–22). Many described offending prior to the first recorded offence. They committed a diverse range of offences that increased in severity. Their index offences were predominantly murder, manslaughter, extremely violent assaults, rape or sexual assault. Most committed more than one such offence. One man was serving a determinate sentence and the rest were serving life sentences. The mean time each man had spent in prison prior to the start of treatment was 17 years (range 5–26 years).

Personality assessments

Personality pathology is measured using the IPDE and the PCL-R. The findings for this cohort are in Tables 1 and 2.

On average most men met probable diagnosis for three personality disorders. As expected almost all the men reached criteria for Antisocial Personality Disorder (ASPD). Of the two who did not do so, one had a probable diagnosis of ASPD and both scored particularly highly on the personality factors of the PCL-R. The other most common personality disorders were borderline, paranoid and narcissistic. This has also been the pattern for each subsequent cohort of men who reached criteria for treatment.

Results: post-treatment measures

Risk measures are used at the beginning of assessment and, staff allowing, the dynamic aspects of the measures are repeated at three years and at the end of therapy. The aim was to do repeat measures each year but staffing levels have prevented this being viable. The Risk Matrix 2000, being an actuarial static measure, is only carried out in assessment but the finding for this cohort are shown to indicate the level of risk that these men are deemed to pose (see Table 3).

Reduction in risk as measured by formal risk measurement tools

The VRS (Wong & Gordon, 1999–2003) was designed to assess the risk of violent recidivism for incarcerated offenders. The dynamic factors can be used to measure changes in risk level as a result of treatment. Dolan and Fulham (2007) researched the predictive validity of this tool. The results indicated that those with lower scores on dynamic factors were less likely to reoffend in the 12 months post-treatment. Table 4 shows a reduction in scores following treatment.

The HCR-20 is a violence risk assessment scheme intended for use in forensic settings. Its purpose is to structure clinical decisions about the likelihood of violent

Table 1. Range of personality disorders as assessed using IPDE ($n = 18$).

	Definite diagnosis	Probable diagnosis
Obsessive-compulsive	3	1
Dependant	2	0
Avoidant	4	1
Narcissistic	5	1
Histrionic	4	2
Borderline	10	3
Antisocial	16	1
Paranoid	9	3
Schizotypal	2	1
Schizoid	4	0

Table 2. Range of PCL-R scores ($n = 18$).

Range of PCL-R scores	21–23	24–26	27–29	30 +
Number of prisoners in that range	1	3	6	8

behaviour. The HCR-20 is a Structured Professional Judgement (SPJ) risk assessment instrument. Clinicians gather qualitative information about the person being assessed, guided by the HCR-20, and the results are used to make treatment decisions. Whilst the historical factors cannot change, the clinical and risk factors can change; the lower the score, the lower the risk of violence. In a prospective study of 41 long-term sentenced offenders in two high-security prisons, Belfrage, Fransson, and Strand (2000) found that the historical scale had little predictive validity for high-risk men, but that there was a high predictive value for the clinical and risk management scales. Table 5 indicates the change in HCR-20 scores over the period of treatment on the unit. All bar two men showed reduction in the clinical and risk scales on the HCR-20 over the period of treatment.

Attendance at therapy sessions

People with a diagnosis of personality disorder are difficult to sustain in therapy, particularly in an emotionally meaningful way. This is one of the characteristics that gave them the oft-quoted if debatable label, ‘untreatable’ (see Salekin, 2002). The prisoners who completed treatment, however, were highly engaged in therapy and their attendance exceeded what would be predicted for this complex and damaged client group, ranging from 95% for individual therapy to 81% [Offence Focused Therapy Group (OFTG)]. Indeed, six men had an attendance rate of over 95% in all interventions. There is an expectation but no compulsion to attend the sessions. As is characteristic of this client group, some of the men withdrew for periods of varying length and then re-engaged. Such ruptures in therapy are predictable and, for many may be necessary to achieve sustained change. It is hypothesised that the high attendance rate is, in part, attributable to the slow build-up of formal interventions. Developing an appropriate individual therapeutic relationship, can form the ‘secure base’ which supports engagement for the gradual introduction of therapeutic interventions; for the first year three per week then four per week to a maximum of five formal therapy sessions per week for the last two years (see Figure 1).

Change in behaviour

The interpersonal difficulties that these men have are more intensified within a prison environment. This can lead the men to belligerence, refusing orders and verbal and

Table 3. Risk as measured by risk matrix 2000 ($n = 18$).

	Violent	Sexual	Sexual and violent combined
Very high	7	5	6
High	10	6	7
Medium	0	2	0

Table 4. Change in Violence Risk Scale (Wong & Gordon, 1999–2003).

Score range on VRS	45–49	50–55	56–60	61–65	66–70
Number of prisoners in that range pre-treatment	0	4	2	8	4
Number of prisoners in that range post-treatment	2	5	5	6	0

physical aggression and violence. Several of the men have also previously taken hostages. The first cohort of men almost all came to the unit after being in repeated or constant segregation for several years. Once on the unit, using the relationship strategies previously described, the interpersonal behaviours of these men improved and the number of incidents dramatically reduced. It has been suggested that the reduction in number of adjudications can, in-part, be accounted for by a greater level of tolerance to verbal abuse. However, officers are constantly observing prisoners and will challenge even minor incidents of verbal aggression that may not be seen on other wings. Therefore, only serious incidents involving violence were included when comparing behaviour prior to coming onto the unit, whereas all refusals to follow a direct order, serious verbal aggression and all violence, against others or against property, are deemed incidents after coming onto the unit.

The available figures for incidents prior to coming onto the unit are almost certainly an underestimation due to unavailability of all records, whereas on the unit, every incident is recorded. Nevertheless, even counting those incidents that were previously recorded, it can be seen that there is a highly significant reduction in such incidents per year after transferring to the unit. Prior to coming onto the unit these prisoners were jointly responsible for a mean of at least 18.4 violent incidents (range 2–64) per person per year. After coming onto the unit and beginning treatment, the same prisoners were jointly responsible for a mean of 2.4 violent incidents per person per year; almost all occurred during the first two years of treatment. This, of course, represents a significant reduction in both the costs of suffering, to officers, other prisoners and the prisoners themselves and also a large financial saving in terms of cost for staff sickness and replacing property and compensation.

Post-treatment pathways

All men in the first cohort came into the unit from high-secure (Category A) prisons, many from segregation. After treatment, only three will remain in high-secure prisons these men being able to survive without recourse to segregation and able to engage in programmes from which they were previously excluded. One man has been

Table 5. Change in HCR-20.

Score on HCR-20	17–19	20–22	23–25	26–28	29–31	32–34	35+
Number of prisoners in that range pre-treatment	0	4	2	5	4	2	1
Number of prisoners in that range post-treatment	6	5	1	3	2	1	0

placed in hospital and one has been discharged into the community. The other men have been placed in Category B (medium secure) prisons. The man who was discharged spent most of his sentence in segregation prior to coming onto the unit. He has now lived safely in the community for over three years. There is no evidence that any of the men who completed therapy 18 months ago have regressed, indeed two men have already been re-categorised to Category C (low secure).

Discussion

The Fens Unit at HMP Whitemoor has worked, and continues to work, therapeutically with some of the most dangerous and problematic prisoners who have a diagnosis of severe personality disorder. These men, previously considered 'untreatable' and who regularly dropped out, or gave only surface compliance to interventions, have engaged well in treatment. There is also evidence from both current and continuing behaviour that the risks that they posed in prison have significantly reduced and, in addition, recognised risk measures show noteworthy reductions associated with a reduction in risk of re-offending.

Importantly, the quality of these men's lives has been greatly improved. The treatment has brought to many of these extremely troubled and troubling men, a better quality of life in that it has treated their psychological distress that previously they managed by self-medicating with drugs or equally addictive behaviours such as sex and violence.

It is the experience of the Fens Unit that the key issue in bringing about lasting change has been in ensuring treatment of the trauma and attachment disorders that are fundamental to the aetiology of personality disorders. Without addressing these issues, the prisoner is left vulnerable at times of stress to returning to using dysfunctional coping strategies, including re-offending. Interestingly, men with the highest scores on the PCL-R were found to have the most early and profound experiences of neglect. It has been hypothesised as to whether the behaviours that we have come to know as psychopathy are a survival response to very early severe neglect (see Saradjian et al., 2010). It is these men with whom it is the most difficult to form emotionally intimate attachment relationships; whilst they appear prepared to cope with aggression, they are terrified by closeness and intimacy. When each man was asked at the end of treatment what he believed was the most significant factor in bringing about change every man stated in some guise that it is the forming of these close relationships that is fundamental to bringing about change.

Financial saving by treating these prisoners

Despite the apparent high cost, the unit constitutes a considerable saving when measured against the cost to the public of keeping such prisoners in custody prior to their transfer to the unit. The cost of a place on the unit is cheaper than keeping a prisoner in segregation or in a Close Supervision Centre to which many of the men in this first cohort were destined had they not been placed on the unit. If these prisoners had not received treatment, the ongoing cost to the public would almost certainly have included costs of replacing broken or burnt property, cost of staff time due to recovery from injury and related stress, cost of regularly moving these prisoners as most prisons did not hold them for long periods. Thus, there are considerable savings made to public finance by treating these men on the unit and by reducing their risk so that post-treatment they can be held in lower levels of security.

Critiques of the DSPD service

There have been specific opponents of the DSPD services (e.g. Tyrer et al., 2010) but many of these critiques have been based on the early days of DSPD before any treatment services had been set-up. They are also based on hospital services as the authors have had little, if any, direct experience of DSPD services in the prisons.

It is, however, agreed that it is early days to draw significant conclusions about the success of the treatment, nevertheless early findings from the Fens Unit are very promising in terms of (1) risk reduction and improved mental health for the individual prisoners and (2) cost effectiveness.

References

Belfrage, H., Fransson, G., & Strand, S. (2000). Prediction of violence using the HCR-20: A prospective study in two maximum security correctional institutions. *The Journal of Forensic Psychiatry, 11*, 167–175. doi:10.1080/095851800362445

Blackburn, R. (1995). Psychopathy and personality disorder: Implications of interpersonal theory. *Issues in Criminological & Legal Psychology, 24*, 18–23.

Burns, T., Yiend, J., Fahy, T., Fitzpatrick, R., Rogers, R., Fazel, S., & Sinclair, J. (2011). Treatments for dangerous severe personality disorder (DSPD). *Journal of Forensic Psychiatry & Psychology.* Retrieved from http://www.rogerslab.org.uk/wp-content/uploads/downloads/2011/11/Treatments-for-dangerous-severe-personality-disorderDSPD.pdf

Cozolino, L. (2002). *The neuroscience of psychotherapy:Building and rebuilding the human brain.* New York, NY: Norton.

Daffern, M., Jones, L., & Shine, J. (2011). *Offence paralleling behaviour: Acase formulation approach to offender assessment and intervention.* Chichester, UK: Wiley, Blackwell.

Dolan, M., & Fullam, R. (2007). The validity of the Violence Risk Scale Version 2 (VRS-2) in a British forensic inpatient sample. *The Journal of Forensic Psychiatry and Psychology, 18*, 381–393. doi:10.1080/14789940701489390

Evans, J., & Watson, N. (2010). Assessing personality disorder within a formulation framework. In N. Murphy & D. McVey (Eds.), *Treating personality disorder: Creating robust services for people with complex mental health needs* (pp. 99–157). London: Routledge.

Fox, S. (2010). The role of the prison officer (dangerous and severe personality disorder in the prison system). In N. Murphy & D. McVey (Eds.), *Treating personality disorder: Creating robust services for people with complex mental health needs* (pp. 378–409). London: Routledge.

Hare, R. (2003). *The Hare psychopathy checklist-revised* (2nd ed.). Toronto: Multi-Health Systems.

Harris, A. J. R., Phenix, A., Hanson, R. K., & Thornton, D. (2003). *Static-99 coding rules.* Ottawa: Department of the Solicitor General of Canada.

Linehan, M. M. (1993). *Skills training manual for treating borderline personality disorder.* New York: Guilford.

Loranger, A. (1999). *International personality disorder examination manual: DSM-IV module.* Washington, DC: American Psychiatric Press.

Magnavita, J. (2000). *Relational therapy for personality disorders.* New York, NY: Wiley.

Meares, R. (2003). *Intimacy & alienation.* London: Routledge.

MOJ/DH (2002, 2007). *Dangerous and severe personality disorder (DSPD) high secure services for men: Planning & delivery guide.* Retrived from http://www.personalitydisorder.org.uk/news/wp-content/uploads/High_Secure_Services_for_Men.pdf

Murphy, N., & McVey, D. (2010). Fundamental treatment strategies for optimising interventions. In N. Murphy & D. McVey (Eds.), *Treating personality disorder: Creating robust services for people with complex mental health needs* (pp. 157–229). London: Routledge.

Salekin, R. T. (2002). Psychopathy and therapeutic pessimism. Clinical lore or clinical reality? *Clinical Psychology Review, 22*, 79–112. doi:10.1016/S0272-7358(01)00083-6

Saradjian, J., Murphy, N., & McVey, D. (2010). Delivering integrated treatment to people with personality disorder. In N. Murphy & D. McVey (Eds.), *Treating personality disorder: Creating robust services for people with complex mental health needs* (pp. 99–157). London: Routledge.

Seigal, D. (2001). Toward an interpersonal neurobiology of the developing mind. *Infant Mental Health Journal, 22*(1–2), 67–94. Retrieved from http://www.robsilvermancounseling.com/images/siegel-interpersonal-neurobiology.pdf

Thornton, D. (2002). Constructing and testing a framework for dynamic risk assessment. *Sexual Abuse: A Journal of Research and Treatment, 14*, 139–153.

Thornton, D. (2003). *Scoring guide for the Risk Matrix 2000* (4th version). Unpublished manuscript.

Tyrer, P., Duggan, C., Cooper, S., Crawford, M., Seivewright, H., Rutter, D., . . . Barrett, B. (2010). The successes and failures of the DSPD experiment: The assessment and management of severe personality disorder. *Medicine, Science and the Law, 50*, 95–99. doi:10.1258/msl.2010.010001

Webster, C. D., Douglas, K. S., Eaves, D., & Hart, S. D. (1997). *HCR-20 assessing risk for violence.* Burnaby BC, Canada: Simon Fraser University.

Wong, S., & Gordon, A. (1999–2003). *The violence risk scale.* Unpublished manuscript. Available from authors. Department of Psychology. University of Saskatchewan, Canada S7N 5A5 or Retrived from http://www.psynergy.ca

Resettle: a significant new step in an emerging pathway that manages risk and addresses need in high-risk personality disordered offenders on their release into the community

V. Baker, D. Johnson and S. Oluonye

Resettle, Merseyside, UK

This paper will describe an innovative UK service development, Resettle, which is designed to address the needs and risks of personality disordered offenders who are released into the community from prison and whose high risks of harm and re-offending are linked to their personality disorder (PD). All the cases worked with are subject to Multi-Agency Public Protection Arrangements (MAPPA). This non-residential, intensive community-based service is nationally funded jointly by the Department of Health and Ministry of Justice, originally as part of the Dangerous and Severe Personality Disorder (DSPD) programme for high-risk offenders. Resettle became operational in 2008. It is currently being independently evaluated via a randomised control trial that is due to complete in March 2013. Formal outcome data are, therefore, not yet available, however, the developing model of intervention based on experience and learning to date is described alongside the policy and service context for this area of work.

Introduction: the historical and policy context

These are changing times in England and Wales for personality disordered offenders and those who work with them. Over the past 10 years, there has been increasing recognition of the needs of those with personality disorder (PD) and the gaps in provision. The publication of the Department of Health (2003) document *Personality disorder: No longer a diagnosis of exclusion* placed individuals with PD firmly within the remit of mental health services from which they, particularly those who commit serious offences, had previously been largely excluded. This document was followed in 2009 by a 10-year plan for mental health provision (*New horizons*, Department of Health, 2009) which, along with the subsequent publication of *No health without mental health* (Department of Health, 2011) recognised the social costs of unaddressed mental health issues, including PD, and their potential links with social exclusion and offending: not the least of which is the negative impact of these factors on society, individuals and their families. These documents made a commitment to improving the mental health and well-being of the population including, explicitly, offenders.

A major driver within the Criminal Justice System (CJS) was the publication of the Bradley Report (2009), commissioned by the government to enquire into and make recommendations for improved provision within the CJS for those with mental health issues and learning disabilities. This significant and seminal report recognised the high number of prisoners with PD (e.g., 66% of the prison population compared to 5.3% of the general population; Singleton, Meltzer, Gatward, Coid, & Deasy, 1998), the majority of whose needs are not currently being assessed or met within mainstream prison provision, nor on release from custody. The Bradley Report called for improved recognition of the needs of offenders with PD within all agencies interfacing with, and within, the CJS, in order to support more sensitive and appropriate decisions in relation to processing and sentencing, including potential diversion into more appropriate services than are currently widely available.

Historically, in England and Wales, only a small proportion of those offenders with a PD either have been identified as having mental health needs or have received specialist input. It has been something of a lottery as to who is offered any mental health assessment and even more so as to who is assessed as having 'treatable' mental health issues that would enable them to access highly specialist treatment provision (Duggan, 2007). Those in the majority are not assessed and are deemed 'bad' rather than 'mad' and are thus dealt with within the CJS: ending up in either mainstream prison or probation. In these settings, the most complex cases are often not offered, or are unable to take up, specialist provision or interventions to address their health or criminogenic needs. This may be as a direct result of a PD diagnosis (which can be used as an exclusion criterion for some provision such as offending behaviour programmes) or because of behaviour that precludes or interferes with their engagement with the services on offer.

In order to attempt to address some of the identified gaps in provision for this population, in the late 1990s there was a significant development with the advent of the Dangerous and Severe Personality Disorder (DSPD) programme, the history and operationalisation of which has been reviewed previously in this journal (Hogue, Jones, Talkes, & Tennant, 2007). A number of services were funded to develop a range of treatment programmes as pilot projects which would subsequently be evaluated in order to further develop the evidence base as to 'what works' with this population. This open remit was a reflection of the wide acknowledgement that, whilst the existing literature about what works in addressing the needs and risks of offenders with PD was (and remains) thin, the historical view that PD could not be successfully treated needed to be superseded by an exploration of what works, for whom and under what circumstances (Day & Bryan, 2007).

Despite this investment, although perhaps not surprisingly given the challenges presented by this population and their heterogeneity, there has been no single 'breakthrough' in terms of a treatment model that works to treat the high-risk offender. Indeed, Ward and Maruna (2007) suggest that the question 'What Works?' may not be the right one, particularly with this most complex and risky group. They suggest instead that we ask 'What Helps?' in acknowledgement of the fact that, within the CJS, the medical model of 'treatment' is not the most appropriate. They call for a move towards a rehabilitation agenda within which all needs (biopsycho-social) are considered and addressed.

The criteria for entry to DSPD services have been that participants have a 'severe' PD, are deemed to present a high risk of harm and that there is a functional link between their PD and risk. Historically, the bulk of provision has been in high secure settings – prison and special hospitals – for which the exit criteria, though not clearly articulated, have been assumed to be that the problems associated with the PD and related risks are sufficiently reduced to allow for a step down in security level, leading eventually to release into the community. And yet, it is very difficult to truly determine risk when this cannot be fully tested out safely (i.e., in the community in which there is exposure to the triggers for previous offending such as drugs, relationship or accommodation instability; Duggan, 2007; Whittington & Logan, 2011). As a result, the experience to date from the DSPD pilots has been that it is difficult for those overseeing treatment to plan effectively for discharge into lower levels of security and, ultimately, movement back to community and mainstream services, particularly in the absence of adequate community provision to which to 'step down', leading to some support for the view that 'without a clear exit protocol . . . the whole system will inevitable silt up and thereby fail to meet the expectations of service provider and user alike' (Duggan, 2007, p. 114).

Duggan's suggested solution to this problem was that services be planned and developed from the 'bottom up', with the focus being on the return to the community within which there is scope for both need and risk to be fully assessed and addressed safely so long as there are appropriate services to move offenders on to. The Resettle project described here is one such service.

The investment in DSPD provision in the UK has recently been subject to review which has sought to address these issues and improve the targeting and spread of resources for this population, in recognition of the large number of prisoners with PD who would meet the DSPD criteria, yet who are not currently being catered for. Following a consultation period, a new strategy and implementation plan was endorsed in October 2011 which includes a requirement for health and criminal justice agencies to work together to identify those with PD at an early stage in their journey through the CJS. The intention of this new strategy is to better provide for their needs at all stages and to develop a more coherent, appropriate and joined up pathway in and out of services. The intention is that more services will be developed, including those which will allow for swifter progression out of high secure services and back into the community: a 'community to community' pathway. The aspiration is for all stages of the pathway to be psychologically informed and tailored more specifically to the needs of this population: for example, by attending to issues of engagement, the maintenance of safe and therapeutic relationships and the social context from which the offender originates and to which they will return. In this way the aspiration is for all needs – social, mental and physical health related as well as those relating directly to risk – to be met within multi-disciplinary and multi-agency services furnishing the pathway.

The Resettle project was established and has been operating within the principles, practices and aspirations outlined above and which have now been ratified by the DSPD review and aforementioned offender PD strategy, as a more effective way of working with this population. It, therefore, represents an important piece of innovation and learning which it is hoped will provide a foundation for the next steps in these exciting developments, once outcome data are available. This paper outlines progress to date on the development and delivery of the programme.

The target population

Consistent with other services funded under the DSPD programme, the entry criteria for Resettle are that the individual has a 'severe' PD, is deemed to present a high risk of harm and that there is a functional link between the PD and the risk. As a community project, it must also be the case that the risk can be safely managed in the community. Numbers in the project are small: we work with up to 15 men in the community at any one time, alongside work with men accepted into the project but currently in prison, either yet to be released or having been recalled. These small numbers allow for intensive and highly responsive intervention tailored to an assessment of the needs of the individual.

Given the high prevalence rates of PD in the offender population, referrals are accepted on the basis of a 'suspected' PD from Offender Managers (OMs), who have been given information about indicators to look out for (e.g., history of trauma, relationship instability, emotional dysregulation, substance misuse issues, etc.). High risk of harm is operationally defined as being subject to the Multi-Agency Public Protection Arrangements (MAPPA) and managed at level 2 or 3. MAPPA aims to identify those offenders who are at high risk of causing harm as a result of their potential to further offend, level 3 applying to the 'critical few', who present an exceptionally high risk and level 2 those cases where multiple agency involvement is required to manage their risk – which is deemed to be high or very high.

All referrals come from the OMs: Probation Officers with little or no specialist training in PD. This, alongside the fact that the majority of high-risk offenders will never have been assessed for PD or other mental health issues, presents a challenge in relation to the identification of suitable cases for referral into the project. A further challenge, albeit to the benefit of the project, is that Resettle is being evaluated via an randomised control trial (RCT) which, in order to allow for blind and random allocation into the control and treatment groups, requires that no contact is made by project staff with the referees prior to randomisation. Having sought the individual's consent to take part in the research, the researchers conduct an assessment of PD and other issues. It is only following randomisation into the Resettle group that we begin our contact with the offender, and our own assessment of their needs and risk, give them information about the project, gain their consent to take part and seek to develop a therapeutic alliance and their engagement. Once consent has been given, attendance at the project becomes a condition of their post-release licence. All cases at Resettle are subject to supervision on licence, and on release from custody this supervision is transferred from the OM to Resettle staff. Depending on risk issues, additional licence conditions may be applied: for example to reside as directed (including at a probation run hostel), not to have contact with a former victim, or to address substance misuse issues.

Thus, the high level of support, monitoring and supervision offered at Resettle should allow for an earlier release than would otherwise be possible under mainstream probation supervision. Whilst available as a 'step down' service from the high-secure DSPD provision, to date we have had only one case via this route. The majority have come from non-specialist prisons where needs associated with the PD have remained unrecognised and unaddressed. In the absence of specialist resources, difficulties have often been played out in a number of ways including, for example, highly conflictual relationships with prison officers. It is not uncommon for the men referred into the project to have spent extended periods in the segregation units of the prison estate.

All participants are male and are aged 18 or over. The mean age of participants in the programme is 33 years, with a range from 18 to 45. To date, 87.5% have self-defined as white British and 12.5% as black British. All have long and diverse offending histories and have served significant prison sentences. Many have spent the majority of their adult lives in prison. In relation to current index offences, 50% of these are for violence, 25% robbery and the remaining for sexual and drug offences. To date, there have been 30 men through the programme.

Mean psychopathy checklist screening version (PCL-SV) scores are equivalent to 23.0 on the *Psychopathy checklist-revised* (PCL-R: Hare, 2003), indicating a high level of interpersonal and social difficulties. An assessment of PD is done using the *International personality disorder examination* (IPDE; Loranger, 1999) as part of the RCT. The majority of our participants have personality traits consistent with meeting the diagnostic criteria for antisocial and borderline personality disorder. In addition, most have substance misuse issues of varying severity and some would meet the criteria for a learning disability. Many have spent the bulk of their adult lives in prison and have few, if any, sources of community or family support.

The service delivery model

The overall aim of Resettle is to improve participants' well-being, facilitate rehabilitation back into the community and to reduce the risk of further offending and thus protect the public from harm. A model of service delivery has been developed which both proactively assesses and manages risk in the community whilst also offering psychologically based interventions to address needs related to PD and other mental health, social and criminogenic needs. This is achieved through the creation of a therapeutic milieu. Here, interpersonal and practical skills can be developed, and targeted and individualised interventions (both group and individual) delivered. This milieu also provides a robust basis for proactive risk management strategies. Interventions are planned to address both the difficulties arising from the PD and those related to risk of further offending based on a detailed understanding of the individual and their needs (Livesley, 2007).

The core model within which targeted interventions are offered at Resettle is 'sociotherapy'. This has been successfully developed within the Van de Hoeven clinic in Holland, albeit within a different social and legislative context (De Boer-van Schaik & Derks, 2010). One of the distinguishing characteristics of this model is that the social context and relationships within it are seen as important mechanisms for learning about oneself and others and for motivating and facilitating change. Individuals are given as many opportunities as possible to take responsibility for their own lives and for contributing to the maintenance of a positive and safe social learning environment within which any issues, including those around risk, are addressed collaboratively with staff as far as is possible.

Although the level of contact is high – up to six days a week initially plus access to a 24-hour telephone helpline – Resettle is a non-residential service. There is a daily community meeting attended by both staff and participants at which all tasks required for the running of the project are shared. Tasks range from the complex such as chairing the morning community meeting, involvement in the selection of staff and greeting visitors to the more straightforward such as assisting with the planning and making of lunch or watering of plants. This wide range of tasks allows all participants to play a part whilst also allowing for progression, with support if needed, onto more complex and responsible tasks: 'learning by doing'. In this way participants are able to begin to develop a different experience of themselves: as, for example, competent, helpful and trustworthy. Twice a week there is an extended community meeting during which personal hopes, goals, achievements and setbacks are discussed in a group. Feedback is given and received by both staff and participants. The planning, preparation and sharing of communal activities such as lunch involves all in the community (i.e., staff and participants alike) and thus allows for social learning and mutual support and feedback. At Resettle, all social interactions are seen as opportunities for learning and for the development of humanising, productive and respectful relationships. Expectations of behaviour are explicit and responsibility for maintaining a safe and calm environment is shared.

This model is consistent with the emerging notion of an 'Enabling Environment' (Johnson & Haigh, 2011), a psychologically informed environment within which psychological and emotional needs are recognised and addressed. This attention to psychological processes is important not only for participants, but also for staff, in order to enable them to work positively and productively with this most demanding and complex of groups. Regular supervision for staff to support reflective practice is recognised as an essential component and this is prioritised at Resettle. A range of supervision is offered, including fortnightly group supervision for all clinical staff, provided by an external and psychodynamically trained supervisor; supervision of the three keyworkers allocated to each case, offered jointly by a psychologist and a senior probation officer; supervision of group facilitators by a psychologist; and individual supervision which focuses on personal and professional development needs. We have found this level of supervision to be essential in developing a thoughtful, resilient and truly integrated staff team who seek to understand and survive the challenges they face in their relationships with participants, and avoid being drawn into unhelpful interactions. Personal and professional differences and views are acknowledged and valued and seen as contributing in their diversity to a coherent whole team approach.

The aim is for interventions to be offered according to individual need, guided by a psychological formulation of the impact of past formative experiences on current functioning and needs. A menu of interventions is available within the project. These range from practical support, development of living skills (cooking, budgeting, etc.), activities relating to employment training and further education (ETE), to more formal therapeutic interventions such as lifeline work. The latter aims to help the individual to develop an understanding of how they have got to where they are: the choices they have made and the things that have happened to them alongside a sense of empowerment and personal efficacy about their future choices.

In addition a number of groups are offered, the overall aims of which include developing relationship and emotional literacy skills, tolerating and learning from others and the development of knowledge and life skills. Groups have included psycho-education about PD and mental health issues, social problem solving, good lives, healthy living, emotional self-management, mentalisation and mindfulness, victim awareness, masculinity and creativity.

The aim is for interventions to be offered within the project when an individual is first released from prison, with a view to the frequency of attendance reducing over time. Activities are included to support social integration and to increase capacity to access community-based interventions, which can then be sustained once attendance at the project comes to an end.

Because Resettle is non-residential, it is necessary to work closely with accommodation providers, including probation-approved premises, to find suitable accommodation placements both on release from prison and in the longer term. Project participants and accommodation providers are offered support in order to try to avoid these arrangements breaking down. These close working relationships and open communication channels also allow for additional monitoring of risk and need.

Risk management

In line with recommendations for best practice, risk management is done in collaboration with the offender as much as is possible and attends to risk to both self and others. Multiple views and perspectives are sought and valued and risk assessment and management is seen as an integral part of good quality care rather than something separate or specialised (NICE Clinical Guidance 77, 2009; Whittington & Logan, 2011). At Resettle, adhering to these recommendations is possible both as a result of the high level of contact we have with participants, and the multi-disciplinary nature of the staff team, which includes probation officers, mental health nurses, psychologists, specialist substance misuse workers and a police officer.

Every morning starts with a staff meeting at which summaries of behaviour in the project the previous day are discussed and any other dynamic information relevant to risk shared. The information discussed may relate, for example, to the individual's mood, practical or relationship issues within or outside the project, any police or victim concerns and feedback received from other services (e.g., accommodation providers). In addition, discussions are informed by feedback from the member of staff responsible for the out of hours crisis line the previous night. This telephone line is staffed by Resettle staff who are familiar with (and to) the participants and knowledgeable about their circumstances, needs and any risk issues. Our experience to date supports previous findings associated with the provision of Dialectical Behaviour Therapy: a crisis line can be very helpful for project participants in encouraging and supporting their self-management (Linehan, 1993).

The information outlined above is used alongside our in-depth knowledge of individuals and their history to further inform planned work in the short-term and to feed into longer-term sentence and intervention planning. Our knowledge and understanding about a participant is regularly and systematically reviewed during case formulation meetings, led by a psychologist and contributed to by the whole multi-disciplinary team. Sentence plans, their implementation and any obstacles relating for example to issues of engagement are discussed and reviewed during at least 12 weekly keyworker case supervision meetings, led by a psychologist and senior probation staff. These discussions are informed by input from the participants. Three keyworkers are allocated to each case with at least one being an offender manager and at least one from a health background. Other staff such as the police officer,

ETE specialist and support staff become involved with individual cases as indicated by risk and need.

Ward and Maruna (2007) emphasise the need to see risk as multi-facetted; any risk assessment should contain individual, social, physical situational and cultural components and should be contextually and temporally tagged. This view was supported by research undertaken by Craissati and Beech (2005) which suggested that situational triggers, psychological difficulties linked to PD and a history of childhood trauma were most associated with further offending on release in a group of sexual offenders. Given the high level of contact we have with participants at Resettle, we are in a strong position to make informed judgments about which situations and contexts are likely to trigger an increase in risk, the likelihood of this happening, as well as who may be at risk and under what circumstances. Such judgments about dynamic risk factors are based on a number of ongoing assessments. These include their capacity to self-manage within their relationships either with staff or their peers within or outside the project, detailed knowledge of their interests and activities outside of the project, any emerging relationships or stressors, any substance misuse or financial issues or any other factors which may relate to risk either directly of indirectly. We seek to address any increase in risk, for example, by offering a higher level of targeted support, restating expectations of behaviour (including the use of behavioural contracts), increasing monitoring and intervention for example in relation to escalating substance misuse. In addition to standard probation sanctions we have developed a system of Resettle warnings and sanctions – such as more frequent drug testing, change in curfew, invested attendance at the project – which can be helpful to support re-engagement and avoid recall.

Recalls and in reach work in prison

A key aim of all the risk assessment and management activities undertaken at Resettle is to ensure that risk can continue to be safely managed in the community and the risk of harm to others reduced, including to previous victims. If risk escalates to an unmanageable level we can and do initiate recall to prison. Whilst striving to avoid the need for recall, a proven track record of timely recall has helped the project to win the confidence of key stakeholders including the Parole Board who make decisions about future release. Nevertheless recalls can present a psychological challenge for the staff team whose level of commitment to working with this population in the community is high. Whole team clinical supervision provides an important space to discuss and process the emotional impact of this process, and other aspects of the work.

At the time of writing only 7 of 18 active cases had never had a period of recall during their time in the project (39%). Two cases currently in the community have been recalled four times during their time in the project; one is on his third re-release and two on a second re-release. Those familiar with the UK parole system will know that it is unusual under normal provision for parole to be granted after this number of apparent 'failures' on licence. However, both desistance research (McNeill & Weaver, 2010) and our clinical experience would suggest that progress with this population can be slow and non-linear. Indeed a period of recall, during which work is done to develop understanding and ownership of the reasons for the recall and a plan developed collaboratively for addressing those, maybe an important part of the offender journey towards reduction in and ultimately desistance from offending. Reports we receive from prisons support this view. For example, in a number of cases there has been a significant reduction in disruptive behaviour and an improvement in relationships with prison staff following time in the project, and this progress has been maintained or developed further even after repeat recalls. In one case an offender who had previously been deemed unmanageable by a particular prison was recalled to the same prison, and posed no management problems during the recall. For those recalled from the project, the average time in prison following first recall was 6 months and this reduced to 3.5 months on second recall.

Given this likelihood of recall as part of the pathway out of prison, we dedicate a significant level of resource to in reach work following recall. In addition, we work with men prior to first release in order to prepare them for the transition into the community. This commitment allows for the development and maintenance of an ongoing therapeutic alliance and a consistent therapeutic process. These are the 'non-specifics' of any therapeutic process, which are recognised in the psychotherapy literature and within NICE guidance for working with people with antisocial and borderline PD as the most important predictor of positive outcomes for those with a PD and an essential foundation for any other work to address personality functioning and stability (Livesley, 2007). We find the Good Lives Model (Ward & Maruna, 2007) helpful at this stage as a framework for setting small, achievable short-term goals as a first step towards longer-term goals and aspirations. These are then revisited throughout subsequent time in the project.

We do not see risk management activities, including any necessary recall to prison, as being in conflict with a therapeutic agenda. This stance is consistent with Livesley's (2003) model of different phases of treatment: the first two of which are safety and containment. This needs to be achieved before progression is possible onto later phases of treatment: targeting emotional regulation, working towards changes in cognitions and behaviour and, finally, interventions to assist the individual to develop a more integrated and stable sense of self. Our experience to date would support the view that the challenge with this population of personality disordered offenders is to keep them engaged in treatment for long enough to progress beyond crisis management and into these later phases of intervention and change.

Both offending and PD are associated with high levels of drop out from, and low engagement with, programmes of intervention. This phenomenon is of particular concern for a number of reasons. Firstly, the evidence base suggests that those people who start, but fail to complete, interventions, have higher recidivism rates that those who do not start the intervention (Howells & Day, 2007). Secondly, it is likely that the very difficulties that characterise PD: a poor sense of self-efficacy; little sense of hope for, or faith in the possibility of, positive change; a sense of failure; and a wish for others to provide solutions or to take the blame for difficulties; may be compounded by uncompleted interventions (Jones, 2007). It may also be the case that, for this population, precipitating a rupture in a working relationship may be psychologically protective in the short term: yet, ultimately, unhelpful for them (Safran, Crocker, McMain, & Murray, 1990). These men may typically have histories of unstable or abusive relationships within which they have not experienced adequate care or protection. This can lead to a difficulty in trusting others to be helpful and non-abusive. As a result, the individual may attempt to reject helpers as a way of guarding against anticipated rejection by them: or even anticipated abuse or exploitation. Cordess (2002) suggests that this process may also be precipitated by the anxiety and uncertainty that is produced from an unfamiliar glimmer of hope experienced as a result of therapeutic engagement. Hope may elicit feelings, for example, of guilt, unworthiness, mistrust or even anger towards the object of hope, leading to an unconscious wish to reject the help or helper.

A further factor for this group of men who have offended against others may be a wish to avoid remaining in a relationship within which the consequences of, and personal responsibility for, inappropriate or harmful behaviour have to be faced. These men may have histories of relationships with others who are initially idealised and then, when they do not live up to unrealistically high expectations, denigrated, with all the blame for difficulties, including the perpetrator's own abusive behaviour, attributed to the other. In this way the offender is able to split off, and not take responsibility for, his abusive offending behaviour. Maintaining a relationship in which such behaviours can be discussed, understood and addressed is, therefore, critical both for reducing future risk and for enabling a more integrated experience of self in which responsibility for past actions can be faced. This then allows for hope for the future to be fostered and a less polarised, more integrated and realistic view of themselves and others to be developed (NICE Clinical Guidance 77, 2009).

For all the reasons outlined above, surviving ruptures in the therapeutic relationship is crucial in order for any therapeutic process to remain helpful, and indeed in order to avoid unhelpful patterns being repeated. This is increasingly accepted within probation practice, encapsulated by McNeill and Weaver (2010, p. 4) in their work on overcoming offender desistance: 'because the journey is likely to be a long and difficult one . . . pit stops are likely to be necessary – checking direction, re-fuelling, maintaining or maybe repairing the relationship'.

Summary and conclusion

Given the nature and complexity of personality disordered offenders, and the multiple domains in which their difficulties manifest, successful interventions need to draw upon a range of theoretical models and to address difficulties and skills deficits across a range of contexts and modalities and over an extended period of time, withstanding crises and ruptures along the way (Hogue et al., 2007; Livesley, 2007). This view is echoed by the review of treatments for ASPD undertaken by NICE Clinical Guidance 77 (2009) which concludes that interventions need to be guided by an individualised understanding of offenders, and their needs and risks, and is likely to include both group and individual work.

A range of interventions is offered at Resettle, all underpinned and guided by a psychological formulation of the individual, which determines the pace and nature of these and any risk management decisions. At the foundation of these targeted interventions is the therapeutic environment, and the breadth, quality and ongoing nature of the therapeutic relationships within which they are delivered. For these to be established and maintained, staff need a high level of support and supervision; this is complex and demanding work given that the difficulties associated with PD are played out in relationships with others.

Offenders, and particularly those with the most complex needs and highest levels of risk, often do not seek help from traditional mental health-based therapeutic services. Instead, they are largely managed within the CJS, currently often without specialist support around their mental health and PD-related needs. In recognition of this gap, recent policy changes in England and Wales suggest the need for psychology and other health staff to work alongside those in the CJS in order to support and improve their work with offenders who would otherwise not access specialist provisions. The Resettle experience would suggest that this is not only possible but also highly desirable, allowing for a truly integrated model within which multiple needs relating to both risk and need can be monitored and met.

References

Cordess, C. (2002). Building and nurturing a therapeutic alliance with offenders. In M. McMurran (Ed.), *Motivating offenders to change: A guide to enhancing engagement in therapy* (pp. 75–86). Chichester, UK: Wiley.

Craissati, J., & Beech, A. (2005). Risk prediction and failure in a complete urban sample of sex offenders. *Journal of Forensic Psychiatry and Psychology, 16*, 24–40. doi:10.1080/14789940412331313287660

Day, A., & Bryan, J. (2007). Personality change and personality disorder: Some initial thoughts on the application of McAdams' triarchic model to the treatment of personality disorder. *Psychology, Crime & Law, 13*, 19–26. doi:10.1080/10683160600869692

De Boer-van Schaik, J., & Derks, F. (2010). The Van der Hoeven Clinic: A flexible and innovative forensic psychiatric hospital based on therapeutic community principles. In R. Shuker & E. Sullivan (Eds.), *Grendon and the emergence of forensic therapeutic communities: Developments in research and practice* (pp. 45–60). West Sussex, UK: Wiley-Blackwell.

Department of Health. (2003). *Personality disorder: No longer a diagnosis of exclusion – Policy implementation guidance for the development of services for people with personality disorder.* London: TSO.

Department of Health. (2009). *New horizons: A shared vision for mental health.* Retrieved from http://www.dh.gov.uk/en/Publicationsandstatistics/Publications/PublicationsPolicyAndGuidance/DH_109705

Department of Health. (2011). *No health without mental health: A cross-government mental health outcomes strategy.* Retrieved from http://www.dh.gov.uk/en/Publicationsandstatistics/Publications/PublicationsPolicyAndGuidance/DH_123766

Duggan, C. (2007). To move or not to move – That is the question! Some reflections on the transfer of DSPD patients in the face of uncertainty. *Psychology, Crime & Law, 13*, 113–121. doi:10.1080/10683160600869874

Hare, R. (2003). *The hare psychopathy checklist-revised* (2nd ed.). Toronto: Multi-Health Systems.

Hogue, T. E., Jones, L., Talkes, K., & Tennant, A. (2007). The peaks: A clinical service for those with dangerous and severe personality disorder. *Psychology, Crime & Law, 13*, 57–68. doi:10.1080/10683160600869791

Howells, K., & Day, A. (2007). Readiness for treatment in high risk offenders with personality disorders. *Psychology, Crime & Law, 13*, 47–56. doi:10.1080/10683160600869767

Johnson, R., & Haigh R. (2011). Social psychiatry and social policy for the 21st century: New concepts for new needs – the "enabling environments" initiative. *Mental Health and Social Inclusion, 15* (1), 17–23. doi:10.5042/mhsi.2011.0054

Jones, L. F. (2007). Iatrogenic interventions with personality disordered offenders. *Psychology, Crime & Law, 13*, 69–79. doi:10.1080/10683160600869809

Linehan, M. (1993). *Cognitive-behavioral treatment of borderline personality disorder.* New York: Guilford.

Livesley, W. J. (2003). Diagnostic dilemmas in the classification of personality disorder. In K. Phillips, M. First, & H. A. Pincus (Eds.), *Advancing DSM: Dilemmas in psychiatric diagnosis* (pp. 153–189). Washington, DC: American Psychiatric Association.

Livesley, W. J. (2007). The relevance of an integrated approach to the treatment of personality disordered offenders. *Psychology, Crime & Law, 13*, 27–46. doi:10.1080/10683160600869734

Loranger, A. (1999). *International personality disorder examination manual: DSM-IV module*. Washington, DC: American Psychiatric Press.

Lord Bradley. (2009). *The Bradley Report: Lord Bradley's review of people with mental health problems or learning disabilities in the criminal justice system*. Retrieved from http://www.dh.gov.uk/publications

McNeill, F., & Weaver, B. (2010). *Changing lives? Desistance research and offender management* (Report no. 03-2010). Scottish Centre for Crime and Justice Research. Retrieved from http://www.sccjr.ac.uk/pubs/Changing-Lives-Desistance-Research-and-Offender-Management/255

NICE Clinical Guidance 77. (2009). *NICE guidance for antisocial personality disorder: Treatment, management and prevention*. Retrieved from http://www.egap.evidence.nhs.uk/antisocial-personality-disorder-cg77

Safran J. D., Crocker, P., McMain, S., & Murray, P. (1990). Therapeutic alliance rupture as a therapy event for empirical investigation. *Psychotherapy: Theory, Research, Practice, Training*, *27*, 154–165. doi:10.1037/0033-3204.27.2.154

Singleton, N., Meltzer, H., Gatward, R., Coid, J., & Deasy, D. (1998). *Psychiatric morbidity among prisoners in England and Wales*. London, UK: Office for National Statistics.

Ward, T., & Maruna, S. (2007). *Rehabilitation*. Oxon, UK: Routledge.

Whittington, R., & Logan, C. (Eds.) (2011). *Self harm and violence: Towards best practicein managing risk in mental health services*. Chichester, UK: Wiley-Blackwell.

The Violence Reduction Programme: a treatment programme for violence-prone forensic clients

Stephen C.P. Wong[a,b,c] and Audrey Gordon[b,c]

[a]*Institute of Mental Health, University of Nottingham, Nottingham, UK;* [b]*Department of Psychology, University of Saskatchewan, Saskatoon, Canada;* [c]*Psynergy Consulting, Saskatoon, Canada*

The Violence Reduction Programme (VRP) is a treatment programme designed to reduce the risk of violence for individuals with antisocial and/or violent histories. The VRP was developed based on integrating the risk, need and responsivity (RNR) principles with contemporary clinical and offender rehabilitation techniques such as using cognitive-behavioural, relapse prevention and motivational interviewing approaches. Further the integration of risk assessment and treatment was achieved within the VRP by using the Violence Risk Scale, also developed based on RNR principles, to assess violence risk, criminogenic needs treatment responsivity and treatment changes. Unlike highly scripted programmes, treatment progress in the VRP is assessed based on achieving specific treatment goals rather than completing a specific number of sessions. As such, the VRP is sufficiently flexible to accommodate participants with quite diverse needs. Results of programme evaluations with long-term follow-up and the inclusion of control groups indicates that programme participation was linked to the reduction of general and violent reoffending. The programme also appears to be effective in treating offenders with significant psychopathic traits.

The World Health Organization has identified violence as a public health issue and has urged 'the health sector (in conjunction with the criminal justice sector)...to take a much more proactive role in violence prevention...' (Krug, Dahlberg, Mercy, Zwi, & Lozano, 2002, p. 246). While primary violence prevention can be undertaken through early intervention for at-risk families, the present paper focuses on tertiary prevention. We describe a treatment programme, the Violence Reduction Programme (VRP), for forensic clients with a history of violent behaviours.

Programme objectives

The VRP was developed to provide a theoretically based and empirically validated treatment programme to address explicitly the causes or associates of antisocial and violent behaviours in individuals in order to reduce the risk of similar behaviours occurring in the future. The programme strongly advocates the need to work collaboratively with programme participants, to assist them in identifying and mitigating criminogenic factors associated with violence such as antisocial beliefs and attitudes, substance use and criminal associates while enhancing their strengths by acquiring pro-social inter-personal, cognitive and vocational skills that are effective in reducing the frequency and intensity of future violence (Andrews & Bonta, 1994–2010; Gendreau, Little, & Goggin, 1996). Essential attributes of the VRP include assisting programme participants to work on their criminogenic needs and to enhance their strengths, while putting into practice what they learn in treatment in their day-to-day activities and interactions with others.

Development of the VRP

The forerunner of the VRP, the Aggressive Behavioural Control (ABC) Programme, was developed in the mid-1990s at the Regional Psychiatric Centre in Saskatoon, Canada, by a mental health team, including the first author, to provide an intensive treatment programme for high-risk and personality disordered offenders[1] in a correctional cum mental health setting. It then evolved based on research and developments in the field and contributions from both authors. The VRP, described herein, is based on an updated version of the ABC programme, lessons learned in the delivery of the ABC programme and recent developments in the field. As such, the VRP is different (and hopefully better!) in many respects from the ABC programme, which, due to a changing client profile,[2] is no longer being offered.

Theoretical underpinning of the VRP

For some of those with entrenched patterns of violence or aggression, behavioural intervention is one of the few options available for their rehabilitation. There is no universally accepted method of intervention to reduce violence and reoffending, in part, because of the heterogeneity of these individuals. No one approach would likely provide all the answers as 'one size doesn't fit all'. The VRP was developed by incorporating key principles of offender rehabilitation from a number of theoretical or evidence-based approaches discussed below.

The Psychology of Criminal Conduct (PCC) and the risk, need and responsivity principles

The PCC is an approach to understand the criminal behaviours of individuals through empirical research, the construction of rational explanatory systems, attending to individual differences and the application of this knowledge to reduce the human and social costs of crime (Andrews & Bonta, 1994–2010). The risk, need and responsivity (RNR) principles form part of a model of correctional assessment and rehabilitative programming derived from the PCC. The PCC and RNR provide the central conceptual underpinnings for the VRP. The extensive 'What Works' literature has indicated that RNR-based treatment approaches are generally more effective in reducing the risk of recidivism in adult and young offenders than non-RNR-based approaches (see Andrews, Bonta, & Wormith, 2010). The intensity of treatment should match the clients' risk level (risk principle). The individual's criminogenic needs linked to violence or criminality (e.g., criminal attitudes and peer groups) must be identified and targeted for treatment (need principle). Service delivery must accommodate the clients' idiosyncratic characteristics (e.g., their learning style, readiness for treatment and cultural background; the general and specific responsivity principles).

The VRP is a treatment regime designed for medium- to high-risk offenders (risk principle). The VRP uses the Violence Risk Scale (VRS; Lewis, Olver, & Wong, 2012; Wong & Gordon, 1999–2003, 2006; Wong & Parhar, 2011) to assess systematically the level of risk and criminogenic needs linked to violence – which become treatment targets (risk and need principles) – and also to assess the offender's readiness for change (responsivity principle). The VRP also recognises the heterogeneity of violence-prone offenders and acknowledges that one size does not fit all. For example, the VRP uses a goal-based rather than session-based approach in treatment delivery. Since everyone is not expected to progress at the same rate, those who complete certain programme requirements (intermediate goals) can progress while others may need more time.

Like RNR, the VRP also recognises and strongly supports focusing on the offender's strengths, which can be used together with risk reduction work in helping the offender progress towards building a repertoire of pro-social behaviours (see the Good Lives Model, Ward & Brown, 2004: also see Andrews, Bonta, & Wormith, 2010, for a comparison of the two models). For example, low scores on the VRS risk factors highlight the offender's strengths and both strengths and deficits are considered together in the assessment of treatment changes (also see the section *From talking the talk to walking the walk*).

Recently, the UK National Institute of Health & Clinical Excellence (*NICE*; 2009) published a set of guidelines for the treatment of antisocial personality disorder (APD) and psychopathy based on a review of the literature. The VRP treatment approaches are consistent with *NICE* recommendations such as focus on offence reduction work, adjusting treatment intensity to client's needs, providing staff support, training and so forth.

Multisystemic Therapy (MST)

MST is a social–ecological and evidence-based intervention to reduce antisocial behaviours among high-risk youths (see Henggeler, Schoenwald, Borduin, Rowland, & Cunningham, 1998). MST focuses on mobilising positive social influences such as family, school, home and community within the youth's natural environment, in order to affect change. A key feature of MST is to provide assistance to the youth '. . . 24 hours a day and seven days a week . . .' using these change agents (Henggeler et al., 1998, p. 43). The Assertive Community Treatment (ACT) approach for the seriously mentally ill (Marx, Test, & Stein, 1973; Stein & Santos, 1998) shares similarities with MST; both use a team approach and provide services 24 hours per day, and 7 days per week.

The VRP, like MST and ACT, also emphasises the importance of social influences in an offender's treatment environment. All VRP and allied staff (e.g., mental health staff, correctional officers, work supervisors, teachers, probation officers) are potential agents of change. Allied staff often have more day-to-day contact with the offenders than core treatment staff and can model pro-social behaviours and support skill generalisation to everyday situations. The VRP similarly emphasises the importance of all staff working collaboratively 24 hours a day, seven days a week to support VRP objectives.

Aggression Replacement Training (ART)

Skillstreaming – the learning of new skills through modelling, role-playing, performance feedback and generalisation training (Goldstein, 2004) – is useful for those with particular skill deficits in certain areas such as dealing with stress or group pressures. Similar to ART, VRP also uses modelling, role-playing, performance feedback and generalisation to address deficits linked to violence.

Relapse Prevention (RP)

RP, first applied in substance use and sex offender treatment, is about recognizing and anticipating precursors of problem behaviours so as to better manage lapses (minor infractions) when they invariably occur (Laws, 1998; Marlatt & Gordon, 1985) with the overall goal of preventing relapse (major infractions). In the VRP, behavioural logs and development of the offence cycle are used to identify internal (e.g., negative feelings, stress, etc.) or external (e.g., interpersonal conflicts) precursors of lapses so that an RP plan can be formulated to prevent lapses and relapses. Reducing the frequency and severity of relapses, a harm reduction approach, rather than complete desistance, is also implicit in the RP approach.

The Transtheoretical Model (TM) of change

The TM (Prochaska & DiClemente, 1984; Prochaska, DiClemente, & Norcross, 1992) is a widely used model to conceptualise behaviour change and improvement. The model proposes that in the change process, individuals progress from the less advanced to more advanced stages of change. The VRP also conceptualises changes similar to that of the TM and the VRS is used to operationalize and measure relevant risk reduction-related behavioural changes and progress through the stages as follows based on staff ratings rather than a questionnaire metric: pre-contemplation (denial of problems), contemplation (acknowledgement of problem but no relevant behavioural changes to reduce risk), preparation (inconsistent or very recent relevant behavioural changes), action (consistent demonstration of relevant behavioural changes) and maintenance (maintaining and generalising relevant behavioural changes). As offenders progress through the stages of change, there should be a corresponding reduction in violence risk (see Lewis et al., 2012; Wong & Gordon, 2006).

Motivational Interviewing (MI)

MI approaches are often used by staff to facilitate the engagement of resistant and unmotivated clients by attending to four key principles: expressing empathy, developing discrepancies, rolling with resistance and supporting self-efficacy (Miller & Rollnick, 2002). Many forensic clients, in particular those with personality disorders, are often resistant to treatment and have high dropout rates. The VRP strongly encourages the use of the MI approach to engage and motivate participants throughout the programme; MI is particularly beneficial during the early stages (i.e., Phase 1) of the VRP.

In sum, the VRP draws from all the above approaches to provide an integrated delivery of treatment to address violence-related criminogenic needs. The VRP also underscores the importance of maintaining treatment integrity; in essence how to make 'what works' work in the field by doing what we say we do. These issues are discussed in more detail in the following sections.

Target population

The VRP is designed to address the treatment needs of medium- to high-risk non-sexual violent offenders and forensic patients, including those with psychopathic traits or APD and those with mental health needs who are sufficiently stabilised to participate in the programme. With appropriate modifications, using a format more akin to MST but obviously directed towards adult rather than juvenile offenders, the VRP can be applied to offenders and forensic patients recently released to the community. Some sexual offenders with a history of non-sexual violence can also benefit from participating in the VRP.

Treatment of offenders with psychopathic traits

Many offenders with psychopathic traits are referred for treatment because of their violent behaviours. The Psychopathy Checklist-Revised (PCL-R; Hare, 2003) is the most widely used assessment tool for psychopathy and has two factors and four facets. Factor 1 (F1 and facets 1 and 2) assesses core affective and interpersonal personality traits, such as callousness, shallow affect and manipulativeness, and Factor 2 (F2 and facets 3 and 4) assesses dysfunctional lifestyle and antisocial behaviours such as irresponsibility and criminal versatility. Recent meta-analytic evidence (Yang, Wong, & Coid, 2010) has suggested that F2, the social deviancy factor can significantly predict violence but not so for F1, the affective and interpersonal factor. In reviewing the literature on the causal link between personality disorders and violence, Duggan and Howard (2009) also found no strong evidence to suggest such a link. There are, however, consistent evidence to suggest that F1 characteristics are closely linked to treatment interfering behaviours (e.g. see Wong, Gordon, Gu, Lewis, & Olver, 2012). The evidence suggests that in treating psychopathic offenders to reduce their risk of violence, one should focus on mitigating their violence-linked criminogenic needs as indicated by F2 while carefully managing their treatment interfering behaviours that are linked to F1 characteristics to maintain programme integrity. This conceptualization of the treatment of psychopathy is consistent with what the VRP advocates. For illustration, the criminogenic need profile of a sample of psychopaths was identified using the VRS and compared to that of a representative sample of moderate-to-high-risk male offenders (see Figure 1 and the section on *Treatment targets for violence-prone offenders* for additional discussions of Figure 1).

The VRP recognises the need to make special efforts to engage and motivate offenders with psychopathic traits in treatment as well as to better manage and to reduce treatment interfering behaviours. As discussed earlier, MI approaches ought to be used extensively throughout the programme especially at the early stages of treatment when engagement and the building of working alliances with psychopathic offenders are key and risk of dropout is high (see Wong, forthcoming, for further discussion on these issues).

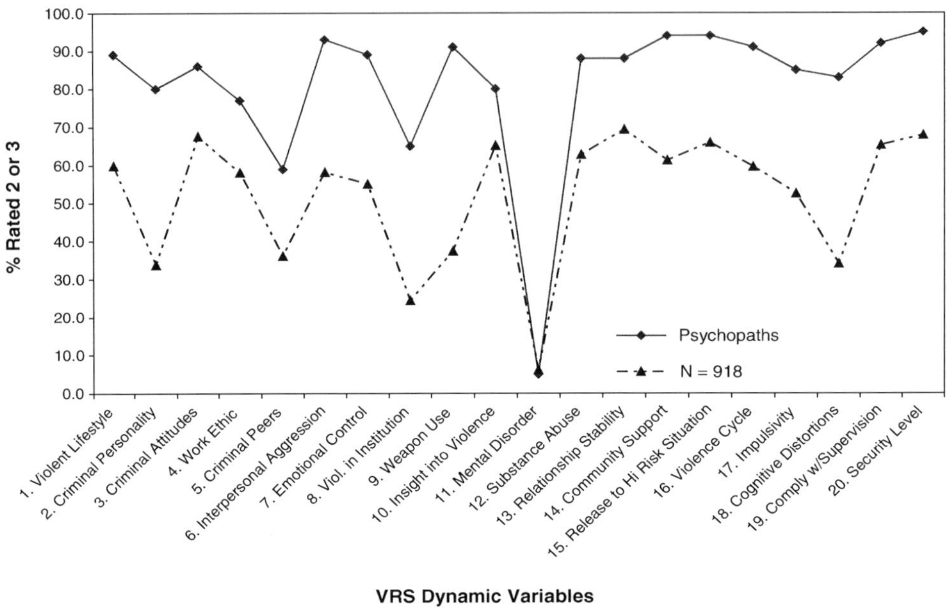

Figure 1. Dynamic risk profile of a general offender and a psychopathic sample assessed using the VRS.
Note: The comparison sample (n = 918) is a sample of federal offenders in Canada. Figure adapted from Wong and Gordon (2006).

Programme design, content and delivery

As described above, the programme uses cognitive-behavioural approaches and social learning principles within a relapse prevention model to assist offenders to make changes. More specifically, the VRP helps offenders identify and modify their cognitions, emotions and behaviours that influence and maintain violence and aggression. Lapses during the programme are used as opportunities to learn to interrupt their dysfunctional cognitive and behavioural patterns linked to violence. Within the VRP, specific cognitive skills (e.g., perception checking, thought stopping and cognitive restructuring), emotional regulation skills (e.g., time outs and stress management skills) and behavioural self-management skills (e.g., de-escalation techniques, effective communication and problem-solving skills) are provided in groups or individually as appropriate. Offenders are then provided with opportunities and strongly encouraged to practice and generalise these skills to their day-to-day functioning and interactions with staff and peers. Where appropriate, interventions that are currently being delivered and are consistent with VRP programme content, such as using Dialectical Behaviour Therapy (Linehan, Armstrong, Suarez, Allmon, & Heard, 1991) to address emotional dis-regulation problems, can be incorporated within the VRP to substitute for or expand on VRP teaching and learning.

Unlike some highly scripted programmes that are quite rigid and inflexible in their delivery, thus assuming that all participants are progressing at about the same rate, progression through the VRP depends on achieving specific goals and objectives, which are assessed based on structured observations using tools provided within the VRP programme manuals. The VRS can be used to assess pre- and post-treatment changes in risk level (see next section). The use of a goal-based design of treatment delivery and evaluation provides needed flexibility that is essential when working with a highly heterogeneous group of offenders.

The VRP is delivered in a three-phase format based on an incremental learning approach, that is, learning takes place in small steps and reinforcement of small incremental improvements is key. There are different tasks and objectives for both participants and programme deliverers in each of the three phases. Phase 1 (programme entry) focuses on enhancing the participant's understanding of the origins and maintenance of violence, assessment and identification of behavioural patterns and precursors of violence (i.e., identify treatment targets) and, of key importance, the development of working alliances. MI is particularly important in Phase 1, which may require considerable time investment for more resistant and unmotivated participants. Phase 2 focuses on the acquisition of relevant skills to effectively manage thoughts, feelings and behaviours associated with destructive patterns and cycles linked to violence. During Phase 2, with typically a better established working alliance with staff than in Phase 1, treatment is more closely focused on skills acquisition and the direct addressing of the offender's risk factors linked to violence and aggression, as well as the development of an offence cycle to examine in detail factors linked to criminality and violence. Phase 3 focuses on over-practice of skills learned in Phase 2, formulating a relapse prevention plan, and the generalisation of learned skills across situations to mitigate future risk of violence. Throughout the VRP, naturally occurring or planned activities are used to promote learning, practice and generalisation of all learning to address problems and challenges as they occur in day-to-day living and in future hypothetical high-risk situations: a very important point that will be further elaborated later. Both the *Facilitator's Manual* and the *Participant's Workbook* are organised into Phases 1–3 to provide a shared VRP pathway for both staff and participants. Activities in the three Phases build on one another and can overlap as the individual progresses through the programme.

Ideally, coming to the end of Phase 3 signals the completion of all aspects of the VRP but, in practice, the offender may need to leave the programme earlier because of various programme or non-programme-related reasons. Such arrangements are appropriate if the receiving agencies (such as lower security institutions or community service agencies) can continue with providing necessary services. There can be a myriad of reasons for treatment termination, a very important issue that, unfortunately, cannot be addressed in detail here because of space limitation (but see Beyko & Wong, 2005; Olver & Wong, 2011; Olver, Stockdale, & Wormith, 2011). The VRP can be run as a closed programme with all intakes admitted at about the same time. However, it is sufficiently flexible to accommodate some participants taking short 'breaks' from the programme or being re-admitted for a 'refresher' that can be fast-tracked through the programme or even admission at various points in the programme.

Assessment of pre-treatment risk, identification of treatment targets and post-treatment changes in risk

The VRS, a valid and reliable dynamic risk assessment tool (VRS; Wong & Gordon, 1999–2003, 2006), is an integral part of the VRP. The VRS, which has 6 static and 20 dynamic risk predictors, is used to assess the risk of violence (risk principle), treatment targets (need principle), treatment readiness (responsivity principle) and to measure risk change; recognising risk is dynamic. Staff ratings of the dynamic predictors (0, 1, 2, 3) indicate the relative strength of association between the predictor (e.g., as criminal attitudes) and violence with ratings of 2 and 3 indicating a moderate or strong association, respectively, and therefore, relevant treatment targets. The individual's readiness for treatment for each treatment target is then assessed by staff using a modified version of the Stage of Change Model (Prochaska et al., 1992) to establish a pre-treatment baseline measure (e.g., at the contemplation stage pre-treatment). At the conclusion of treatment, the Stage of Change for each treatment target is re-assessed (e.g., now at the action stage post-treatment). Risk reduction is indicated by progression through the stages of change (e.g., from contemplation to action) and is translated into a quantitative reduction in violence risk. The pre-treatment stage of change can be used to guide the selection of appropriate intervention strategies matched to the individual's ability and the level of treatment readiness: the post-treatment risk level and the stage of change can also be used to guide post-treatment risk management (Wong & Gordon, 2004).

Treatment targets for violence-prone offenders

The profiles of treatment targets of 918 medium- to high-risk non-sexual Canadian federal offenders[3] and 65 psychopaths (PCL-R > 25) assessed using VRS dynamic predictors (shown on the *x*-axis) are presented in Figure 1. The two profiles show the percentages of offenders in the two samples with each of the treatment targets (dynamic predictors rated 2 or 3) in question. Other than the mental disorder predictor,[4] in the general offender sample, there is a 30–65% prevalence of the treatment targets identified by the VRS. As expected, the psychopathic sample has a much higher prevalence of the same treatment targets. Obviously, not all potential treatment targets can be identified by the VRS; additional clinical investigations should be undertaken as required.

Case formulation

The main objective of case formulation is to abstract key features of a case to guide the selection of the most effective treatment for each individual (Haynes & O'Brien, 2000; Sturmey, 2010). However, research on forensic case formulation is very limited and reliability studies of non-forensic case formulation are also inconsistent (Sturmey, 2010). Until forensic case formulations are better researched, dynamic risk assessment tools such as the VRS can be used as an aid to systematically identify treatment targets. For offenders with complex or highly unusual problems, that is, the outliers of the general offender population, general clinical case formulation guided by a dynamic risk assessment tool may assist in identifying treatment needs.

From talking the talk to walking the walk

The breaking of behavioural patterns associated with aggression and violence are highlighted and addressed throughout the programme. The incremental learning principle of strengthening small improvements must take place both inside and outside the formal treatment sessions. In essence, a central VRP principle is that ideally, treatment should take place 24 hours a day and 7 days a week and not just within formal treatment groups or individual therapy sessions. Observations of the behaviours of offenders in informal day-to-day contacts and interactions with all staff and peers are crucial in assessing the veracity of apparent behavioural changes as allied staff often have more opportunities to observe offenders relative to core treatment staff. As such, the VRP recognises the important roles of both the clinical/treatment and the allied staff in monitoring and addressing the offender's negative behaviours and in facilitating and rewarding positive behaviours. It is recognised that staff have their prescribed roles and are different in their training and experience. Nonetheless, all staff should work as a coherent team towards a common goal of violence reduction rather than in silos, as the latter can lead to giving offenders contradictory messages, staff splitting, or worse, undermining one another's efforts.

Offence Analogue Behaviours (OABs) are defined as offenders' negative offence-linked behaviours such as aggression and intimidation, while Offence Replacement Behaviours (ORBs) are the positive, violence-reducing behaviours such as assertiveness and conflict resolution skills (see Gordon & Wong, 2010). An OAB and ORB Guide has been developed to assist staff in monitoring and addressing these behaviours. The Guide helps staff identify, address and document the offender's everyday OABs that are linked to criminogenic factors identified by the VRS. Similarly, ORBs are identified, reinforced and documented. The gradual replacement of the 'bad' by the 'good' behaviours should be a valid and objective indication of violence reduction related treatment improvements.

Delivery format

The VRP is primarily designed for delivery in a group format supplemented by individual work when necessary. However, the VRP can also be delivered in a one-on-one format to participants who are not yet amenable to group programming, such as those who are behaviourally unstable, rejected by the group, held in isolation, have intermittent acute mental health problems or are cognitively compromised: all of which are specific responsivity issues. In line with the responsivity principle, the VRP is flexible enough to accommodate these issues as it is organised in a goal oriented rather than a session-oriented format: in short, many roads can lead to Rome.

In sum, the VRP is designed to meet the treatment needs of a heterogeneous group of violence-prone forensic clients and can be implemented in a variety of mental health and prison settings. Individual or group delivery length is based on client responsivity. For example, individuals with attentional or cognitive deficits may require shorter but higher frequency sessions.

Staff training

A treatment programme is only as good as the programme staff! Both initial and in-service staff training is vital to implement and sustain the VRP. The VRP was developed based on psychological principles, thus, to maintain programme integrity, that is, doing what we say we do, it is best led and supervised by an appropriately trained and experienced mental health professional, such as a psychologist. It is desirable to have programme staff who are human service oriented and informed about clinical or psychological principles. Multidisciplinary treatment teams that can work collaboratively towards VRP objectives can greatly enrich the programme.

Careful staff selection based on local needs and availability is key; these issues are discussed in more details in the VRP *Programme Management Manual*. Where feasible, a 24-hour-a-day and 7-days-a-week treatment approach is highly desirable. VRP staff training entails training both core clinical/treatment staff as well as allied staff (as much as possible), who will likely have significant meaningful contacts with the treatment participants. The type of training is contingent on the role and type of contacts staff are expected to have with programme participants, ranging from brief VRP awareness training to more intensive facilitator training. Other than programme content-specific training, the use of social learning approaches such as the modelling of pro-social behaviours, the use of reward and punishment contingencies and MI approaches are important. Further realignment of the VRP to local needs, resources and organisational structures, is best accomplished through additional consultation and staff training undertakings prior to the formal implementation of the programme. As the saying goes: prepare, prepare, prepare!

VRP implementation

The VRP is designed such that the programme can be implemented in a variety of settings. Effective implementation depends on a thorough appraisal of the treatment environment, target population, resources, staffing, existing treatment interventions and so forth that may be unique to the setting. A *VRP Implementation Checklist* has been developed to guide implementation, along with a series of *Programme manuals and materials*; see Appendix 1. For example, programme duration and the amount of group vs. individual work would vary with staffing levels. The overall goal is to ensure core programme integrity is maintained (see Livesley, 2007; Wong, forthcoming).

Length of programme

The VRP is not organised in a highly scripted format with a defined number of 'lessons' to be covered within a fixed time period because of participants' responsivity issues. It is also recognised that different organisations may have different treatment objectives that may require varying comprehensiveness or intensity of treatment. Programme length is also contingent on staffing levels, operational or security issues that may limit access to the programme, as well as the need to attend to certain specific programme objectives such as facilitating community release or reduced security. These are participant and site-specific variables that are best dealt with on a case-by-case basis. Thus, it is difficult to specify a priori the programme length. Past research has shown that significant reductions in violent reoffending and institutional misconduct can be demonstrated after participating in a programme of about eight months in duration (see section on VRP outcome evaluations).

A synopsis of outcome evaluations of VRP

Most outcome research was carried out based on the ABC programme because of its more extensive history but should be generalizable to the VRP given the overall similarity of the two programmes and target population. A sample of 31 offenders who were residing in a super-maximum security prison because they had committed very serious violent offences such as murders and hostage taking during their incarceration were admitted to the ABC Programme for treatment, with the aim of reintegrating them to a regular lower security prison post-treatment. Over 80% of the offenders were reintegrated successfully into a low security facility without returning to the super-maximum institutions within a follow-up period of over 20 months. They also have lower institutional offence rates post-reintegration compared to pre-reintegration (Wong et al., 2005).

A number of officially identified gang members who had committed serious offences were treated in the ABC programme. A case matched control design was used to compare recidivism in the community of a treated gang group and matched controls with little or no treatment after about 24 months follow-up. Members of both groups (n =40, respectively) were about 24 years of age, with about 20 criminal convictions pre-treatment, of comparable recidivism risk (assessed with General Statistical Information on Recidivism tool; Bonta, Harman, Han, & Cormier, 1996) and were serving, on average, six-year sentences. After being in treatment for about eight months, the treated gang group had significantly lower incidence of court adjudicated violent and non-violent recidivism, significantly fewer major institutional misconducts and, if they had recidivated violently, committed significantly less serious violent offences than the matched controls (Di Placido, Simon, Witte, Gu, & Wong, 2006).

A follow-up study extended the above findings by assessing the impact of treatment on institutional security placements, segregation time and institutional misconduct of gang-affiliated offenders. Gang members (n =68) who completed treatment were compared to a matched group (n =56) with the same demographic and criminological characteristics but had received significantly less treatment. Members of both groups had extensive criminal, violent and incarceration histories with no significant difference between groups. Almost 90% of both groups were also diagnosed with substance use disorder and similarly about 75% with APD. While there were minimal differences in their security placement in the three years pre-treatment, in the three years post-treatment, treatment completers were housed in lower security levels, received less segregation time and had less serious institutional offences than non-completers (Brulotte, Di Placido, Gu, Witte, & Wong, in preparation).

In another treatment outcome study (Wong et al., 2012), 34 treated psychopaths were matched with 34 untreated controls (mean PCL-R ratings of 28.6 and 28.0, respectively). The two groups were matched on race, age, PCL-R, F1 and F2 scores and followed up in the community (both for a mean of 7.4 years). All were high-risk violence-prone offenders with significant psychopathic traits. On follow-up, the treated and matched group were equivalent in the number of violent, and non-violent re-convictions and sentencing dates, as well as time to first re-conviction: although the trends were in the expected direction, that is, better performance for the treated compared to the match group. However, compared to the untreated group, the treated group had a significantly less serious re-offences as indicated by the significantly shorter aggregated sentences they received (27.7 vs. 56.4 months, respectively, p <.05). Sentence length has been shown to be a reasonable proxy for the level of violence or severity of offending (see Di Placido et al., 2006). Treatment appeared to reduce the degree of violence or severity of reoffending: a harm reduction effect for these high risk psychopathic offenders. For the highly psychopathic offenders, eight months of treatment is probably not long enough to produce the optimal outcome. Despite the less than optimal treatment 'dosage', the results support the contention that risk reduction programmes such as the VRP can reduce violent recidivism, even among particularly high-risk individuals and that treatment definitely did not make them worse (see Rice, Harris, & Comier, 1992).

A sample of 150 male mostly high-risk violent offenders with significant psychopathic traits (mean VRS score = 60; about 1 *sd* above the normative sample mean; mean PCL-R = 26, 64% > 25) was treated in the ABC programme for about eight months. They were released and followed up for approximately five years in the community to determine if risk reductions observed in the treatment programme were linked to reduction in violent recidivism. The amount of treatment improvement as indicated by risk reduction assessed with the VRS were linked to the amount of reduction in violence recidivism in the community (Lewis et al., 2012; Olver, Lewis, & Wong, 2012). Such changes were still evident after controlling for psychopathy and recidivism risk.

The VRP has been implemented in a number of prison and forensic mental health hospitals in the UK. An independent evaluation of the efficacy of a small pilot VRP ($n = 4$) conducted at a super-maximum prison was commissioned and reported (see Fylan & Clarke, 2006). All four prisoners who participated in the VRP were extremely difficult to manage offenders who had to be kept in isolation as they had committed very violent acts while incarcerated, such as homicide involving prison officers or fellow inmates. The small sample size precluded quantitative analyses of the data. However, the authors of the report did note prisoners' behaviour showed marked improvement based on staff observations – violent behaviour had decreased and inter-personal skills had improved – and noted that such observations appeared to have been maintained in less supportive and non-treatment oriented environments. Obviously, this can only be deemed a pilot programme with such a small sample size.

Summary

The VRP is designed to provide treatment to forensic service users to reduce the risk of violent recidivism and institutional misconduct. The VRP was designed by integrating a number of different theoretically derived and evidence-based approaches in offender rehabilitation, together with the lessons learnt by the authors in its development and implementation, into a (hopefully) coherent and understandable whole. Outcome evaluations indicate that treatment participants show reductions in violent recidivism and institutional misconduct even when offenders have significant psychopathic personality traits. By helping these violence-prone individuals manage their lives better, there should be a corresponding improvement in their general well-being and in their impact on people they come into contact with, not to mention significant savings in management and incarceration costs. It is our hope that treatment programmes such as the VRP can be accepted and implemented by correctional authorities as being just as essential for good correctional practice as is good security.

Future directions

A randomised controlled trial of the VRP is highly desirable but, understandably, difficult and costly to conduct. A second line of inquiry is to identify the necessary and sufficient components of the VRP for the different client groups with a view to delivering only what is necessary to effect positive change and violence reduction. Under development is a short version of the VRP (the VRP-SV) appropriate for moderate risk offenders. It is less intensive and requires less time to complete, and is therefore likely applicable to a wider range of offenders than the VRP full version.

Research since the 1970s has provided a reasonably good empirical understanding of the risk and need domains of the RNR. No doubt more research is required but, at least, there is more clarity as to what and where to look. The responsivity prong of the triad with respect to offenders and staff and the many obstacles in maintaining programme integrity are, to us, the main challenges for the future. More qualitative and quantitative research is needed to unravel these issues.

Notes

1. The term offender is used generically to indicate individuals held under the criminal justice or forensic mental health jurisdictions.
2. Seriously mentally disordered or learning disabled offenders, rather than personality disorder offenders, have been given priority to treatment at the Regional Psychiatric Centre.
3. They have a mean 2.58 violent and 15.59 non-violent convictions over a 10-year criminal career.
4. This sample consisted of very few offenders with major mental illnesses that are associated with violence and thus the low endorsement of the Mental Disorder item.

References

Andrews, D. A., & Bonta, J. (1994–2010). *The psychology of criminal conduct* (1st to 5th ed.). Cincinnati, OH: Anderson Publishing.

Andrews, D. A., Bonta, J., & Wormith, J. S. (2010). Does adding the Good Lives Model contribute to crime prevention. *Criminal Justice & Behavior, 38*(7), 735–755.doi:10.1177/0093854811406356

Beyko, M., & Wong, S. C. P. (2005). Predictors of treatment attrition as indicators for programme improvement not offender shortcomings: A study of sex offender treatment attrition. *Sexual Abuse: A Journal of Research and Treatment, 17*, 375–389. doi:10.1177/107906320501700403

Bonta, J., Harman, W. G., Han, R. G., & Cormier, R. B. (1996). The prediction of recidivism among federally sentenced offenders: A re-validation of the SIR scale. *Canadian Journal of Criminology, 38*, 61–79. Retrieved from http://search.ebscohost.com/login.aspx?direct=true&db=a9h&AN=9601316043&site=ehost-live

Brulotte, J., Di Placido, C., Gu, D., Witte T., & Wong, S. C. P. (in preparation). Treatment can reduce security requirements for gang members.

Di Placido, C., Simon, T., Witte, T., Gu, D., & Wong, S. C. P. (2006). Treatment of gang members can reduce recidivism and institutional misconduct. *Law and Human Behavior, 30*(1), 93–114. doi:10.1007/s10979-006-9003-6

Duggan, C., & Howard, R. (2009). The 'functional link' between personality disorder and violence: A critical appraisal. In M. McMurran & R. Howard (Eds.), *Personality, personality disorder and violence* (pp. 19–37). Chichester: Wiley-Blackwell.

Fylan, F., & Clarke, J. (2006). *Violence reduction strategy: Final report*. Unpublished internal report.

Gendreau, P., Little, T., & Goggin, C. (1996). A meta-analysis of the predictors of adult offender recidivism: What works! *Criminology, 34*, 575–607. doi:10.1111/j.1745-9125.1996.tb01220.x

Goldstein, A. P. (2004). Skillstreaming: the behavioural component. In A. P. Goldstein, R. Nensen, & B. Daleflod (Eds.), *New perspectives on aggression replacement training* (pp. 21–29). Chichester: Wiley.

Gordon, A. (2009). *Violence reduction program: Supplementary facilitator's manual.* Retrieved from http://www.psynergy.ca/.

Gordon, A., & Wong, S. C. P. (1999–2009). *Violence reduction program: Facilitator's manual.* Retrieved from http://www.psynergy.ca/.

Gordon, A., & Wong, S. C. P. (2010). Offence analogue behaviours as indicator of criminogenic need and treatment progress in custodial settings. In M. Daffern, L. Jones, & J. Shine (Eds.), *Offence paralleling behaviour: An individualized approach to offender assessment and treatment* (pp. 171–183). Chichester: Wiley.

Gordon, A., & Wong, S. C. P. (2011). *Offence Analogue Behaviour (OAB) and Offence Replacement Behaviour (ORB) Rating Guide.* Retrieved from http://www.psynergy.ca/

Hare, R. D. (2003). *The Hare psychopathy checklist-revised* (2nd ed.). Toronto, ON: Multi-Health Systems, Inc.

Haynes, S. N., & O'Brien, W. H. (2000). *Principles and practice of behavioural assessment.* New York: Plenum.

Henggeler, S. W., Schoenwald, S. K., Borduin, C. M., Rowland, M. D., & Cunningham, P. B. (1998). *Multisystemic treatment of antisocial behaviour in children and adolescents.* New York, NY: Guildford.

Krug, E. G., Dahlberg, L. L., Mercy, J. A., Zwi, A. B., & Lozano, R. (2002). *World report on violence and health.* Geneva: World Health Organization.

Laws, R. (1998). *Relapse prevention with sex offenders.* New York, NY: Guildford.

Lewis, K., Olver, M., & Wong, S. C. P. (2012). The Violence Risk Scale: Predictive validity and linking changes in risk with violent recidivism in a sample of high risk offenders with psychopathic traits. *Assessment.* Published online May 3, 2012. doi:10.1177/1073191112441242

Linehan, M. M., Armstrong, H. E., Suarez, A., Allmon, D., & Heard, H. L. (1991). Cognitive-behavioural treatment of chronically parasuicidal borderline patients. *Archives of General Psychiatry, 48*, 1060–1064. doi:10.1001/archpsyc.1991.01810360024003

Livesley, J. (2007). The relevance of an integrated approach to the treatment of personality disordered offenders. *Psychology, Crime & Law, 13*(1), 27–46. doi:10.1080/10683160600869734

Marlatt, G. A., & Gordon, J. R. (1985). *Relapse prevention: Maintenance and strategies in the treatment of addictive behaviours.* New York, NY: Guildford.

Marx, A. J., Test, M. A., & Stein, L. I. (1973). Extrahospital management of severe mental illness, feasibility and effects of social functioning. *Archives of General Psychiatry, 29*, 505–511. doi:10.1001/archpsyc.1973.04200040051009

Miller, W. R., & Rollnick, S. (2002). *Motivational interviewing.* New York, NY: Guildford.

National Institute of Clinical Excellence. (2009). *Antisocial personality disorder: Treatment, management and prevention.* London: National Collaborating Centre for Mental Health.

Olver, M., Lewis, K. & Wong, S. C. P. (2012). Risk reduction treatment of high-risk psychopathic offenders: The relationship of psychopathy and treatment change to violent recidivism. *Personality Disorder: Theory, Research and Treatment.* doi:10.1037/a0029769

Olver, M. E., Stockdale, K. C., & Wormith, J. S. (2011). A meta-analysis of predictors of offender treatment attrition and its relationship to recidivism. *Journal of Consulting and Clinical Psychology, 79*, 6–21. doi:10.1037/a0022200

Olver, M., & Wong, S. C. P. (2011). Predictors of sex offender treatment dropout: Psychopathy, sex offender risk, and responsivity implications. *Psychology, Crime & Law, 17* (5), 457–471. doi:10.1080/10683160903318876

Prochaska, J. O., & DiClemente, C. C. (1984). *The transtheoretical approach: Crossing traditional boundaries of therapy.* Homewood, IL: Dow Jones-Irwin.

Prochaska, J. O., DiClemente, C. C., & Norcross, J. C. (1992). In search of how people change: Applications to addictive behaviours. *American Psychologist, 47*, 1102–1114. doi:10.1037/0003-066X.47.9.1102

Rice, M. E., Harris, G. T., & Cormier, C. A. (1992). An evaluation of a maximum security therapeutic community for psychopaths and other mentally disordered offenders. *Law and Human Behavior, 16*, 399–412.

Stein, L. I., & Santos, A. B. (1998). *Assertive community treatment for people with severe mental illness.* New York, NY: W.W.Norton & Company.

Sturmey, P. (2010). Case formulation in forensic psychology. In M. Daffern, L. Jones, & J. Shine (Eds.), *Offence paralleling behaviour: An individualized approach to offender assessment and treatment.* Chichester: Wiley-Blackwell.

Ward, T., & Brown, M. (2004). The good lives model and conceptual issues in offender rehabilitation. *Psychology, Crime & Law, 10*, 243–257. doi:10.1080/10683160410001662744

Wong, S. C. P. (1999). *Violence reduction program: Program management manual.* Retrieved from http://www.psynergy.ca/

Wong, S. C. P. (forthcoming). Violence reduction treatment for individuals with psychopathic personality traits: Towards an integration of research & practice. In W. J. Livesley, G. Dimaggio, & J. F. Clarkin (Eds.), *Integrated modular treatment for personality disorders.* Guilford.

Wong, S., & Gordon, A. (1999–2003). The Violence Risk Scale. Retrieved from http://www.psynergy.ca/

Wong, S. C. P., & Gordon, A. (2004). A risk-readiness model of post-treatment risk management. *Issues in Forensic Psychology, 5*, 152–163.

Wong, S. C. P., & Gordon, A. (2006). The validity and reliability of the violence risk scale: A treatment friendly violence risk assessment scale. *Psychology, Public Policy and Law. 12*(3), 279–309. doi:10.1037/1076-8971.12.3.279

Wong, S. C. P., Gordon, A., Gu, D., Lewis, K. & Olver, M. (2012). The effectiveness of violence reduction treatment for psychopathic offenders: Empirical evidence and a treatment model. *International Journal of Forensic Mental Health, 11*(4), 336–349. doi.org/10.1080/14999013.2012.746760

Wong, S. C. P., & Parhar, K. (2011). Evaluation of the predictive validity of the Violence Risk Scale in a paroled offender sample: A seven-year prospective study. *Journal of Forensic Psychiatry and Psychology, 22*(6), 790–808.

Wong, S. C. P., Van der Veen, S., Leis, T., Denkhaus, H., Gu, D., Liber, E., . . . Middleton, H. (2005).Reintegrating seriously violent and personality disordered offenders from a super maximum security institution into the general offender population. *International Journal of Offender Therapy and Comparative Criminology, 49*(4), 362–375. doi:10.1177/0306624X05274501

Yang, M., Wong, S. C. P., & Coid, J. (2010). The efficacy of violence prediction: A meta-analytic comparison of nine risk assessment instruments. *Psychological Bulletin, 136*(5), 740–767. doi:10.1037/a0020473

Appendix 1
Programme manuals and materials

The following programme materials have been developed for the VRP:

VRP Implementation Checklist is a self-assessment tool used to assess the organisation's readiness for programme implementation and delivery such as considerations regarding human resource, the physical environment, staff training and data collection procedures etc.

Programme Management Manual (Wong, 1999) provides the rationale and theoretical bases of the programme, describes the programme design and addresses the management issues in the programme implementation, such as staff and resource considerations.

Facilitator's Manual (Gordon & Wong, 1999–2009) guides the programme facilitator(s) on the delivery of the intervention by specifying the rationale, objectives of the interventions, group work and assignments for each of the VRP modules etc. Also included in the manual are handouts to illustrate and supplement the session content as well as session and Phase evaluation forms.

Supplementary Facilitator's Manual (Gordon, 2009) provides additional materials, activities and handouts to extend and supplement the Facilitator's Manual.

Participant's Workbook (Wong, 1999) which parallels the *Facilitator's Manual* in topics covered and is written in a simple, user-friendly language (suitable for those with only five to six years of schooling) to facilitate participants' comprehension of the programme material.

Offence Analogue Behaviour (OAB) and Offence Replacement Behaviour (ORB) Rating Guide (Gordon & Wong, 2011) was developed to assist staff in identifying, monitoring and documenting OABs and ORBs.

Violence Risk Scale (Wong & Gordon, 1999–2003, 2006) is an integral part of the VRP and is used as described above.

VRsoft©: an Access® based software programme has been developed for the collection of VRS and VRP related data.

A description and research review of the Clearwater Sex Offender Treatment Programme

Mark E. Olver[a] and Stephen C.P. Wong[a,b]

[a]*Department of Psychology, University of Saskatchewan, Saskatoon, Saskatchewan, Canada;* [b]*Institute of Mental Health, University of Nottingham, Nottingham, UK*

This article provides a description and research review of an in-patient sex offender treatment programme, the Clearwater Sex Offender Treatment Programme, over its history of more than two decades of operation at the Regional Psychiatric Centre (RPC) in Saskatoon, Saskatchewan, Canada. We begin by reviewing the Clearwater Programme referral criteria and mandate, its methods of assessment and evaluation and the programme content, structure, treatment philosophy and model of change. A review of applied research undertakings of the Clearwater Programme follows, including past treatment outcome evaluations, examinations of therapeutic change and attention to responsivity considerations (e.g. treatment attrition). We finish with some conclusions, comment on programmatic developments taken by the Clearwater Programme and anticipated future research directions.

Sexual offender treatment programmes serve an extremely important purpose, both to those in treatment and society at large by providing effective assessment, treatment and risk management services to reduce sexual victimisation and to promote successful community reintegration of offenders after treatment. To achieve these stated objectives, the interventions have to comply with evidence-informed forensic and correctional practices. Andrews and Bonta's (2010) principles of risk (i.e. match service intensity to offender risk level), need (i.e. target criminogenic needs for treatment) and responsivity (i.e. use of cognitive behavioural treatment approaches, known as *general responsivity*, and skilfully adapting service delivery to unique client characteristics such as motivation and learning style, known as *specific responsivity*) have important implications for effective forensic service delivery to reduce recidivism and hence, enhance client well-being (Andrews, Bonta, & Wormith, 2011). Applications of what have become known as Risk Need Responsivity (RNR) principles have been demonstrated to reduce recidivism in various offender groups (Andrews & Bonta, 2010), including sexual offenders (Hanson, Bourgon, Helmus, & Hodgson, 2009). In a recent meta-analysis of sex offender treatment outcome studies, Hanson et al. (2009) obtained evidence to show that adherence to a greater number of RNR principles generated larger reductions in recidivism, with the largest reductions observed in adherence to three principles, versus two, one or none.

This article provides a description and research review of an in-patient sex offender treatment programme, the Clearwater Sex Offender Treatment Programme (referred herein as the Clearwater Programme for short) over its history of more than two decades of operation at the Regional Psychiatric Centre (RPC) in Saskatoon, Saskatchewan, Canada. We begin by reviewing the Clearwater Programme referral criteria and mandate, its methods of assessment and evaluation and the programme content, structure, treatment philosophy and model of change. It is important to note that in preparing this programme overview, the Clearwater Case File (Correctional Service of Canada, 2004), prepared, revised, updated and maintained by a legion of service providers (the first author of the present article included) for accreditation reviews was a key information source; the hard work of Clearwater Programme service providers and the RPC in general in developing the Case File document (Correctional Service of Canada, 2004) must be acknowledged. The present article then provides a review of applied research undertakings of the Clearwater Programme including past treatment outcome evaluations, examinations of therapeutic change and attention to responsivity considerations, in particular, treatment attrition from the Clearwater Programme. We finish with some conclusions, a summary of programmatic developments taken by the Clearwater Programme, and anticipated future research directions.

Clearwater Programme referral criteria and mandate

In Canada, offenders serving sentences of less than two years are held under the jurisdictions of the provinces, while those serving sentences of two years or longer are held under that of the federal government. The Correctional Service of Canada (CSC), a Canadian federal correctional department, is responsible for the administration of all offenders serving sentences of at least two years. When a convicted sex offender is admitted to CSC, an intake assessment is conducted (generally by a psychologist) to assess risk, identify treatment needs and ascertain the programme intensity suited to the individual. An institutional parole officer will also develop a correctional plan to address the appropriate criminogenic needs for the offender. Different levels of intensity are offered for sex offender programmes in CSC including low, moderate and high-intensity programmes as well as the institutional and community maintenance sex offender treatment programmes (Correctional Service of Canada, 2009).[1]

The Clearwater Programme is currently a 48-bed in-patient sex offender treatment programme located within a multilevel security mental health facility, the RPC, an accredited hospital and one of five specially designated treatment facilities or regional treatment centres within each of the five Canadian regions (Pacific, Prairie, Ontario, Quebec, Atlantic). The RPC is the regional treatment centre for CSC Prairie Region, which includes Alberta, Saskatchewan, Manitoba, Northern Ontario, Northwest Territories and Nunavut. The RPC provides a range of forensic mental and physical health services to a wide range of clientele in addition to the Clearwater Programme.

Historically, the Clearwater Programme has been classified as a high-intensity programme, which is typically recommended for offenders assessed as at least moderate to high risk for sexual violence. With high-intensity programmes, the programme modules should be presented daily with a programme duration of typically 8 months and a minimum 15 contact hours of therapy per week. If an offender is assessed during the intake process as high risk for sexual violence or has specific criminogenic needs or responsivity issues that may impact his response to treatment, a referral package is completed and the individual may be referred to the Clearwater Programme. The applications are then screened by Clearwater staff to determine suitability, interest and need for treatment. Applicants for treatment are prioritised according to their risk (with high-risk applicants given higher priority) and expected release dates.

In recent years, the Clearwater Programme mandate has changed to focus on learning disabled, brain injured or seriously mentally ill patients as the delivery of sex offender programmes in CSC for offenders without such special needs has tended to be prison-based. The data on these new admissions and programme operation are not presently available given the recentness of these developments, although Table 1 provides a patient profile of Clearwater Programme participants sampled over the years from 1983 to 2007. As these data are drawn from several published and unpublished sources and have not necessarily been collected continuously throughout the programme's history of operation (with many of these data being gathered retrospectively), the *N*'s vary considerably for some of the patient variables. The mean Static-99 score of 4.84 (SD $=2.04$, $N=514$), corresponding to medium–high risk (Hanson & Thornton, 1999), corroborates the higher risk nature of the clientele referred to this programme. As seen in this table, Clearwater Programme referrals tend to have extensive criminal histories (both sexual and non-sexual) and may be serving fairly lengthy sentences. Over the time frame of the programme, approximately 40% of the clients self-identified as being of Aboriginal ancestry and a similar proportion have never been married. On average, participants have had less than a Grade 10 education and tend to be a younger adult male population but vary considerably in age. Table 1 also presents psychiatric information, with the caveat that the diagnostic variables (with the exception of the psychopathy and Psychopathy Checklist-Revised (PCL-R) data) represent the 1983–1997 time period of the programme from the intake assessments completed by RPC psychiatrists on all admissions. From that time period, roughly one-half of programme participants had a Diagnostic and Statistical Manual (III or III-R) diagnosis of a substance use disorder, a similar proportion had a diagnosis of antisocial personality disorder or (when not meeting full criteria for the disorder) antisocial personality disorder traits, more than three quarters any personality disorder or personality disorder traits, and only a small proportion had a major (i.e. Axis I) mental illness. The psychopathy data, gathered from two datasets spanning 1983–2005 (DeSorcy, Olver, & Wormith, 2011; Olver & Wong, 2006) will be discussed later in this article.

Assessment and evaluation

Following admission to the Clearwater Programme, a comprehensive intake assessment is conducted by the treatment team using a collection of risk assessment and other psychological measures (e.g. personality, cognitive) to assess the individual's pre-treatment risk, identify criminogenic needs to be prioritised for treatment and identify responsivity factors that may impact treatment (e.g. learning style, cognitive ability). Included among the measures employed in the pre-treatment evaluation is the Violence Risk Scale-Sexual Offender version (VRS-SO; Wong,

Table 1. Clearwater Programme and patient characteristics.

Measure	*N*	Mean (SD)	Frequency% (*N*)
Demographics			
Education (years)	603	9.56 (2.75)	–
Age at programme admission	623	34.90 (9.84)	–
Aboriginal descent	740	–	40.68 (301)
Single/never married	620	–	42.90 (266)
Offence variables			
Index sentence (years)	540	5.06 (2.96)	–
Prior sex offences	547	1.12 (1.67)	–
Prior non-sexual violence	546	1.60 (2.29)	–
Prior convictions	547	11.38 (12.50)	–
Programme variables			
Programme length (months)	623	7.59 (3.10)	–
Successful completion	740	–	87.16 (645)
Non-completion	740	–	12.84 (95)
Sex offender type	414		
Rapist		–	51.69 (214)
Mixed		–	14.25 (59)
Extrafamilial child molester		–	19.32 (80)
Intrafamilial child molester		–	14.01 (58)
Exhibitionist		–	0.72 (3)
Risk characteristics			
Static 99	514	4.84 (2.04)	–
VRS-SO static	510	10.82 (3.74)	–
VRS-SO dynamic	507	26.95 (7.54)	–
VRS-SO total	507	37.66 (10.02)	–
Sexual Deviance	507	7.18 (4.09)	–
Criminality	510	9.45 (3.60)	–
Treatment responsivity	511	7.17 (2.29)	–
Psychiatric			
PCL-R total score	236	21.78 (6.79)	–
Psychopathy (25-pt cut-off)	236	–	36.44
Psychopathy (30-pt cut-off)	236	–	13.56
ASPD or traits	316	–	52.22
Personality disorder or traits	316	–	78.80
Substance use disorder	314	–	50.63
Major mental illness	316	–	11.07

Note: These data are drawn from several published and unpublished sources of Clearwater Programme participants sampled over the years from 1983 to 2007 and have not necessarily been collected continuously throughout the programme's history of operation with many of these data being gathered retrospectively from samplings of patients from different time periods of the programme. As a result, the *n*'s vary considerably for the variables and measures reported above. The PCL-R data are based on two separate samples (Olver & Wong, 2006, $N=156$ and DeSorcy, 2012, $N=80$) to generate a weighted average and pooled standard deviation. ASPD, Antisocial Personality Disorder.

Olver, Nicholaichuk, & Gordon, 2003), which was adopted into regular use in the Clearwater Programme in 2000. Comprised of 7 static and 17 dynamic items rated on a four-point (0, 1, 2, 3) scale, the VRS-SO is designed to assess sex offender risk, identify targets for treatment and evaluate changes in risk from treatment or other change agents. The dynamic items can be grouped into three broad factors labelled

Sexual Deviance (e.g. deviant sexual interests, sexual compulsivity), Criminality (e.g. substance abuse, interpersonal aggression, impulsivity) and Treatment Responsivity (e.g. cognitive distortions, lack of insight). Total scores (i.e. static + dynamic) range from 0 to 72 and can be grouped into risk categories of low (0–20), moderate-low (21–30), moderate-high (31–40) and high (40–72). VRS-SO descriptive data from the Clearwater Programme (Olver, Nicholaichuk, Kingston, & Wong, 2012; Olver, Wong, Nicholaichuk, & Gordon, 2007) are presented in Table 1. The mean VRS-SO total score of 37.66 (SD = 10.02) corresponds to moderate-high risk on average and also reaffirms the higher risk-need nature of programme participants.

In cases where the pre-treatment assessment provides some evidence of deviant sexual arousal, either because of self-report or offence history, a voluntary phallometric assessment is also completed; if necessary, the phallometric technician will conduct control sessions to assist and evaluate clients in their ability to control deviant arousal. Given the heterogeneity of sexual offenders, each client is expected to have a unique profile of criminogenic needs and the treatment plan will be tailored accordingly. For instance, as seen in Table 1, approximately one-half of patients would be classified as rapists (i.e. adult, generally female victims only), while the other half are fairly evenly divided among offenders with a child victim, with a slightly higher proportion of extra-familial child molesters. VRS-SO research has shown that these Clearwater patients have different profiles of criminogenic needs. For instance, Olver et al. (2007) found rapists and mixed offenders had significantly higher Criminality scores than offenders with exclusively child victims, while extra-familial and mixed offenders had higher Sexual Deviance scores (and hence, a greater number of criminogenic needs in this area) than all other offender groups. Given that other programmes targeting broad criminogenic needs (e.g. substance abuse, criminal peers) as they relate to offending in general exist in CSC, the priority of the Clearwater Programme has been on targeting criminogenic needs (both general and specific) in terms of their links to sexual violence.

The results of the pre-treatment assessment provide direction to the treatment team about appropriate therapeutic techniques and strategies for each client. For instance, for an offender who is functionally illiterate, the completion of therapeutic assignments might involve the use of pictures rather than written words or the use of other audio media. Based on the offender's level of cognitive ability, treatment staff might choose to present information in a more concrete or abstract manner or (for learning disabled clients) to provide repetition and numerous opportunities for practice. Treatment plans are continuously evaluated in terms of a client's progress and adjusted accordingly. When necessary, additional psychological or psychiatric assessments are completed to identify possible factors that may be impeding treatment progress. As clients approach the end of treatment a comprehensive final post-treatment assessment is conducted to evaluate risk-related changes inform post-treatment risk, supervision and risk management strategies to help ensure continuity of care and ultimately successful reintegration.

Programme structure, treatment philosophy and model of change

The Clearwater Programme was developed and has been in existence at the RPC since the early 1980s, emerging from the efforts of Dr Arthur Gordon who was the psychologist instrumental in the development of the programme. Although the programme has evolved and changed over the years, in size (increasing from 12 to 24 to 48 beds), content and structure, it has been consistent in its adherence to a cognitive behavioural model of treatment (see Gordon & Nicholaichuk, 1996) and has continually incorporated new knowledge and practice developments in offender assessment and treatment such as the RNR principles (Andrews et al., 1990) and later, elements from the Good Lives Model (Ward, Mann, & Gannon, 2007). The Clearwater Programme is currently structured as two units of 24 patients each (an upper unit and a lower unit), operating simultaneously. A rolling cohort format is employed in which approximately two dozen new admissions are brought in and integrated with the client cohort on each unit who are halfway through the programme (e.g. 3–4 months), filling the spots of the remaining individuals who have completed the programme. This model enables new clients to be therapeutically mentored by individuals who are now accustomed to the programme who can assist in group exercises and provide support.

The length of the Clearwater Programme has ranged from 6 to 8 months in duration with an average length of 7.59 months (SD = 3.10). In some cases, patients may start late in the programme but could be allowed to 'catch up' and successfully complete the programme. In other cases, patients who fall behind or who have particularly complex needs could be given the opportunity to stay longer to complete the programme providing they have been identified as making progress or demonstrated a commitment to do so. Programme intensity and duration may vary by diagnosis or other presenting responsivity issues. For instance, offenders of higher intellectual ability may be delivered programme information at an accelerated rate, while offenders with lengthy offending histories, limited intellectual ability, mental illness or lengthy periods of incarceration may receive an extended programme (e.g. an additional 4 months).

A multidisciplinary treatment team including psychologists, psychiatrists, psychiatric nurses, social workers, Aboriginal Elders, occupational therapists, correctional and parole officers staffs the Clearwater Programme. Treatment is delivered in both individual and group formats. Each client is assigned a primary therapist (e.g. often a psychiatric nurse, social worker or occupational therapist) who helps teach the client in developing new cognitive and behavioural skills individually during day-to-day interactions, for instance, through modelling, roleplaying, written assignments and specific skill building groups. More complex cases may also be seen for individual services from the unit psychologist(s).

The treatment modules are delivered in groups of 10–12 participants each by programme facilitators with a co-facilitator (e.g. primary therapist or another programme staff member as available). The group treatment modules are offered on a continual basis and target many domains of sex offender functioning linked to risk (e.g. attitudes and cognitions, intimacy skills deficits, developing healthy relationships and sexuality). Programme facilitators can vary the pacing of programme delivery given that the programme emphasises a skills-based, process-oriented treatment focus. The number of sessions devoted to a given module can vary depending upon the skill level and responsivity of group members.

Treatment involves a combination of didactic instructions to provide a basic working framework, then group discussion, paper and pencil exercises and audio/video media. A skills-based approach to cognitive, affective and behavioural change is utilised in which specific skills designed to impact particular treatment targets are employed. Cognitive techniques are supplemented with a number of focused skills-oriented exercises involving a high level of interpersonal interaction to put learned concepts into practice. Therapists also role model appropriate interpersonal skills and problem-solving techniques and are appropriately attentive to responsivity issues. Moreover, clients are expected to learn from other clients. For instance, the disclosure groups (discussed in further detail below) are larger groups attended by all Clearwater Programme participants. As referenced above, in the disclosure groups newly admitted clients are able to observe clients who have been in the programme for a longer period of time (e.g. observing how a crime cycle and relapse prevention (RP) plan is developed). The group environment is intended to be supportive but also challenging such that offenders can examine, with honesty and in detail, the pattern and themes of their sexual offending towards the formulation of a RP plan. Towards the end of the treatment programme, one component is devoted to discussing lapses and practicing behavioural management strategies to deal proactively and positively with stressful situations and lapses.

The specific group treatment modules employed in the Clearwater Programme have varied over the years but broadly include: (1) disclosure groups, which are conducted in the form of two-hour groups held twice weekly throughout the duration of treatment. The disclosure groups consist of three sets of therapeutic activities: the preparation of a personal autobiography, offence cycle (an examination of the cognitive, affective and behavioural dynamics of current and previous sexual offences) and RP plan (developing a comprehensive RP plan, including outlining offence pathways, coping skills and personal and community resources to prevent relapse), which the patient presents at the beginning, middle and end of treatment, respectively; (2) groups targeting antisocial attitudes and cognitions to assist clients in identifying, confronting and challenging the distorted cognitions linked to their sexual offending behaviour, including psychoeducation around sexual fantasies and self-management strategies for deviant fantasies; (3) emotional regulation skills groups with a focus on emotional self-management, particularly anger and developing cognitive and behavioural strategies to manage and reduce anger intensity and its associated negative consequences; (4) social skills groups, focusing particularly on the skill of assertiveness, and learning and roleplaying behavioural skills and strategies to respond prosocially to provocative interpersonal situations; (5) intimacy and relationships skills, to develop an understanding of the client's own relationship functioning, acquire coping skills to manage jealousy, rejection and loneliness and roleplaying to improve communication and problem-solving skills; and (6) groups focusing on empathy and victim awareness provide an opportunity for the client to address his own victimisation, and arrive at a greater appreciation of the impact of his sexual offending behaviour on his victim; the module content is also frequently used to challenge offence supportive attitudes and cognitions. In addition to the core group treatment modules, clients may also participate in addictions programming or support groups [e.g. Alcoholics Anonymous (AA), Narcotics Anonymous (NA)], educational upgrading, or work programmes to enhance work skills and attitudes including responsible work behaviour, accepting direction, cooperation with authority and independent work skills.

Finally, efforts are made to ensure continuity of care upon the completion of the Clearwater Programme. When patients are referred for follow up services in the community or their parent institution, the Clearwater treatment team provides a final treatment report that clearly outlines the progress the client has made in addressing his dynamic-risk factors and thus the overall reduction in his risk for sexual or violent recidivism. This report includes the psychologist's opinion about the manageability of the client's risk in the community and the means required to manage the individual's risk. This report is also used by the Parole Board of Canada when reviewing the client for decision purposes (e.g. conditional release). The client's crime cycle and RP plan are included among the documents to inform future service providers working with the individual and may be used for on-going supervision and monitoring. The treatment team will also liaise with community agencies or other institutions to increase the consistency and continuity of aftercare.

Outcome evaluations of the Clearwater Programme

Over the Clearwater Programme's history a body of research has accumulated examining the efficacy of the programme for promoting treatment related change and reducing sexual offence recidivism. The first outcome examination of the Clearwater Programme was conducted by Nicholaichuk, Gordon, Gu, and Wong (2000) who compared the recidivism rates of a sample of 296 treated and released Clearwater patients to a control group of 283 untreated sex offenders matched on offence history and age.[2] The control sample was selected from a pool of more than 3000 federally incarcerated sex offenders from the CSC's Prairie region who had not received treatment services from the Clearwater Programme, although they may have received services elsewhere. Followed up an average 6 years post-release in the community, treated offenders had significantly lower rates of sexual reconviction (14.5%) in contrast to the controls (33.2%), equating to a reduction of more than 50%. In follow-up analyses, Nicholaichuk et al. (2000) observed a recidivism treatment effect when the offender groups were disaggregated into first time versus repeat (i.e. having a prior sex conviction) offenders.

Olver, Wong, and Nicholaichuk (2009) subsequently conducted an updated outcome examination of the Clearwater Programme on the original sample plus a number of new programme admissions who had attended since the original investigation. The same control sample as in Nicholaichuk et al. (2000) was used and the recidivism outcome data were updated to add another 4 years follow-up for an average of 10 years. To increase methodological rigour, Olver et al. (2009) included only those participants who had a minimum of two-years offending opportunity in the community, removed any cases from the control sample that had release dates earlier than the treated group and used techniques to control for individual differences in the follow-up time, as well as risk-related confounding variables (e.g. age, offence history). In total, 176 new treatment cases were added (increasing the total N to 472) compared to 265 controls. As the new admissions tended to have more serious offence histories but were somewhat older on average upon release, age at release and sexual offence history were separately controlled through cox regression survival analysis. The results demonstrated treatment participation to be associated with significant reductions in sexual offence recidivism after controlling for these risk-related confounds. Additionally, sexual recidivism rates were examined between treatment and comparison groups over 2-, 3-, 5- and 10-year fixed follow-up periods, with odds ratios of 0.40 to 0.63 obtained over these follow-ups interpreted to mean that for every 100 untreated offenders who sexually re-offend, approximately 40–63% of treated offenders would sexually re-offend. Use of logistic regression examining the relationship of treatment participation to recidivism at each fixed follow-up period controlling for age and sexual offence history upheld the findings.

Evaluating therapeutic change in the Clearwater Programme

While single treatment outcome studies perform an obvious important function, not every offender who completes sex offender treatment, completes it well (Abracen & Looman, 2005). The men who participate in these programmes may make substantial risk-reducing changes and embark on a change trajectory that continues after treatment onward into subsequent programmes and eventual release into the community. Others, however, may demonstrate inconsistent progress or staggered levels of improvement or encounter substantial difficulties and even fail to complete treatment. Suffice it to say, simply attending or completing a sex offender treatment programme is not necessarily a mark of improvement or risk-reduction. Moreover, the picture also changes considerably when the individuals who fail to progress happen to be higher, rather than lower, risk in keeping with the RNR principles (Andrews & Bonta, 2010).

As such, therapeutic change in the Clearwater Programme is routinely monitored through clinical observation, evaluation of homework assignments and consultation with team members. Programme staff are able to observe programme participants throughout most of the day and team members are able to directly observe progress both within the various groups and in other situations (e.g. meal times, mingling with other offenders, leisure times, etc.). Through regular consultation with other team members (i.e. shift change, ward rounds, progress notes, etc.), information can be transmitted. As a result, the entire team has an awareness of how each individual is progressing and what treatment needs require further attention. As the client approaches programme completion, the final treatment evaluation includes a post-treatment rating of the VRS-SO to assess possible reductions in the individual's risk level and to identify any outstanding areas of risk and need.

In this regard, a further line of Clearwater Programme research has examined the relationship of risk-related treatment changes as assessed by the VRS-SO to sexual and violent recidivism occurring post-release into the community. In a sample of 321 treated Clearwater patients (which included the Nicholaichuk et al., 2000 cohort), Olver et al. (2007) found measures of risk change on the VRS-SO to be significantly associated with reductions in sexual recidivism after controlling for actuarial risk. Follow-up examinations of therapeutic or risk-change on the VRS-SO in this treated patient cohort has found change scores to be associated with reductions in sexual and violent recidivism after controlling for scores on the Hare PCL-R (Hare, 1991, 2003; Olver & Wong, 2009), as well as significantly lower rates of sexual recidivism among offenders with high Static-99 scores who demonstrated above average amounts of change compared to offenders with high Static-99 scores who made little change (Olver & Wong, 2011a).

Olver et al. (2012) examined pre-post treatment changes on a psychometric battery completed on a sample of 257 Clearwater Programme participants. Although some impressive pre-post changes seemed evident (often exceeding $d = 0.50$) in important domains of psychological functioning, many of these changes diminished after controlling for social desirability. A factor analysis of the battery generated three factors, but none of the change scores within these domains were significantly related to reductions in sexual or violent recidivism. Although the changes captured by these psychometric measures may have reflected some improvements in psychological functioning, these changes were not necessarily risk-relevant.

In sum, research findings from the Clearwater Programme suggest that the amount of therapeutic progress made in sex offender treatment, providing it is risk-relevant, does matter and can have an important bearing on recidivism probability after treatment, particularly among high-risk offenders.

Attention to responsivity considerations in the Clearwater Programme

Responsivity considerations have special prominence in the delivery of the Clearwater Programme, specifically, through adapting the content and delivery of therapeutic material, within groups and individually with an eye toward individual client factors that can impact the course of treatment. Indeed, factors such as literacy, intellectual capacity, cognitive abilities, personality (e.g. psychopathic or borderline traits), mental disorder (e.g. mood disorders, psychosis), social skill level and cultural differences must be considered as they could negatively influence a patient's ability to learn within a therapeutic situation. It has always been the mandate of the Clearwater Programme to accommodate the responsivity needs of the client, and attention to responsivity considerations has been particularly paramount with the recent changes in the programme's mandate to provide services to special needs populations. Some of the primary ways the Clearwater Programme has, and continues to, address important responsivity considerations is through intervention and flexible programming including maintaining a therapeutic attitude, use of interventions to enhance motivation, programmatic adaptations geared to the client's learning style or cognitive capabilities and culturally responsive interventions.

First, in terms of therapist attitude, Clearwater treatment staff are respectful of their clients and present as confident, sensitive, caring and committed. Efforts are made to treat everyone in a fair and consistent manner. All team members are also aware of their responsibility to be appropriate role models, and they take this responsibility seriously. Efforts are made to create a supportive atmosphere for both staff and clients and to achieve the best fit between client and primary therapist. Realistically, difficulties can and do occur regarding staff morale and therapist-patient fit, especially given that work with sex offenders, many of whom have psychopathic or personality disorder traits or do not take to the programme well, is frankly difficult, and can be discouraging, physically taxing, mentally gruelling and emotionally draining. Such realities of doing difficult clinical work and engaging a challenging treatment population underscore the necessity of initiatives to promote staff self-care and well-being and reduce turnover and burnout.

Second, efforts are made on a variety of fronts in an effort to mobilise the individual's motivation for change. One vehicle is through the referral process, given that clients voluntarily choose to begin the programme and are free to withdraw from the programme, or any of its components, at any time. This being said, it is recognised that many offenders may feel coerced into treatment, consenting because non-participation in treatment often results in extended periods of incarceration and denial of conditional release. Thus, Clearwater staff expect clients to vary in degree of motivation to change. The philosophy is that minimization and denial are endemic to sex offender populations and are thus not used as exclusionary criteria for the programme. Rather, it is expected that treatment staff will work with and engage their clients to overcome such obstacles. In this regard, treatment staff work to develop and maintain a strong working alliance that focuses on establishing therapeutic goals that are mutually valued and the developing therapeutic tasks that are mutually perceived to be relevant and effective.

Third, programme accommodations are made to be sensitive to the learning style, reading level and cognitive capabilities of their clientele. With a mean education level below Grade 10 (and frequently much lower), Clearwater patients frequently present with a lack of formal education, learning disability, cognitive impairment and academic deficits. As mentioned earlier, a variety of programme accommodations can be made to modify the pacing, content and delivery of interventions.

Finally, despite comprising only 3% of the general Canadian population, Aboriginal people represent approximately 20% of its federal inmate population, and over the years, have represented roughly 40% of the Clearwater population (see Table 1). As such, the Clearwater Programme strives to adapt the content and delivery of treatment to the cultural heritage of its Aboriginal clientele. This adaptation is done by way of a blend of cognitive behavioural and traditional healing approaches, for instance, through employing Aboriginal Elders or programme facilitators who are fully familiar with indigenous culture and language and who can use traditional healing methods (e.g. sweat lodge, smudging) or teachings to maximise therapeutic engagement and gain. Elders/Healers also help promote self-awareness and healing through teachings and ceremonies, encourage the sharing of experiences to promote personal and spiritual growth, provide advice and teaching on issues of Aboriginal spirituality and culture, provide crisis intervention to clients in emergency situations (e.g. death in the family) and can assist with learning the skills and techniques taught in the programme areas to help control inappropriate sexual behaviour. They may also assist with community reintegration initiatives (e.g. accompany Escorted Temporary Absences to develop supportive relationships with community) and attend Parole Board hearings.

Treatment attrition in the Clearwater Programme

The adaptations employed by the Clearwater Programme reviewed above often have an added practical advantage given that they can maximise therapeutic engagement. In turn, the extant literature has also indicated that failure to adhere to important responsivity considerations may be linked to programme non-completion. In their meta-analysis of offender treatment attrition studies, Olver, Stockdale, and Wormith (2011) found that the subset of sex offender programmes examined ($k = 34$, $N =$ 12,878) had an average rate of treatment non-completion of 27.6%. Significant predictors of sex offender treatment non-completion included specific demographic predictors (unemployment, single, low education), indictors of criminality or risk (e.g. non-sexual offence history, Static-99 score), diagnostic indicators (e.g. antisocial personality, psychopathy, any personality disorder) and certain responsivity considerations (e.g. high levels of denial, low motivation, poor treatment engagement). Perhaps most concerning, sex offender treatment non-completion was associated with increases in all recidivism outcomes, including sexual recidivism; across

15 studies and 9837 offenders a mean weighted $r = 0.15$ was obtained, which would represent a 15% difference between treatment completers and non-completers (with non-completers being higher). The implications from this research are that although treatment non-completers tend to be more likely to recidivate, they also tend to be higher risk offenders, and thus risk confounds the interpretation of the relationship of non-completion to recidivism.

As reported in Table 1, the Clearwater Programme has demonstrated a relatively low rate of attrition (12.84%), that is, individuals who fail to successfully complete the programme, over its years of operation. This figure is generated from two non-overlapping Clearwater samples from Olver et al. (2007, $N = 318$, 1983–1997) and DeSorcy et al. (2011, $N = 422$, 1998–2005). A collection of studies of patients sampled from these cohorts has examined the predictors and consequences of non-completion from the Clearwater Programme. Beyko and Wong (2005) compared 32 treatment completers to 32 treatment non-completers who had attended the Clearwater Programme from 1995 to 2001 and found that negative-treatment attitudes, non-violent institutional offences, general criminality, disruptive behaviour and high levels of denial were strong unique predictors of non-completion. In a non-overlapping sample of 60 randomly selected federal offenders admitted to the Clearwater Programme, McKenzie et al. (2002) also found treatment completers to advance to a higher stage of change (Prochaska, DiClemente, & Norcross, 1992), while non-completers demonstrated lower motivation, decreased improvement and were less engaged in therapeutic activities (e.g. completion of homework, meeting treatment goals).

Olver and Wong (2011b) examined predictors of treatment non-completion, specifically, the role of psychopathy as a potential responsivity consideration in a sample of 154 Clearwater participants. While established attrition predictors were observed, consistent with previous findings (Beyko & Wong, 2005; McKenzie et al., 2002), PCL-R psychopathy was a unique predictor of non-completion, particularly the Affective facet of the tool, which was the only independently significant predictor of non-completion among the four PCL-R facets. Olver and Wong (2012) subsequently found, in a sample of 318 Clearwater patients followed up 18 years post-release, treatment non-completion to be associated with significant increases in violent, but not sexual, recidivism after controlling for actuarial risk. Finally, DeSorcy et al. (2011) examined the relationship of working alliance, psychopathy and Aboriginal ancestry to treatment attrition and recidivism in a sample of 422 Clearwater patients. Strength of working alliance, as measured by the Working Alliance Inventory (WAI; Horvath & Greenberg, 1989), was positively associated with successful completion of, and length of stay in, the Clearwater Programme. PCL-R total scores were not significantly associated with strength of working alliance, although high scores on the affective facet were associated with weaker working alliances, including therapeutic bond and goals.

Treatment responses of psychopathic sexual offenders

As seen in Table 1, the psychopathy data from the DeSorcy et al. (2011; original source DeSorcy, 2012) and Olver and Wong (2006) samples demonstrate that around one-third of Clearwater participants qualify for a diagnosis of psychopathy using the PCL-R cut-off of 25 recommended for file-based diagnoses (Wong, 1988), but only 13.6% using the 30-point cut-off, and a mean overall PCL-R total score of 21.78

(SD = 6.79). The programme has thus contained a fairly high proportion of psychopathic offenders over the years, with higher rates of psychopathy tending to be observed among rapists and mixed offenders (Olver & Wong, 2006).

As already discussed above, Clearwater Programme research has found psychopathy, particularly the callous/unemotional traits of the syndrome, to be significantly predictive of treatment non-completion (Olver & Wong, 2009, 2011b). While Olver and Wong (2009) found that psychopathic sex offenders were much more likely than non-psychopathic offenders to fail in treatment, interestingly they found that nearly three quarters (73%) of psychopathic men actually completed treatment; and those who completed treatment had a one-third reduction in their rates of overall violent recidivism post-release. Risk related changes, as captured by the VRS-SO, were also significantly associated with reductions in sexual and violent recidivism after controlling for psychopathy and actuarial risk. The results indicate that while certainly not all psychopathic sex offenders could be considered successfully treated from their involvement in the Clearwater Programme, there was evidence for at least some meaningful risk reduction in the propensity of some of these men for future sexual and general violence.

Conclusions and future directions

As one of the first sex offender treatment programmes in the Correctional Service of Canada, the Clearwater Sex Offender Treatment Programme has a long history of providing assessment, treatment and risk management services to moderate to high risk federally incarcerated sex offenders. These programme developments, its shifts and changes, are summarised by Olver and Wong (2008, pp. 70–71) who note:

> The [Clearwater] programme has evolved and changed over the years: more medium and high risk sex offenders were admitted, programme content was modified to reflect developments in the sex offender literature and best practice principles, programme delivery became more structured, and the programme was accredited twice by international expert panels after making significant changes. The leadership of the programme also had changed many times together with many complete changeovers of line staff. The programme also had its share of ups and downs and had to weather many challenges over the years: not at all unexpected within a large bureaucracy such as the CSC.
>
> What had remained quite consistent from programme inception to the present (other than the programme name!) and had become the accepted treatment philosophy of Clearwater is the unwavering focus on risk reduction, intervention using cognitive-behavioural or behavioural treatment approaches, and the targeting of criminogenic factors in treatment; in essence, what the "What Works" principles advocate. Despite the coming and going of programme directors and clinical leads with varying trainings, skills, professional backgrounds, personalities and management styles, the overall programme philosophy remained fairly constant, withstood the challenges of time and had become the backbone of the Clearwater programme. (pp. 70–71)

The body of research reviewed in the present article indicates that treatment participation in the Clearwater Programme is associated with a 20–50% reduction in the probability of future sexual violence compared to untreated controls (Nicholaichuk et al., 2000; Olver et al., 2009), and for greater risk-related changes made in treatment to be associated with reductions in sexual and violent recidivism, particularly among higher risk offenders (Olver & Wong, 2009, 2011a; Olver et al.,

2007). The findings indicate that the amount of change made, provided it is risk-relevant, can and does matter in terms of the likelihood of being successfully reintegrated into the community versus returning after committing a new sexual or otherwise violent crime.

The ongoing body of applied research supporting the efficacy of the Clearwater Programme for reducing sexual and violent recidivism, promoting risk-related change in its offender clientele, and demonstrating relatively low rates of attrition have many important implications. First, the programme, its dedicated staff, and its patients striving to make personal changes have likely prevented new incidents of sexual re-victimisation. In addition to helping promote public safety, the programme has likely also helped improve the lives of its offender clientele, who not only learn to manage their dynamic-risk factors but develop new skill sets, and some cases likely move on to more satisfying lives and relationships that are, in some cases, free of sexual or other forms of interpersonal violence.

It seems to us that an important challenge facing service providers in the Clearwater Programme is to continue to meet the therapeutic demand presented by the changing client profile and to maintain service integrity, via adherence to RNR, with an eye toward specific responsivity considerations (as detailed above) in the face of these and other challenges often facing large organisations such as staffing shortages and cutbacks. Accordingly, we also believe it will be important to continue the process of programme evaluation and clinical research collaboration, specifically: to obtain mental health, risk and demographic profiles of its changing patient population; to monitor attrition, scrutinise the reasons for its occurrence and takes steps to minimise it; and to examine aggregations of risk-related change of programme participants and if such changes continue to be linked to reductions in sexual and violent recidivism post-release. Such collaborative links between research and practice we believe have the potential to forge increasingly productive partnerships to better inform strategies for the prevention of sexual violence.

Acknowledgements

The authors would like to acknowledge the hard work of Clearwater Programme service providers and the RPC in general in developing the Clearwater Case File document, which was a key information source in preparing the programme overview for the present article. We also thank Dr Terry Nicholaichuk for some of the historical details he provided on the Clearwater Programme.

Notes

1. The continuation of the low intensity programme has been under review. A listing of CSC's sex offender programmes may be found at: http://www.csc-scc.gc.ca/text/prgrm/cor-pro-2009-eng.shtml
2. Dr Terry Nicholaichuk succeeded Dr Arthur Gordon as the Clearwater Programme's director and chief psychologist in the early 1990s.

References

Abracen, J., & Looman, J. (2005). Developments in the assessment and treatment of sexual offenders: Looking backward with a view to the future. *Journal of Interpersonal Violence*, *20*, 12–19. doi:10.1177/0886260504268088

Andrews, D. A., & Bonta, J. (2010). Rehabilitating criminal justice policy and practice. *Psychology, Public Policy and Law, 16*, 39–55. doi:10.1037/a0018362

Andrews, D. A., Bonta, J., & Wormith, J. S. (2011). The risk-need-responsivity (RNR) model: Does adding the good lives model contribute to effective crime prevention? *Criminal Justice and Behavior, 38*, 735–755. doi:10.1177/0093854811406356

Andrews, D. A., Zinger, I., Hoge, R. D., Bonta, J., Gendreau, P., & Cullen, F. T. (1990). Does correctional treatment work? A clinically relevant and psychologically informed meta-analysis. *Criminology, 28*, 369–404. doi:10.1111/j.1745-9125.1990.tb01330.x

Beyko, M., & Wong, S. C. P. (2005). Predictors of treatment attrition as indicators for program improvement not offender shortcomings: A study of sex offender treatment attrition. *Sexual Abuse: A Journal of Research and Treatment, 17*, 375–389. doi:10.1007/s11194-005-8050-8

Correctional Service of Canada. (2004). *Clearwater Sex Offender Treatment Program case file May 2004*. Regional Psychiatric Centre: Saskatoon, Saskatchewan, Canada.

Correctional Service of Canada. (2009). *Sex offender programs*. Retrieved from http://www.csc-scc.gc.ca/text/prgrm/cor-pro-2009-eng.shtml

DeSorcy, D. (2012). *Working alliance and its relationship with treatment outcome, Aboriginal ancestry, and psychopathy in a sample of federal sex offenders* (Unpublished raw dissertation data). University of Saskatchewan, Saskatoon, Canada.

DeSorcy, D., Olver, M. E., & Wormith, J. S. (2011, June). *The impact of the therapeutic relationship on treatment completion and recidivism in a sample of sex offenders*. Presented at the 72nd annual meeting of the Canadian Psychological Association, Toronto, ON.

Gordon, A., & Nicholaichuk, T. P. (1996). Applying the risk principle to sex offender treatment. *Forum on Corrections Research, 8*, 36–38. Retrieved from http://www.csc-scc.gc.ca/text/pblct/forum/e082/082j_e.pdf

Hanson, R. K., Bourgon, G., Helmus, L., & Hodgson, S. (2009). The principles of effective correctional treatment also apply to sexual offenders. *Criminal Justice and Behavior, 36*, 865–891. doi:10.1177/0093854809338545

Hanson, R. K., & Thornton, D. (1999). *Static 99: Improving actuarial risk assessments for sex offenders* (User Report 99-02). Ottawa: Department of the Solicitor General of Canada.

Hare, R. D. (1991). *The psychopathy checklist revised*. Toronto, ON: Multi-Health Systems.

Hare, R. D. (2003). *The psychopathy checklist revised* (2nd ed.). Toronto, ON: Multi-Health Systems.

Horvath, A. O., & Greenberg, L. S. (1989). Development and validation of the working alliance inventory. *Journal of Counseling Psychology, 36*, 223–233. doi:10.1037/022-0167.36.2.223

McKenzie, K, Witte, T., Beyko, M., Wong, S., Olver, M., & Wormith, J. S. (2002). *Predictors of attrition in a sex offender program*. Poster presented at the 63rd annual meeting of the Canadian Psychological Association, Vancouver, British Columbia.

Nicholaichuk, T. P., Gordon, A., Gu, D., & Wong, S. (2000). Outcome of an institutional sexual offender treatment program: A comparison between treated and matched untreated offenders. *Sexual Abuse: A Journal of Research and Treatment, 12*, 139–153. doi:10.1177/107906320001200205

Olver, M. E., Nicholaichuk, T. P., Kingston, D. A., & Wong, S. C. P. (2012). *The Violence Risk Scale-Sexual Offender version: A multisite examination of sexual offender risk and therapeutic change* (Unpublished raw data). University of Saskatchewan and the Regional Psychiatric Centre, Saskatoon, Canada.

Olver, M. E., Nicholaichuk, T. P., & Wong, S. C. P. (2012). *The predictive and convergent validity of a psychometric battery used to assess sex offenders in a treatment program: An 18-year prospective study*. Manuscript under review.

Olver, M. E., Stockdale, K. C., & Wormith, J. S. (2011). A meta-analysis of predictors of offender treatment attrition and its relationship to recidivism. *Journal of Consulting and Clinical Psychology, 79*, 6–21. doi:10.1037/a0022200

Olver, M. E., & Wong, S. C. P. (2006). Psychopathy, sexual deviance, and recidivism among sex offenders. *Sexual Abuse: A Journal of Research and Treatment, 18*, 65–82. doi:10.1007/s11194-006-9006-3

Olver, M. E., & Wong, S. C. P. (2008). Evaluating sex offender treatment efficacy: A review of research findings from a high intensity sex offender program (pp. 68–72). In G. Bourgon,

R. K. Hanson, J. D. Pozzulo, K. E. Morton-Bourgon, & C. L. Tanasichuk (Eds.), *The proceedings of the 2007 North American Correctional & Criminal Justice Psychology Conference*. Ottawa: Public Safety Canada.

Olver, M. E., & Wong, S. C. P. (2009). Therapeutic responses of psychopathic sexual offenders: Treatment attrition, therapeutic change, and long term recidivism. *Journal of Consulting and Clinical Psychology*, *77*, 328–336. doi:10.1037/a0015001

Olver, M. E., & Wong, S. C. P. (2011a). A comparison of static and dynamic assessment of sex offender risk and need in a treatment context. *Criminal Justice and Behavior*, *38*, 113–126. doi:10.1177/0093854810389534

Olver, M. E., & Wong, S. (2011b). Predictors of sex offender treatment dropout: Psychopathy, sex offender risk, and responsivity implications. *Psychology, Crime, & Law* *17*, 457–471. doi:10.1080/10683160903318876

Olver, M. E., & Wong, S. C. P. (2012). Sexual offender treatment attrition, risk, and recidivism: An 18-year follow-up (Unpublished manuscript). University of Saskatchewan and the Regional Psychiatric Centre, Saskatoon, Canada.

Olver, M. E., Wong, S. C. P., & Nicholaichuk, T. (2009). Outcome evaluation of a high intensity sex offender treatment program. *Journal of Interpersonal Violence*, *24*, 522–536. doi:10.1177/0886260508317196

Olver, M. E., Wong, S. C. P., Nicholaichuk, T., & Gordon, A. (2007). The validity and reliability of the Violence Risk Scale-Sexual Offender version: Assessing sex offender risk and evaluating therapeutic change. *Psychological Assessment*, *19*, 318–329. doi:10.1037/1040-3590.19.3.318

Prochaska, J. O., DiClemente, C. C., & Norcross, J. C. (1992). In search of how people change: Applications to the addictive behaviors. *American Psychologist*, *47*, 1102–1114. doi:10.1037/0003-066X.47.9.1102

Ward, T., Mann, R. E., & Gannon, T. A. (2007). The good lives model of offender rehabilitation: Clinical implications. *Aggression and Violent Behavior*, *12*, 87–107. doi:10.1016/j.avb.2006.03.004

Wong, S. (1988). Is Hare's psychopathy checklist reliable without the interview? *Psychological Reports*, *62*, 931–934. doi:10.2466/pr0.1988.62.3.931

Wong, S., Olver, M. E., Nicholaichuk, T. P., & Gordon, A. (2003). *The Violence Risk Scale: Sexual offender version (VRS-SO)*. Regional Psychiatric Centre and University of Saskatchewan, Saskatoon, Saskatchewan, Canada.

Challenging the 'urban myth' of psychopathy untreatability: the High-Risk Personality Programme

Nick J. Wilson and Armon Tamatea

Department of Corrections, Psychological Services, Rehabilitation and Reintegration Services, Hamilton, New Zealand

Psychopathy has long been framed as a special challenge in criminal justice contexts, in part due to the supposedly untreatable nature of psychopathic offenders. Indeed, previous failed attempts to 'treat' this particular group have resulted in a widespread pessimism about treatment efficacy amongst correctional professionals. This pessimism has focused on the inherent unchangeable nature of psychopathic traits, especially those associated with Psychopathy Checklist-Revised (PCL-R) Factor 1 items and the challenge of developing an effective therapeutic alliance with hostile, manipulative offenders. It is argued that this negative stance is neither unanimous nor justified because of poor consistency of population definition and methodological problems with structural and functional attributes of traditional treatment approaches. This article describes an experimental intervention – the High-Risk Personality Programme (HRPP) – a New Zealand prison-based group intensive treatment programme designed to reduce violence with a psychopathic group, and create opportunities to devise rehabilitative solutions with a challenging group.

The belief that those assessed as 'criminal psychopaths' are not able to be treated is pervasive among the general public, as well as those involved in the criminal justice system, implying that the most viable 'solution' is indeterminate and high-security incarceration or capital punishment (Hare, 1996). Psychopathic individuals typically are characterised as exhibiting significant qualitative differences from other offenders. For example, psychopathic offenders are identified as having long-term criminal careers, beginning at an early age and their offending is often extensive and versatile (Hare, 2003). They also tend to violate conditional releases much sooner than non-psychopathic offenders; commit reactive violence; exhibit clear external goals as part of their overall offence patterns; derive gratification from inflicting pain on others (Porter & Porter, 2007) and commit a disproportionate amount of serious crime (Cooke, Forth, & Hare, 1998; Hare, 1998; Harris, Rice, & Cormier, 1991; Hart & Hare, 1997; Serin & Amos, 1995). However, it is important to point out that many offenders classified as at high risk of serious reoffending have similar career and offence characteristics captured by Psychopathy Checklist-Revised (PCL-R) Factor 2 items without necessarily having the interpersonal and affective deficits captured by Factor 1 items (Skeem, Polaschek, Patrick, & Lilienfeld, 2011; Wilson, 2004).

Furthermore, there are practical implications of being identified as possessing psychopathic traits in forensic settings (e.g. parole, treatment eligibility, sentence length; Hare, 2003). It is important, therefore, to move beyond diagnostic criteria (and unhelpful stereotypes) when the issue of most concern is risk of reoffending. Instead, the focus should be on specific interpersonal and affective differences that relate to deviant social and criminal behaviour of the psychopathic offender (Skeem, Polaschek, & Manchak, 2009).

The literature in regard to the use of therapy to change the antisocial behaviour associated with high-risk psychopathic offenders has resulted in a bleak picture, suggesting that the attitudes and behaviours of psychopathic offenders are difficult or impossible to modify – or even worsened – with traditional forms of therapeutic intervention (Dolan & Coid, 1993; D'Silva, Duggan, & McCarthy, 2004; Hare, 1998; Lösel, 1998; Millon, Simonsen, & Birket-Smith, 1998). Ironically, this perceived untreatability led many clinicians and corrections authorities to avoid attempts to treat psychopathic offenders (Wong & Hare, 2006).

However, it is not possible to review the research literature on the treatment of adult psychopathy without finding investigations with this group that are of generally poor quality, in which no conclusive evidence of improvement has been shown. On a fundamental level, the therapeutic pessimism has been based on studies that use differing definitions of psychopathy and targets for treatment that may not address the maintaining factors for antisocial behaviour (Salekin, 2002). Other methodological limitations in past psychopathy treatment include a lack of adequate control groups, failure to control for heterogeneity within treatment groups, lack of attention to developmental factors, inadequate definition and implementation of treatment and restricted outcome criteria (Harris et al., 1991; Hemphill & Hart, 2002; Salekin, 2002). Finally there is a need to consider the growing literature on crime desistance and the need to follow offenders over time capturing the transition to less serious and frequent offending rather than only focusing on recidivism (Serin & Lloyd, 2009).

Is treatment possible?

Historically the evidence of effective treatment is limited. Salekin (2002) while reporting on 42 relevant studies found few regarded as having sound methodology. It is therefore encouraging that research carried out since Salekin's review has been more robust in terms of diagnosis and stated outcomes. Recent research into the treatment of psychopathy has followed the core principles of risk, need and responsivity (RNR; Andrews, 1995) that have become the most prominent corrections therapy model (Cullen & Johnston, 2010). The research supporting success from adherence to these principles while modest (effect sizes 0.15–0.34) is robust across offenders populations and offence types (Andrews & Bonta, 2010). Although this reduction in reoffending for general offenders in relation to targeted offence-specific behaviours is encouraging, are similar approaches effective with high-risk offenders? High-risk violent offenders are a group that typically contains a larger number of psychopathic offenders (Porter, Birt, & Boer, 2001) and this was found to also be the case in New Zealand research (Polaschek & Bell, 2008; Wilson, 2003).

A recent comprehensive review of psychopathic personality (Skeem et al., 2011) reported on four studies that had addressed the issue of treatment success with psychopathic offenders. Of these, three found some evidence of change in psychiatric, youth and adult offender populations. While the follow-up periods and failure outcomes varied from 10 weeks to 2 years, their limited success is promising. However, it should also be acknowledged that to date there are no randomised control studies (RCT) published with treatment research remaining at the level of case studies, and quasi-experimental designs (Tyrer et al., 2010).

What is less clear is the ability of treatment to reduce psychopathic traits. No evidence has yet been published showing change in traits in part due to the lack of a change sensitive measure (Cooke, Hart, Logan, & Michie, forthcoming). The focus, therefore, in recent years has been on change, not in the psychopathic individual's basic personality structure but rather in the dynamic-risk factors associated with offending. In this regard dynamic need measures such as the Violence Risk Scale (VRS), developed by Wong and Gordon (2000) through their work with high-risk offenders at the Saskatoon Regional Forensic Centre are promising approaches. Olver and Wong (2009) found that reductions in scores for VRS dynamic-risk items for psychopathic sex offenders reduced sexual or violent offending with a further study of violent psychopathic offenders confirming lower scores changed patterns of serious reoffending (Lewis, Olver, & Wong, 2012). The critical factors identified in the success of the Saskatoon programme included (1) strict management of programme integrity; (2) delivery of intensive treatment that is tailored to the individual's ability; (3) cognitive-behavioural therapy (CBT) in group and individual settings; (4) intensive intervention (i.e. 30+ hours per week of treatment related activity); (5) emphasis on the development of working alliances; and (6) use of the stages of change model in the VRS (Wong & Gordon, 2000).

In summary, the treatment or management of psychopathic behaviour is one that is yet to receive rigorous study. While it is important to recognise and plan to overcome the barriers that psychopathy (and other severe personality disorder [PD]) presents to treatment, the focus on criminogenic factors appears to be a promising direction for psychopathy 'treatment' and the development of innovative programmes (Wong & Hare, 2006).

New Zealand context

Psychopathy as a forensic construct has had a relatively late impact in New Zealand correctional practice and hence, research is limited. However, a study using data from the late 1990s validated the utility of the PCL: SV (Hart, Cox, & Hare, 1995). Wilson (2003) found high scorers (16 plus) on this measure tended to be reimprisoned six times more rapidly than non-psychopathic offenders. However, those classified as 'false positives' (25%) based on high PCL: SV scores and no reported reimprisonment within five years post-release were found to have changed their adaptive responses to their environment. This improved risk management (without treatment) was related to geographic isolation, reduced substance abuse, prosocial support and avoidance of antisocial influences (Wilson, 2003).

Prior to the current research there had not been any structured interventions evaluated for psychopathic offenders in New Zealand. However, Corrections psychologists in New Zealand have been treating individuals who would meet the diagnostic criteria for criminal psychopathy for decades; we just did not know they had this classification. The PCL-R (Hare, 1991) and PCL: SV (Hart et al., 1995) were not in regular use in New Zealand until 2000, when Corrections developed regular validated training in these measures. Even then, only those deemed likely to be psychopathic were administered the measure, so most never received the classification and were not excluded or treated differently from other high-risk offenders assessed as in need of treatment (Polaschek & Bell, 2008; Wilson, 2003). Yet some success has been found in New Zealand treatment programmes that followed the RNR principles delivering structured group-based interventions with high-risk violent male offenders (Berry, 1999; Polaschek, Wilson, Townsend, & Daly, 2005; Wilson & Bakker, 2002). However, despite showing promise, more data are required to assess the effects of programmes with psychopathic offenders compared to non-psychopathic high-risk offenders (Polaschek, 2011).

The High-Risk Personality Programme (HRPP) in New Zealand

The HRPP was designed to (1) respond to the risk management needs of an increasingly identified population of psychopathic offenders in New Zealand prisons (Wilson, 2003); (2) reduce the incidence of serious violent offending; (3) pursue promising treatment directions to inform other offender rehabilitation initiatives in New Zealand correctional practice; (4) learn how to meet specific responsivity needs for such offenders; and (5) *not* to treat psychopathy per se, but rather to manage core characteristics while targeting secondary behaviours functionally linked to violent offending. It was recognised that disordered personality reflects failures to adapt appropriately to life challenges (Livesley, 2007), so the relationship between personality and offending behaviour was understood to be complex (e.g. presence of multiple personality pathology, Wilson, 2004), requiring specific attention as an indication of treatment efficacy. The overall treatment philosophy involved transitions from external factors (containment) to developing internal stability and synthesis of self-regulation skills, especially in the face of setbacks and crises and the eventual return to the community (Livesley, 2007, 2012). It was also regarded as important to provide this treatment option in a high security setting, in view of a lack of specialist therapy for New Zealand prisoners held in medium-high and maximum security settings. The typical reasons for not offering specialist treatment in higher security settings in New Zealand have included difficulties in delivering therapy in facilities without dedicated treatment spaces, safety concerns in grouping these men and their low motivation to change.

The HRPP approach

The HRPP was based on a review of other intensive treatment results from Canada (i.e. Saskatoon Regional Forensic Centre; see Wong & Gordon, 2013) and the then newly-created Dangerous and Severe Personality Disorder (DSPD) Units (Tyrer et al., 2010; see also Saradjian, 2013; Tew & Atkinson, 2013). Meta-analyses of factors associated with effective treatment for adult and juvenile offenders indicated that CBT was the most efficacious intervention modality when reducing recidivism was a treatment outcome (Landenberger & Lipsey, 2005). The Saskatoon and DSPD programmes were both largely informed by cognitive-behavioural treatments (and variations, such as Dialectical Behaviour Therapy; Maden, 2006; Maden, Williams, Wong, & Leis, 2004; Warren et al., 2003). Furthermore, New Zealand-based intensive intervention programmes have demonstrated some success using CBT approaches with high-risk violent offenders (Berry, 1999) – many of whom have been identified as having marked psychopathic traits (Polaschek & Bell, 2008). As a result the core treatment model of the programme was cognitive-behavioural in orientation.

Delivery of intensive group and individual therapy was tailored to each individual's ability and need with consideration given to all their personality pathology, not just psychopathy. The inclusion of the VRS dynamic items as an educational and treatment tool allowed the participants an opportunity to 'self-assess' the items they felt were most relevant to them (interestingly, most men self-identified their relevant items). The VRS also informed the creation of relevant post-treatment management plans as well as how final reports of change would inform parole recommendations. The focus was also – with 11 out of the 12 participants identifying as – on developing and maintaining a working alliance with the incorporation of *tikanga*[1] to address resistance and culturally-informed responsivity issues.

The main focus of this paper is to provide an understanding of (1) how the HRPP programme was structured and delivered in a high security prison setting with high-risk violent offenders assessed as psychopathic, and (2) how successful the approach has been in promoting desistance from serious reoffending.

Setting

The HRPP was situated in a medium-high security prison unit in one of a number of wings that formed a high security complex. At the time of the programme, the same unit also housed other prisoners with high security classifications who were segregated from the mainstream prison community: usually due to safety concerns to themselves and other members of the prison community. The HRPP participants were further segregated from the other unit prisoners due to concerns over their high risk of violence to others. In practice this meant the HRPP group only associated with each other for therapy and exercise, spending long periods locked in their single occupant cells. Prison staff in the HRPP unit were provided with training about psychopathy, the programme, their role and the importance of maintaining therapeutic gains in an impoverished and often aversive environment.

Format

The programme was conducted over a 44-week period from late January to early November 2007. This was viewed as long enough to deliver the programme and assess change in the treatment setting and was in keeping with the review of other intensive programmes (Andrews & Bonta, 2010). The programme also served to facilitate progression from higher to lower security classifications for individuals with mainly finite sentences, challenging behaviours (e.g. serious assaults on staff and other prisoners) and a need for access to mainstream rehabilitative interventions. Thus, it was critical that the programme had identified treatment targets and a specified end date. On a given week the men participated in (1) three group therapy sessions (approximately three hours duration); (2) a one-hour individual therapy session; and (3) a two-hour group therapy session that involved culturally-informed therapeutic activities. In summary, the participants were exposed to over 450 hours of direct psychological intervention.

Staff

The programme was delivered by three experienced clinical psychologists employed by the Department of Corrections, who were of mixed ethnicity (i.e. Pasifika, and North American) and gender. In addition, the programme developer (first author), cultural consultant and a forensic psychiatrist were available to assist with case management in the event of emergent pathology or culturally-salient behaviour beyond the expertise of the therapists. The treatment-interfering behaviours that are sequelae of psychopathic traits (e.g. lack of insight and concern for others) can create hazards in therapy with this population (Sheldon & Tennant, 2011; Thornton & Blud, 2007). Therapy staff involved in the programme were trained and supervised in relation to the transference and personality pathology typically displayed by high-risk psychopathic offenders, to ensure the development of an effective and objective working alliance and staff safety (Wong & Hare, 2006).

Content

The programme itself comprised three stages: each about three months long, and separated by a 2–3 week 'holiday from therapy'. These breaks allowed therapists to regroup and plan successive sessions, and participants, to practice acquired skills. The principles for therapy phases and session goals for each phase were created at the beginning of the HRPP. However, sessions were reviewed and modified between phases as required. The first stage addressed past treatment failure, education about therapy and the HRPP approach and the identification of personality issues that served as barriers to entering, engaging and maintaining gains in treatment (e.g. reactive emotionally dysregulated and dissocial interpersonal behaviours). The focus was on creating a collaborative and consultative relationship with shared goals in relation to the treatment of violence. The second phase focused on techniques for understanding and appropriately managing aggression and violence in both community and institutional settings. Personal offending disclosures were used to identify cognitive schemas (Young, Klosko, & Weishaar, 2003) and behaviour patterns that supported violence. Participants were also taught functional analysis: to develop a greater understanding of their past behaviour, and to improve their analysis of future high-risk situations. The third and final phase involved preparing for release or gradual reintegration (including engagement in other treatment) and incorporated the recruitment and assistance of external support people to aid reintegration.

The programme balanced structure (i.e. module objectives) with flexibility. For instance, the second module focused on the 20 VRS dynamic items but also provided opportunities to allow for repetition of past sessions and practice of newly learnt skills. Consistent with this flexibility, therapy staff – while grounded in a CBT approach – utilised other therapies to address the range of participants' treatment and responsivity issues. These included Acceptance and Commitment Therapy (Hayes, 2004) and Dialectical Behaviour Therapy (Linehan, 1998).

The combination of group and individual therapy allowed for flexibility of practice: including use of group dynamics in supporting and challenging shared issues. Individual sessions allowed for a more intimate focus, and were also used to clarify material from group sessions, and to address interpersonal conflict with other group members or therapy and custodial staff.

Participants

Twelve male prisoners were selected via nominations from prison management or self-referrals from a number of New Zealand prisons. Selection criteria included: (1) age 18 or older; (2) high score on the PCL-R (27 plus); (3) index violent offence or history of institutional violence; and (4) sufficient sentence length to complete treatment. The programme was located in an old high-medium-security wing at Waikeria Prison; participants had to volunteer to be placed onto segregation classification to meet the unit management criteria. It was expected that most would be members of criminal gangs (Wilson, 2004) and participants also had to agree to leave gang rivalries outside of the therapy setting.

Measures

PCL-R

The PCL-R is a standardised rating scale of psychopathic personality and is comprised of 20 items rated on a three-point scale (0 = *does not apply*, 1 = *applies in some respects* and 2 = *a good match*; Hare, 2003). Eligibility criteria required participants to have marked psychopathic traits (i.e. PCL-R ≥ 27).

Treatment Readiness, Responsivity, and Gain Scale: Short Version (TRRG: SV)

This scale is a structured clinical judgement measure designed to assess an offender's degree of preparedness and engagement with rehabilitative interventions via a range of motivational anchors, treatment responsiveness indicators and subsequent progress made (i.e. knowledge, participation and competence; Serin, Kennedy, & Mailloux, 2005). Higher scores on the readiness (eight items, range 0–24) and responsivity (eight items, range 0–24) scales indicate greater amenability for treatment engagement.

VRS

The VRS is a structured professional judgement measure comprised of both static (e.g. age at first violent conviction) and 20 dynamic (e.g. cognitive distortions, insight into violence) variables (Wong & Gordon, 2000). It is designed to assess risk for general violence as well as changes in risk over time. Items are rated on a four-point scale reflecting the presence or absence of the item criteria. Higher scores reflect presence of risk factors.

Millon Clinical Multiaxial Inventory – 3rd Edition (MCMI-III)

The MCMI-III is a widely-used multiple-choice, self-report instrument designed to provide diagnostic and treatment information in the areas of PDs and clinical syndromes, and has applicability with general correctional populations (Millon, Millon, Davis, & Grossman, 2009; Retzlaff, Stoner, & Kleinsasser, 2002; Wilson, 2004). Whilst serving as a general mental health screening measure, the presence of severe PD (i.e. paranoid, schizotypal and borderline PD) is also captured by this instrument. It was expected from research into the characteristics of high-risk offenders or DSPD that most would have the presence of other PD associated with reactive emotionally dysregulated and dissocial interpersonal behaviour (Burns et al., 2011; Wilson, 2004).

Results

Socio-demographic characteristics

The HRPP group comprised of 12 male prisoners. The mean age at the start of the programme was 28.6 years ($SD = 8.4$; range 19–49 years): slightly younger than the general prison population. Ten self-identified as Maori, one claimed New Zealand European descent, and another claimed both and Pacific ancestry. Five participants were serving at least eight years imprisonment with three on indeterminate sentences. All had extensive community and institutional violent offending histories.

All participants had a history of involvement with criminal gangs. To help deal with mix of rival gang-members, group members were provided with a distinctive uniform in gang neutral colours, and were only allowed to associate with other group members and be unlocked with three staff present.

Treatment engagement

Readiness

Contrary to expectations, participants exhibited a high degree of preparedness for treatment ($M = 17.45$, $SD = 3.56$) which did not significantly change between pre- and post-treatment.

Responsivity

Similarly, the group reported a high degree of responsiveness for treatment at the start of the HRPP and scores were not significantly higher at the end of treatment (pre-$M = 12.18$, $SD = 6.32$, range 0–24; post-$M = 17.02$, $SD = 5.45$).

Change in dynamic risk during treatment

Change-related information on the HRPP participants was obtained from group and individual session case notes. In addition, daily brief meetings with custodial staff were held before group to gain information on custodial staff observations of participant behaviour. Although the participants were largely segregated from themselves and others, the multiple formats for treatment (group, individual and cultural sessions) as well as staff interactions and observations of exercise and self-care provided opportunities for participants to demonstrate observable change.

The primary focus of the treatment programme itself concerned change in violent behaviour. The mean VRS total score (pre-treatment) was high: 60.42 ($SD = 5.33$).

Common items for participants included violent lifestyle, criminal personality, attitudes, peers, interpersonal aggression, emotional control, substance abuse, stability of relationships and discernible violence cycles. At post-treatment, dynamic scores were observed to have collectively reduced across all dynamic factors (post-total $M = 52.70$; $SD = 5.97$; difference *ns;* see Figure 1).

Personality pathology

Psychopathy

The mean PCL-R scores was 32.13 ($SD = 2.21$); all programme participants all met the diagnostic criteria for psychopathy (see Table 1). The Factor scores revealed that interpersonal and affective deficits (Factor 1) typical of psychopathic individuals were not as high as those for antisocial and deviant lifestyles (Factor 2). The high Factor 2 scores reflect participants' pervasive criminal histories and serious violent offending rather than psychopathy as such.

Other PDs

Scores on the MCMI-III indicated the marked presence (or 'prominence') of advanced personality pathology amongst eight participants. Six revealed core traits of borderline PD; nearly half reported primary features of paranoid PD; and four reported schizotypal features. However, post-treatment administration of the MCMI-III revealed a decline in overall severe personality pathology scale scores across the group, with only four participants reporting symptoms consistent with severe PD (see Table 2).

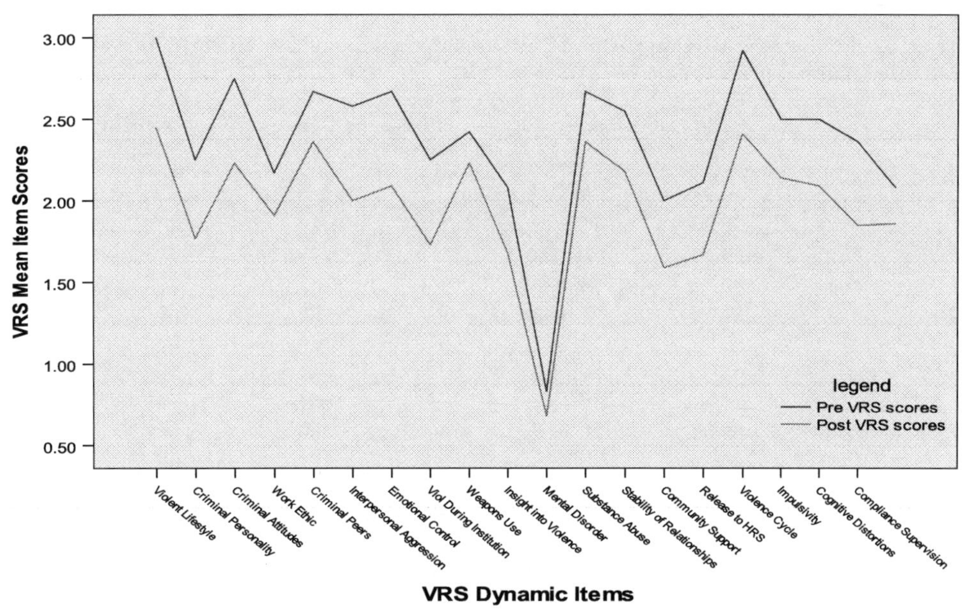

Figure 1. Comparison pre- and post-HRPP for VRS dynamic item mean scores.

Table 1. PCL-R factor, facet and total scores for the HRPP sample ($N = 12$).

PCL-R	Min	Max	Mean	SD
Factor 1	10	14	12.08	1.24
Facet 1	4	7	5.25	0.87
Facet 2	5	8	6.83	0.72
Factor 2	14	20	17.88	1.66
Facet 3	6	10	8.82	1.21
Facet 4	6.2	10	8.82	1.07
Total score	28.4	36	32.13	2.21

Post-programme observations and reoffending follow-up

Only one participant failed to complete the HRPP; he was removed from the programme to facilitate lengthy court appearances for past offending. For the 11 who completed progress was certainly not linear, but they all reduced scores on dynamic violence risk measures and on measures of personality pathology relating to control over unstable emotions and impulses. No violent misconducts were reported during the 44-week programme; three were incurred in the six months post-programme, when all were in other prisons units; a marked reduction from the months before the programme. In addition, prison staff – whose previous experiences with these prisoners made them initially sceptical – reported positive changes in behaviour, that continued into their in new units. Eighty per cent reduced their pre-programme security rating; half achieved minimum security within six months, some for the first time. Forty per cent went on to engage in additional intensive group therapy.

In terms of reoffending it is, as expected, a mixed picture. Ten of the 11 treatment completers have been released at some point in the last four years. Some returned to prison for less serious offences and were released once again or indeed on multiple

Table 2. Pre- and post-treatment severe personality pathology for HRPP participants using MCMI-III base rate scores.

	Paranoid PD		Borderline PD		Schizotypal PD	
Participant	Pre	Post	Pre	Post	Pre	Post
1	78*	12	85**	19	74	62
2	64	0	90**	39	71	0
3	95**	74	66	63	70	65
4	64	53	69	25	69	5
5	63	–	10	–	65	–
6	63	0	62	40	20	60
7	80*	70	77*	63	94**	80
8	69	70	84*	60	62	65
9	64	30	60	26	40	6
10	79*	78*	68	49	88**	79
11	86**	73	80*	57	70	72
12	74	24	87**	70	82*	60

*Indicates the *presence* of the disorder [base rate (BR) = 75–84].
**Indicates the *prominence* of the disorder (BR = 85 +).
***Post MCMI-III scores were not available for this case as this offender did not complete the programme.

occasions: a pattern typical of unstable desisters (fluctuating but less serious and frequent offending, Laub & Sampson, 2003). However, as Table 3 shows when the pattern of reoffending (prison and the community) is considered, most are either stable desisters (46%, $n=5$) or unstable desisters (18%, $n=2$). Stable desisters had either no further reoffending or infrequent less serious offending (institutional or community based) while unstable desisters had fluctuating reoffending that represented a change in frequency or seriousness compared to past offence patterns.

Table 3. Four year post-treatment behaviour follow up across the 11 HRPP completers in regards to pattern of desistance.

	Index offence	One year	Two years	Three years	Four years	Desistance category
1	GBH with knife	Released	Reimprisoned serious violence-six years	Violent misconducts	Violent misconducts	Persister
2	Murder	No issues	Minor misconduct	Viol misconduct	No issues	Desister
3	Aggravated robbery	No issues	Prosocial leader	Prosocial leader	Work release	Desister
4	Wounds, GBH, torture/ kidnap	No issues	Released	Domestic violence, breach, stalking	Domestic violence (× 3) reimprisoned	Persister
5	Rape, GBH	Minor issues	Violence misconducts	Released, minor offences	Disorder offences, 2 month reimprisonment	Unstable
6	Aggravated robbery, injures	Released reimprisoned theft	Minor issues sought trt re-released	Assaults (× 3), EBA, reimprisoned	Released, reimprisoned serious assault	Persister
7	Aggravated robbery, kidnap	Minor issues released	Released, reimprisoned 1 year	Model prisoner released	Minor offending, family focused	Desister
8	Aggravated robbery, assault	No issues	Released, good behaviour noted	Reimprisoned assault police	Released, threat offence	Unstable
9	Injures with intent	Minor issues	Released	Minor offences	Minor offence	Desister
10	Wounds, robbery	No issues	Release-recalled minor breach conditions	Released	No issues	Desister
11	Aggravated robbery, assault	Released reimprisonment theft	Serious prison issues	Released, convicted domestic violence	Reimprisoned repeat breach, drunk driving	Persister

GBH, grevious bodily harm; EBA, excess blood alcohol.

For behaviour in the community, 'serious' was defined as reoffending leading to imprisonment for periods of two years or more. In prison, 'serious' represented assaults on staff or other violence resulting in new criminal convictions.[2] Changes in frequency were based for each participant on a comparison of new offences with those during their last similar period in the community post-release or if the current prison sentence was lengthy, with misconducts recorded during an equivalent amount of time immediately pre-programme. Analysis of participants' reoffending based on interview and a review of probation records found that efforts to desist were undone by unstable environments, maladaptive schema, active gang membership and poorer release plans.

When their risk and need profile based on their past criminal histories and institutional behaviour records are considered this is an encouraging result for a group considered prior to treatment to be unable to desist. While the study did not include a control group previous research by the lead author into desistance by those with high psychopathy scores found 25% desisted from serious or frequent reoffending without attending treatment over a five-year period post-release (Wilson, 2003).

Discussion

This paper presents an overview of an experimental treatment programme for high-risk violent psychopathic offenders designed to inform other offender rehabilitation initiatives in New Zealand correctional practice. Capitalising on the accomplishments, challenges and experiences of psychopathy-specific initiatives in other jurisdictions, the HRPP was informed by (1) an established model of psychopathy (Hare, 2003); (2) a theory of criminal behaviour (Andrews & Bonta, 2010); (3) a theory of behaviour change (Prochaska & DiClemente, 1984); and (4) measurable behavioural outcomes (Serin et al., 2005; Wong & Gordon, 2000). Psychopathic traits were treated as responsivity issues, consistent with Andrews and Bonta's (2010) reconfiguration of PCL-R factors in a RNR-compliant arrangement, rather than as the actual focus of treatment. In other words, the goal was to reduce *violence* in a psychopathic group, rather than reduce *psychopathy* in a violent group. Measurable goals related to violence recidivism (e.g. VRS dynamic items) were more central to the programme than personality change per se, despite some notable change across a range of pathological presentations (i.e. MCMI-III).

The treatment of those with severe PD requires the establishment of emotional and behavioural stability before it is possible to address maladaptive behaviour, in the case of the HRPP violence (Livesley, 2012). The changes in personality pathology in participants across the approximately year-long therapy suggest that the HRPP was successful in bringing about safety, through programme structure and group and individual therapeutic support. The programme was also effective in containing and managing unstable emotions and impulses in the therapy setting. These changes are in keeping with the first two stages of Livesley's (2012) integrated domain-focused model of PD treatment.

The modest success of the programme may be attributed to realistic and narrow aims compared with the more ambitious focus of previous initiatives: changing personality pathology. For instance, 'success' – a major conceptual challenge (Harris & Rice, 2006; Salekin, 2002) – was defined from the outset as assisting participants to change institutional behaviour and access mainstream interventions (i.e. manage violent behaviour – particularly behaviour driven by reactive and explosive aggression). So, the participants' ability to lower their security classification was a definitive and measurable index of 'success'. Any further reductions in their institutional aggression, security classification, or even post-release violence were viewed as additional and very welcome benefits. The measures revealed change across a range of empirically-supported factors related to violence – as well as treatment gains and responsiveness – suggesting that treatment of psychopathic offenders is justifiable because they can change established patterns of interpersonal violence.

Despite mixed reoffending results and the limitations of one small sample, the HRPP outcomes appear promising, suggesting that not only do psychopathic offenders – as a group – appear to benefit from correctional programmes (Polaschek et al., 2005), but they may further benefit from purpose-built interventions designed to target specific features.

Resources for the HRPP were comparatively modest in relation to overseas initiatives (Tyrer et al., 2010) although they were higher than those typically provided for the treatment of high-risk offenders in New Zealand. However, the programme was not able to be housed in a dedicated space, but was based in an environment that served multiple prisoner categories. Although the arrangement was not particularly desirable, it was able to be used to advantage, to greatly reduce contact with members of the prison gang community. It also had unexpectedly fortuitous consequences. For example, the provision of a distinctive uniform for HRPP men avoided both issues associated with rival gang colours, and also made them readily identifiable to others who had sought segregation on the wing because they needed protection from the types of participants in the treatment group. The special management regime that saw HRPP participants having increased cell time created an increased opportunity for study and homework.

That psychopathic offenders are one of the most challenging populations in corrections environments has been a long-held reality by many workers and researchers in the field, not least because the inherent nature of psychopathic traits have been viewed as incommensurate with goals and processes of traditional therapeutic programmes. In contrast many HRPP participants maintained apparent genuine high regard for each other – despite some very real past and future rivalries (e.g. gangs) – and continued to ask after each other in the years that followed, in a manner suggesting a degree of social attachment not driven by external goals. This success in maintaining 11 out of the 12 participants until the completion of therapy is a significant result when one considers the high drop-out rate by psychopathic offenders (Olver, Stockdale, & Wormith, 2011). This result is unexpected. PCL-R Factor 1 scores for HRPP participants are usually associated with selfish, callous and remorseless use of others, and in particular, with poor group and prison wing behaviour (Hobson, Shine, & Roberts, 2000).

Limitations

The HRPP was an experimental treatment programme that involved 12 men. The problems of over-generalising the outcomes of this programme to high-risk psychopathic populations are obvious. The promising results are hampered by the small sample size and lack of a matched comparison group. The relationship between the programme and each participant's apparent desistance behaviour is still imprecise and would need to be demonstrated empirically.

The HRPP had clear success in being able to bring together participants from four separate gangs with long histories of violent warfare, and maintain them safely in group therapy. This success may in part result from shared ethnicity, and shared sense of belonging to an economically and politically disadvantaged group. We were able to use Māori concepts to reinforce the ability for rivals to come together and leave gang differences outside of the therapy room. Thus the treatment room could be regarded as a *Marae*, a place where the culture can be celebrated, where the Māori language can be spoken, where inter-tribal obligations can be met, where customs can be explored and debated by participants in a safe prescribed and indeed 'sacred place'. We also had some senior gang members in the group whose presence was a curb on the junior members. No gang colour and signs were tolerated during treatment. However, we did not insist that members left the gang before treatment. They were instead expected to put membership 'on hold' during therapy, and make a commitment to the therapy group. On the other hand, frequent rotations of unit custodial staff during treatment resulted in the loss of staff initially trained to understand psychopathy and the aims and structure of the programme. This loss affected staff expertise, and cooperation with the programme goals.

Impact of the HRPP and future research directions

Following the HRPP group over time is important in understanding desistance by high-risk psychopathic offenders, especially in terms of the level of support needed to maintain stability and to address issues for those 'zigzagging'. The assessment of reoffending detailed in Table 3 covering a four-year post-completion follow-up of the programme indicates why a desistance framework is needed to understand success and failure in such offenders. The preliminary analysis of reoffending by participants found that the men in the HRPP were similar to other high risk violent recidivists: desistance efforts were undone by poor release plans (Dickson, Polaschek, & Casey, 2012), unstable environments, maladaptive schema and active gang membership (Jones, Brown, & Zamble, 2010). Thus, creation of high quality release plans coupled with the active management of fluctuations in dynamic risk by probation staff is likely to increase the success of future treatment initiatives with psychopathic offenders.

However, one thing is clear, the group did make measurable positive changes both during the programme and in the follow-up period, with the majority showing either stable or unstable desistance from crime. Although the HRPP was treated as an experiment, the lessons learnt in delivering the programme are being used to align Corrections' other intensive-treatment programmes (see Polaschek & Kilgour, 2013; Wilson, Kilgour, & Polaschek, 2013) to better address the needs of high-psychopathy participants. For instance these other programmes now (1) provide structured individual therapy sessions; (2) provide support for a reduced reliance on highly manualised programme material, and an increased focus on principle-based treatment that takes into account learning and responsivity barriers.

The other noted impacts of the HRPP on New Zealand Corrections' service delivery included increased acceptance by Department psychologists and staff in probation and prison settings that those high in psychopathy are able to be treated and should not be eliminated from other intensive therapy options. There was also increased awareness of the heterogeneous nature of those meeting the diagnostic criteria for psychopathy. The 12 men, although presenting similar high PCL-R scores, behaved very differently from each other, suggesting different needs and responsivity considerations (Skeem et al., 2011). Some were able to engage effectively in treatment and use the knowledge and skills learned to establish a pathway out of offending. The more we understand these offenders in terms of their functional differences the greater our ability to assist those able to change and to identify those who, at this stage, remain a significant risk to others if released (Camp, Skeem, Barchard, Lilienfeld, & Poythress, in press). The HRPP outcomes while positive should be interpreted as small steps towards understanding this population as a group defined by challenging behaviours.

Notes

1. Referring to traditional Māori cultural worldviews to promote a culturally-informed treatment philosophy.
2. Most incidents of prison violence are dealt with through established policies for processing institutional misconducts. New criminal convictions only result in rare cases; when the incident is sufficiently serious to warrant prosecution through the (external) court system.

References

Andrews, D. (1995). The psychology of criminal conduct and effective treatment. In J. McGuire (Ed.), *What works: Reducing reoffending* (pp. 35–62). Chichester: Wiley.

Andrews, D. A., & Bonta, J. (2010). *The psychology of criminal conduct* (5th ed.). Cincinnati, OH: Anderson.

Berry, S. (1999). *Montgomery house evaluation* (Unpublished report). Department of Corrections, Wellington, New Zealand.

Burns, T., Fazel, S., Fahy, T., Fitzpatrick, R., Rogers, R., Sinclair, J., . . . IDEA group. (2011). Dangerous Severe Personality Disordered (DSPD) patients: Characteristics and comparison with other high-risk offenders. *International Journal of Forensic Mental Health, 10*, 127–136. doi:10.1080/14999013.2011.577139

Camp, J., Skeem, J., Barchard, K., Lilienfeld, S., & Poythress, N. (in press). Psychopathic predators? Getting specific about the relation between psychopathy and violence. *Psychological Assessment*.

Cooke, D. J., Forth, A. E., & Hare, R. D. (1998). *Psychopathy: Theory, research and implications for society*. Dordrecht, The Netherlands: Kluwer.

Cooke, D. J., Hart, S. D., Logan, C., & Michie, C. (forthcoming). Towards a clinically informed and comprehensive model of psychopathic personality. Manuscript under review.

Cullen, F. T., & Johnston, C. L. (2010). Rehabilitation and treatment. In J. Q. Wilson & J. Petersilia (Eds.), *Crime: Public policies for crime control* (3rd ed., pp. 293–344). New York: Oxford University Press.

Dickson, S. R., Polaschek, D. L. L., & Casey, A. R. (2012). Can the quality of high-risk violent prisoners' release plans predict recidivism following intensive rehabilitation? A comparison with risk assessment instruments. *Psychology, Crime & Law*. doi:10.1080/1068316X.2011.640634

Dolan, B., & Coid, J. (1993). *Psychopathic and antisocial personality disorders*. London: Gaskell.

D'Silva, K., Duggan, C., & McCarthy, L. (2004). Does treatment really make psychopaths worse? A review of the evidence. *Journal of Personality Disorders, 18*, 163–177. doi:10.1521/pedi.18.2.163.32775

Hare, R. D. (1991). *The Hare Psychopathy Checklist-Revised*. Toronto, ON: Multi-Health Systems.

Hare, R. D. (1996). Psychopathy: A construct whose time has come. *Criminal Justice and Behavior, 23*, 25–54. doi:10.1177/0093854896023001004

Hare, R. D. (1998). Psychopaths and their nature: Implications for the mental health and criminal justice systems. In T. Millon, E. Simonsen, M. Birket-Smith, & R. D. Davis (Eds.), *Psychopathy: Antisocial, criminal, and violent behavior* (pp. 188–212). London: Guilford.

Hare, R. D. (2003). *The Hare Psychopathy Checklist-Revised (PCL-R)* (2nd ed.). Toronto, Ontario: Multi-Health Systems.

Harris, G. T., & Rice, M. E. (2006). Treatment of psychopathy: A review of empirical findings. In C. J. Patrick (Ed.), *Handbook of psychopathy* (pp. 555–572). London: Guilford.

Harris, G. T., Rice, M. E., & Cormier, C. (1991). Psychopathy and violent recidivism. *Law and Human Behavior, 15*, 625–637. doi:10.1007/BF01065856

Hart, S. D., Cox, D. N., & Hare, R. D. (1995). *The Hare Psychopathy Checklist: Screening Version*. Toronto, Ontario: Multi-Health Systems.

Hart, S. D., & Hare, R. D. (1997). Psychopathy: Assessment and association with criminal conduct. In D. M. Stoff, J. Breiling, & J. D. Maser (Eds.), *Handbook of antisocial behavior* (pp. 22–35). New York: Wiley.

Hayes, S. C. (2004). Acceptance and commitment therapy, relational frame theory, and the third wave of behavior therapy. *Behavior Therapy, 35*, 639–665. doi:10.1016/S0005-7894(04)80013-3

Hemphill, J. F., & Hart, S. D. (2002). Motivating the unmotivated: Psychopathy, treatment, and change. In M. McMurran (Ed.), *Motivating offenders to change: A guide to enhancing engagement in therapy* (pp. 193–219). New York: Wiley.

Hobson, J., Shine, J., & Roberts, R. (2000). How do psychopaths behave in a prison therapeutic community? *Psychology, Crime & Law, 6*, 139–154. doi:10.1080/1068316000 8410838

Jones, N. J., Brown, S. L., & Zamble, E. (2010). Predicting criminal recidivism in adult male offenders: Researcher versus parole officer assessment of dynamic risk. *Criminal Justice and Behavior, 37*, 860–882. doi:10.1177/0093854810368924

Landenberger, N. A., & Lipsey, M. W. (2005). The positive effects of cognitive-behavioral programs for offenders: A meta-analysis of factors associated with effective treatment. *Journal of Experimental Criminology, 1*, 451–476. doi:10.1007/s11292-005-3541-7

Laub, J. H., & Sampson, R. J. (2003). *Shared beginnings, divergent lives: Delinquent boys to age 70*. Cambridge, MA: Harvard University Press.

Lewis, K., Olver, M. E., & Wong, S. C. P. (2012). The Violence Risk Scale: Predictive validity and linking treatment changes with recidivism in a sample of high risk and personality disordered offenders. *Assessment*. Advance online publication. doi:10.1177/107319111 2441242

Linehan, M. M. (1998). Dialectical behavior therapy. In J. Todd & A. C. Bohart (Eds.), *Foundations of clinical and counseling psychology* (3rd ed., pp. 298–299). Long Grove, IL: Waveland Press.

Livesley, J. (2007). Integrated therapy for complex cases of personality disorder. *Journal of Clinical Psychology, 64*, 207–221. doi:10.1002/jclp.20453

Livesley, J. (2012). Integrated treatment: A conceptual framework for an evidence-based approach to the treatment of personality disorder. *Journal of Personality Disorder, 26*, 17–42. doi:10.1521/pedi.2012.26.1.17

Lösel, F. (1998). Treatment and management of psychopaths. In D. J. Cooke, A. E. Forth, & R. D. Hare (Eds.), *Psychopathy: Theory, research and implications for society* (pp. 303–345). Dordrecht, The Netherlands: Kluwer.

Maden, T. (2006). DSPD: Origins and progress to date. *The British Journal of Forensic Practice, 8*, 24–28. doi:10.1108/14636646200600022

Maden, A., Williams, J., Wong, S. C. P., & Leis, T. A. (2004). Treating dangerous and severe personality disorder in high security. Lessons from the Regional Psychiatric Centre, Saskatoon, Canada. *Journal of Forensic Psychiatry & Psychology, 15*, 375–390. doi:10.1080/ 1478994042000268853

Millon, T., Millon, C., Davis, R., & Grossman, S. (2009). *Millon Clinical Multiaxial Inventory-III (MCMI-III) manual* (4th ed.). San Antonio, TX: Pearson.

Millon, T., Simonsen, E., & Birket-Smith, M. (1998). Historical conceptions of psychopathy in the United States and Europe. In T. Millon, E. Simonsen, M. Birket-Smith, & R. D. Davis (Eds.), *Psychopathy: Antisocial, criminal, and violent behavior* (pp. 3–31). London: Guilford.

Olver, M. E., Stockdale, K. C., & Wormith, J. (2011). A meta-analysis of predictors of offender treatment attrition and its relationship to recidivism. *Journal of Consulting and Clinical Psychology, 79*, 6–21. doi:10.1037/a0022200

Olver, M. E., & Wong, S. C. P. (2009). Therapeutic responses to psychopathic sexual offenders: Treatment attrition, therapeutic change, and long-term recidivism. *Journal of Consulting and Clinical Psychology, 77*, 328–336. doi:10.1037/a0015001

Polaschek, D. L. L. (2011). High-intensity rehabilitation for violent offenders in New Zealand: Reconviction outcomes for high- and medium-risk prisoners. *Journal of Interpersonal Violence, 26*, 664–682. doi:10.1177/0886260510365854

Polaschek, D. L. L., & Bell, R. K. (2008). *Psychopathy Checklist: Screening Version (PCL: SV) project: Retrospective file scoring of PCL: SV measures for VPU evaluation sample* (Unpublished report). Department of Corrections, Wellington, New Zealand.

Polaschek, D. L. L. & Kilgour, T. G. (2013). New Zealand's Special Treatment Units: The development and implementation of intensive treatment for high-risk male prisoners. *Psychology, Crime & Law.* doi:10.1080/1068316X.2013.759004

Polaschek, D. L. L., Wilson, N. J., Townsend, M. R., & Daly, L. R. (2005). Cognitive-behavioral rehabilitation for high-risk violent offenders: An outcome evaluation of the Violence Prevention Unit. *Journal of Interpersonal Violence, 20*, 1–17.doi:10.1177/0886260505280507

Porter, S., Birt, A. R., & Boer, D. P. (2001). Investigation of the criminal and conditional release histories of Canadian federal offenders as a function of psychopathy and age. *Law and Human Behavior, 25*, 647–661. doi:10.1023/A:1012710424821

Porter, S., & Porter, S. (2007). Psychopathy and violent crime. In H. Hervé & J. C. Yuille (Eds.), *The psychopath: Theory, research and practice* (pp. 287–300). Mahwah, NJ: Lawrence Erlbaum Associates.

Prochaska, J. O., & DiClemente, C. C. (1984). *The transtheoretical approach. Crossing traditional boundaries of therapy.* Homewood, IL: Dow Jones-Irwin.

Retzlaff, P., Stoner, J., & Kleinsasser, D. (2002). The use of the MCMI-III in the screening and triage of offenders. *International Journal of Offender Therapy and Comparative Criminology, 46*, 319–332. doi:10.1177/03024X02046003006

Salekin, R. (2002). Psychopathy and therapeutic pessimism: Clinical lore or clinical reality? *Clinical Psychology Review, 22*, 79–112. doi:10.1016/S0272-7358(01)00083-6

Saradjian, J. (2013). Delivering effective therapeutic interventions for men with severe personality disorder within a high secure prison. *Psychology, Crime & Law.* doi:10.1080/1068316X.2013.758972

Serin, R. C., & Amos, L. N. (1995). The role of psychopathy in the assessment of dangerousness. *International Journal of Law and Psychiatry, 18*, 231–238. doi:10.1016/0160-2527(95)00008-6

Serin, R., & Lloyd, C. (2009). Examining the process of offender change: The transition to crime desistance. *Psychology, Crime and Law, 15*, 347–364. doi:10.1080/10683160802261078

Serin, R. C., Kennedy, S., & Mailloux, D. L. (2005). *Manual for the Treatment Readiness, Responsivity and Gain scale Short Version (TRRG: SV).* Ottawa, Ontario, Canada: Carleton University.

Sheldon, K., & Tennant, A. (2011). Considerations for working with personality-disordered patients. *British Journal of Forensic Practice, 13*, 44–53. doi:10.5042/bjfp.2011.0049

Skeem, J. L., Polaschek, D. L. L., & Manchak, S. (2009). Appropriate treatment works, but how? Rehabilitating general psychopathic, and high-risk offenders. In J. L. Skeem, K. S. Douglas, & S. O. Lilienfeld (Eds.), *Psychological science in the courtroom: Consensus and controversy* (pp. 358–384). New York: Guilford.

Skeem, J. L., Polaschek, D. L. L., Patrick, C. J., & Lilienfeld, S. O. (2011). Psychopathic personality: Bridging the gap between scientific evidence and public policy. *Psychological Science in the Public Interest, 12*, 95–162. doi:10.1177/1529100611426706

Tew, J. & Atkinson, R. (2013). The Chromis programme: From conception to evaluation. *Psychology, Crime & Law.* doi:10.1080/1068316X.2013.758967

Thornton, D., & Blud, L. (2007). The influence of psychopathic traits on response to treatment. In D. Thornton & L. Blud (Eds.), *The psychopath: Theory, research, and practice* (pp. 5050–539). Mahwah, NJ, US: Lawrence Erlbaum.

Tyrer, P., Duggan, C., Cooper, S., Crawford, M., Seivewright, H., Rutter, D., ... Barrett, B. (2010). The successes and failures of the DSPD experiment: The assessment and management of severe personality disorder. *Medicine, Science and the Law, 50*, 95–99. doi:10.1258/msl.2010.010001

Warren, F., McGauley, G., Norton, K., Dolan, B., Preedy-Fayers, K., Pickering, A., & Geddes, J. R. (2003). *Review of treatments for severe personality disorder* (United Kingdom Home Office Online Report 30/03). London: Home Office.

Wilson, N. J. (2003). *The utility of the Psychopathy Checklist-Screening Version for predicting serious violent recidivism in a New Zealand offender sample* (Doctoral Thesis). Waikato University, Hamilton, NZ. Retrieved from New Zealand Department of Corrections website http://www.corrections.govt.nz/research/The-utility-of-the-psychopathy-checklist-screening-version.html

Wilson, N. J. (2004). *New Zealand high-risk offenders: Who are they and what are the issues in their management and treatment?* Retrieved from New Zealand Department of Corrections website http://www.corrections.govt.nz/research/high-risk-offenders.html

Wilson, N. J., & Bakker, L. (2002). *Violence prevention unit: Psychological tests of change and recidivism evaluation* (Unpublished report). New Zealand, Department of Corrections.

Wilson, N. J., Kilgour, G., & Polaschek, D. L. L. (2013). Treating high-risk rapists in a New Zealand intensive prison programme. *Psychology, Crime & Law.* doi:10.1080/1068316X.2013.758994

Wong, S., & Gordon, A. (2000). *Violence Risk Scale.* Unpublished manuscript. Saskatoon, SK, Canada, Research Unit, Regional Psychiatric Centre.

Wong, S. C. P., & Gordon, A. (2013). The Violence Reduction Programme: A treatment programme for violence prone forensic clients. *Psychology, Crime & Law.* doi:10.1080/1068316X.2013.758981

Wong, S., & Hare, R. D. (2006). *Guidelines for a psychopathy treatment program.* Toronto, ON: Multi-Health Systems.

Young, J. E., Klosko, J. S., & Weishaar, M. E. (2003). *Schema therapy: A practitioner's guide.* New York: Guilford.

New Zealand's special treatment units: the development and implementation of intensive treatment for high-risk male prisoners

Devon L.L. Polaschek[a] and T. Glen Kilgour[b]

[a]*School of Psychology, Victoria University of Wellington, Wellington, New Zealand;* [b]*Department of Corrections Psychological Service, Hamilton, New Zealand*

In the late 1980s, New Zealand developed two highly innovative residential treatment programmes for serious offenders that blended together the strengths of structured cognitive behavioural group programmes and therapeutic community approaches. Since the mid-1990s this hybrid model – recently advocated as a fruitful direction for future offender programme development – was adopted and further refined for use in New Zealand's four high-risk special treatment units (HRSTUs). We outline the HRSTU model, noting the challenges and potential benefits of providing an intervention that integrates therapy, resocialisation and reintegration experiences for high-risk, high need, low responsivity clients: many with significant psychopathic features. On average, the majority of those referred to HRSTUs complete the programme and make small but significant amounts of change on important treatment goals. But most changes remain tentative, suggesting the importance of more supportive aftercare. Although an earlier evaluation of the first unit to open found the programme to be modestly effective in reducing recidivism, an outcome evaluation currently underway will help establish whether improvements since that time are associated with reductions in disciplinary infractions and recidivism.

The first intensive rehabilitation unit for high-risk prisoners in New Zealand opened in 1998 and targeted repetitively violent offenders: The Rimutaka Violence Prevention Unit.[1] Three similar units opened during 2008 and 2009. This paper focuses on these four 'special treatment units' for high-risk prisoners.

New Zealand has a single, nationalised prison system, currently housing over 8500 prisoners, giving it one of the highest per capita imprisonment rates in the Western world (Walmsley, 2009). Most New Zealand prisoners (94%) are male and aged between 20 and 29 years. Maori comprise 51%, with 34% European New Zealanders and 12% of Pacific nations descent. The most common index offences are violent (41%) and sexual (21%), and at least one-quarter of prisoners are members of criminal gangs (Prison facts and statistics, 2010). Most prisoners (89%) are eligible for release. Those serving more than 2 years imprisonment are usually eligible for early parole when one-third of their sentence has passed. Once released, more than half will return to prison within 5 years: half of those in the first 12 months (Nadesu,

2009). High rates of imprisonment and reimprisonment, and high costs – over $90000 per prisoner per annum – together provide impetus for initiatives that may reduce reoffending.

Prisoners eligible for admission into one of the high-risk special treatment units (HRSTUs) usually have an estimated risk of returning to prison of at least 70% over the 5 years following release, are over the age of 20, have a low-medium or minimum security rating, have sufficient time left on their sentence to complete the programme and agree to be transferred to the unit. Until recently, Te Whare Manaakitanga (TWM; Rimutaka) prioritised referrals from those with more extensive histories of repetitive violent offending, but all four units adopted the same entry criteria in 2011.

Background to the current treatment model

Over the last 3–4 years, the HRSTU treatment model has been evolving into a high-level comprehensive forensic therapy programme. Such programmes work intensively to provide individualised treatment in a group context to high-risk offenders with multiple responsivity difficulties (Polaschek, 2011b). The current treatment model is a hybrid of two earlier therapy traditions: (1) structured, closed-group cognitive-behavioural treatment programmes, in which knowledge and skills are taught directly in a fixed and sequenced number of treatment sessions, and where the context or environment of delivery is not part of the programme itself and (2) democratic therapeutic community programmes, in which involvement in the interpersonal processes of a community of staff and peers is the main mechanism for change (Rawlings, 1999; Ware, Frost, & Hoy, 2010). Integrating these two traditions helps to get around two perennial problems for prison-based programmes: a lack of opportunities to practice and generalise new skills in a change-supportive environment, and limited information from sources, other than self-report, about offender change. A third important benefit of the hybrid model is the resocialisation of men who may have been in prison for long periods. Outcome evaluations are, as yet, few for these types of programmes, but the assumption is that since both intensive cognitive-behavioural psychological treatments for higher risk offenders (Andrews & Bonta, 2010), and to a lesser extent, therapeutic community approaches (Aos, Miller, & Drake, 2006; Lösel & Schmucker, 2005) can on their own demonstrate reductions in recidivism, the combination may further enhance outcomes (Polaschek, 2011b; Ware et al., 2010).

Two important initiatives in the late 1980s were the forerunners of this hybrid treatment model in New Zealand. The high-intensity community-based Montgomery House violence prevention programme (Polaschek & Dixon, 2001) opened in 1987. It brought together several therapeutic elements still regarded more than 20 years later as novel, innovative and theoretically sound (Polaschek, 2011b; Ware et al., 2010). These elements included (1) embedding modular cognitive behavioural skills-based treatment sessions for multiple risk factors (e.g. affect regulation, relationship skills, communication and problem-solving) inside; (2) a therapeutic (residential) community based on democratic principles, within the constraints of offenders' sentencing requirements; (3) the use of Maori cultural values and practices to further enhance and contextualise the therapeutic community for participating offenders; (4) the inclusion of diverse activities to fully reintegrate offenders into positive, fulfilling lives; (5) the provision of aftercare, and brokerage to other services to assist in the post-programme transitions and (6) the involvement of family (whanau) in treatment generalisation and change monitoring.

Soon afterwards, Kia Marama opened as the first high-intensity prison-based programme for child-sex offenders (Hudson, Wales, & Ward, 1998). Although Kia Marama was initially a closed group treatment programme, over time it also developed a democratic therapeutic community within the constraints of a traditional custodial environment; providing a model for the HRSTUs (Frost & Connolly, 2004; B. Rutherford personal communication, October 6, 2011).

The prototype for the HRSTUs was TWM (Rimutaka prison), opened in 1998. However, despite the progress made at Kia Marama and Montgomery House in integrating structured group treatment within an intensive and comprehensive therapeutic environment, TWM at first concentrated only on the development of the structured session-based group therapy programme itself. The intent was to establish the core programme content and then develop the therapeutic community environment. It was initially conceptualised as an intensive treatment programme for violent offending. The programme began by recruiting – for three programme starting dates each year – 10 suitable prisoners who then entered a closed group led by two therapists which met three to four times each week for 3 hours at a time, and worked through a cognitive-behavioural programme manual. The programme was designed for use with Maori and Pacific prisoners – the majority of attendees – and therapy staff also liaised with family (whanau) and planned each prisoner's reintegration.

The core group programme was informed by etiological theories of aggression and violence; particularly the social information-processing and cognitive script models because of their obvious compatibility with cognitive-behavioural approaches to therapy (e.g. Crick & Dodge, 1996; Huesmann, 1988; and later Anderson & Bushman, 2002). However, in time the programme designers and evaluators recognised that these theories – although strong on psychological mechanisms for the development of aggressive behaviour – provided an incomplete account of the likely causes of offending in the target population, because they were not intended to explain the development of violence potential within a wider criminal lifestyle. Furthermore, they de-emphasise genetic, and early developmental neuro-cognitive factors that may also be etiologically relevant (Moffitt, 1993; Raine et al., 2005). The high-risk violent offenders targeted by TWM, like those from several longitudinal studies of high-risk populations (Farrington et al., 2006), were predominantly from low socio-economic backgrounds and were chronic and versatile criminals whose versatility extended to repetitive violence (Polaschek, Wilson, Townsend, & Daly, 2005).

Developmental and life-course criminology theories such as Farrington's Integrated Cognitive Antisocial Potential (ICAP) theory (Farrington, 2003, 2007), and Moffitt's life-course persistent offender theory (Moffitt, 1993) provide a more complete picture of the myriad factors and range of domains that are etiologically relevant for these offenders. Although the relevant psychological mechanisms are generally less well articulated than for the social-cognitive theories of aggression, these theories also have the potential for application to different parts of the lifespan as different factors become more or less relevant, and with further development, may be able to accommodate desistance factors as well. Thus, importantly, they can recognise the phenomenon of assymetric causation (i.e. etiological factors in offending onset differ from those that predict desistance; see Uggen & Piliavin, 1998).

A variety of therapeutic models also contributed components and techniques to the programme manual. Those underpinning the current manual are outlined in a later section.

A recidivism evaluation of treated prisoners in the first 7 years (1998–2005) showed a modest effect for high-risk men (Polaschek, 2011a), but a major review of the programme, also in 2005, identified significant problems with the integrity and quality of treatment delivery.[2] Furthermore, little progress had been made on extending a therapeutic environment outside of group sessions. In practice, the unit operated much like mainstream prison units, except that residents had access to fewer routine adjunct activities (e.g. employment, education and recreation), potentially making the majority of time outside of group criminogenic rather than therapeutic, and effectively resulting in an environment that punished prisoners for consenting to participate. One result of the review was the development of a revised, and highly prescriptive treatment manual (King, Creamer, Tiller, & Williams, 2007) to support a rigorous, content-focused integrity monitoring process. This manual was adopted by the three HRSTUs that opened soon after. The last three years have seen the gradual development of a unit-based therapeutic environment in all four units.

The treatment programme

Referral and initial assessment

Collectively the four HRSTUs offer treatment to approximately 150 male prisoners each year, of whom about two-thirds complete the programme. Potentially eligible prisoners are identified at sentence commencement, and placed on a centralised waiting list. After they become parole-eligible, prisoners are contacted by unit staff to ascertain whether they consent to transfer for assessment when beds become available.

Prior to beginning core group sessions, each man undergoes psychological assessment based on interviews, file records, psychometric tests and staff observations of behaviour in the unit. The main aims are to gain sufficient information to develop a working formulation and preliminary treatment goals, and to identify current engagement in change. The Violence Risk Scale (VRS; Wong & Gordon, 2000) is used to identify treatment targets and aid collaborative case formulation, and later, to monitor and give feedback about progress.

Unit structure and staffing

The programme is based in a standard low-medium security prison unit with additional buildings housing therapy staff offices and treatment rooms. Prisoners reside individually in self-contained cells, with daytime access to recreational areas (including a gym, library, a carving room), and activities (e.g. art classes, music, kapa haka).

In addition to treatment sessions, prisoners may be engaged in employment or education, recreational (e.g. sports, debating, carving and other crafts), spiritual (e.g. Bible study, yoga and meditation), Maori cultural (e.g. kapa haka and te reo Māori) or other rehabilitative activities (e.g. parenting, financial or employment-related skills training and art therapy).

The usual complement of prison officers provides the custodial regime and is ultimately responsible for the daily safety and security of the participants. Prison staff verbalise commitment to working in a therapeutic environment on entry, but do not usually have any previous specialised training and prison rotation policies result in regular entry of staff naïve to the therapeutic milieu. Therapy staff are employed by a separate arm of the Department of Corrections: the Psychological Services. In addition to a psychologist–manager and administrative support person, there are three or four therapist dyads. Each dyad – a psychologist and a programme facilitator (or rehabilitation worker) – becomes the therapy team for the group treatment sessions of each 10-prisoner cohort. In practice, psychologists vary from fully qualified senior clinicians to students in the final-year of clinical training. Programme facilitators may have some university training in psychology, and varied social service and education backgrounds. Specialist Maori/Pacifica cultural advice is also available via either dedicated staff or contracted providers.

The treatment process

The HRSTU treatment model is consistent with the Risk-Need-Responsivity model of offender rehabilitation, and is outlined below. In brief, offenders are provided with individualised opportunities for pro-social change through their involvement in a cognitive-behavioural group treatment programme embedded in a social learning-based therapeutic community. Consistent with the aetiological theories outlined above, prisoners entering these units share features that influence the treatment process, and must be accommodated if HRSTUs are to support and promote change. Typically adverse developmental histories have resulted in myriad risk-related treatment needs and complex responsivity issues. Many have high PCL-R/SV scores and other personality problems, low-average IQs, negative attitudes to 'school' and authority, are involved in ongoing criminal activities in prison, and have difficult temperaments: they may be hostile and suspicious, irritable, anxious, moody, self-absorbed and difficult to influence (Skeem, Polaschek, Patrick, & Lilienfeld, 2011; Wilson, 2004). Although consenting to transfer, they often deny treatment needs (Polaschek & Ross, 2010), and long periods spent in prison have entrenched them in the institutional culture, leaving only weak prosocial community attachments. There is a strong mistrust of other prisoners and staff, and, especially early in treatment, habitual socially harmful and criminal behaviour patterns continue.

The overall theoretical model for the treatment programme, as for the unit itself, is a social learning one. In the context of low readiness for change, entrenched dynamic risk factors, mistrust and attachment difficulties, and high levels of personality pathology, a strong emphasis is placed on developing a strong therapy alliance, and on demonstrating therapist features associated with positive change (Marshall et al., 2003; Marshall, Marshall, Serran, & O'Brien, 2011). Understanding client interpersonal patterns and interactions with therapists is informed by the approaches of Young, Klosko, and Weishaar (2003) and Livesley (2003), and Safran's (1998) model of interpersonal process is also helpful here.

The theoretical underpinnings of the approach to effective treatment process in working with the closed group is most influenced by Yalom's (2005) theory of group stages and tasks. The group is viewed as a social microcosm in order to understand how it can best be used to facilitate learning on what, for most offenders, are interpersonal problems (i.e. their treatment targets are personal and interpersonal).

Specific techniques used to enhance engagement with therapists and change include motivational interviewing (McMurran, 2002; Miller & Rollnick, 2002). Other key approaches to encouraging clients to think about, question and reflect on themselves and the programme material include Socratic Questioning (or Naive Inquiry). Dialectical Behaviour Therapy (Linehan, 1993) also provides a foundation for many parts of the programme, including mindfulness training, and other techniques for increasing distress tolerance, managing affect and impulses and enhancing relationships. A wide variety of other resources for cognitive behavioural treatment also informs the programme. Notably, the preferred approach with entrenched dysfunctional beliefs and attitudes – both criminogenic and not – is based on Padesky and Mooney's (2006) approach, which emphasises generating new beliefs that will ultimately alter personality style, rather than focusing on disputing the old ones. When old beliefs are held inflexibly, such direct challenging may promote resistance as clients attempt to defend ways of thinking that, at one time, served them well. Throughout the programme there is an emphasis on learning by modelling, practice and coaching with positive feedback. The final phase, preparing for the future, draws on traditional relapse prevention approaches, but also on resources developed in-house for reintegration planning.

The most important part of recent practice developments at the HRSTUs has been the transition from delivering a core group treatment programme in a busy, positive unit environment, to a fully integrated therapeutic community, albeit within the constraints of a custodial setting with few specialist rehabilitative staff. These changes can be understood from two angles.

First, the unit environment itself has become more cohesive and focused. Individually, and collectively, staff and prisoners are responsible for upholding core community values of respect, support, self-responsibility, unity and openness (Van Rensburg et al., 2009). The communities promote a philosophy that includes communalism, group decision-making, positive peer-group influence, a focus on interpersonal behaviour (Lipton, 1998), and incorporate Maori and Pacific cultural practices and values. As far as possible, the community parallels the structure and functions of outside community life. It provides offenders with opportunities to resocialise and even reintegrate into a form of community before they are released. There are weekly community meetings, and celebrations and commemorations of important events (e.g. programme completion, Matariki[3] and family days). A structured day includes communal meals and recreation activities, and other activities connect the unit to the outside world (e.g. growing vegetables for Women's Refuge).

Second, for each offender, time outside of the group is individualised to extend the same processes and opportunities that effect change in group sessions. Employment and other activities are aligned with treatment goals. Offenders practice new skills (e.g. problem-solving, conflict resolution) with others who can shape positive behaviour through contingent responses to their conduct. Change monitoring is enhanced; custodial and therapy staff can identify progress or deterioration, and modify treatment plans accordingly. The extension of change processes into the custody environment requires all staff to be familiar with a resident's treatment plan.

Regular case-management meetings, in which individual prisoners meet with several staff, provide important opportunities to review events and participants' behaviour, sanction it (positively or negatively), set new goals and plans, and practice specific interpersonal skills (e.g. job interviews, cases for day paroles).

Therapy within a HRSTU begins when the prisoner enters the unit. After new participants are welcomed, they take part fully in the activities of the community, and attend 'starters' group' weekly until their 10-man cohort begins the main treatment programme. Following completion of the core programme, they may stay in the unit for weeks or months prior to release, or be moved back into a mainstream unit. Graduates who remain in the unit continue to attend a graduates' group, and take leading roles in the unit community. The average stay in one of the units is almost a year and, where possible, men are paroled directly to the community.

Because ongoing antisocial behaviour and disruptive and uncooperative treatment behaviour are understood more as indicators of treatment need than treatment unsuitability, the HRSTUs aim to retain those who commit minor incidents, or who take time to socialise into the treatment and unit culture: responding to their behaviour with refined treatment goals and plans. For minor problem behaviour, staff may request that the prisoner develops a behavioural contract for remediating the problem, apologise or account for his actions at a community meeting, and/or seek help and support from a graduate mentor. Such tasks require prisoners to actively choose whether to demonstrate more commitment to the programme, or to be transferred elsewhere. When prisoners do not respond despite remedial interventions (e.g. continued refusal to undertake required treatment tasks) they will be removed, but treatment terminations of this kind are undertaken as a last resort, with unit staff understanding that assisting offenders to respond to the programme is a primary treatment task. When a prisoner's behaviour poses a significant threat to safety or security, he will normally be immediately transferred, and some prisoners leave the unit at their own request.

Group treatment sessions

Starters' group meets weekly and is attended by all those waiting in the unit to begin the core programme. Its main functions relate to treatment readiness – developing recognition of treatment needs and goals, and socialising men to interpersonal group processes. Graduates' group is optional: determined by availability of beds, and sentence management factors for each prisoner. Graduates' group also meets weekly, and its main function is to support the maintenance of change, and reintegration planning.

The core treatment programme has 99 sessions of 2.5 hours, delivered over 25 weeks. There are three phases: orientation and initial treatment engagement, knowledge and skill-building and preparing for post-treatment transfer/release. Throughout the programme there is a focus on using multiple learning methods that emphasise active participation, pitching complexity at the level of participants' linguistic and cognitive functioning, and on using culturally relevant analogies (e.g. myths, proverbs), concepts, language and examples (especially from Maori and Pacific cultures).

Although readiness to change and responsivity fluctuate throughout the programme, these are often most salient early in treatment. Initial sessions orient prisoners to the programme content and aims, build basic skills needed to undertake treatment (e.g. giving and receiving feedback, mindfulness and distress tolerance) and strengthen group and therapist–offender relationships. Phase I then works on developing engagement, by examining offenders' histories (autobiographies), and key characteristics of their current or intended prosocial identity ('new me'), mapping out offence patterns (common cognitive–affective–behavioural cycles across violent and non-violent offences), and identifying offending-related cognitions, attitudes and beliefs. For most high-risk violent offenders, the ingrained nature of crime-supportive cognitions (Polaschek, Calvert, & Gannon, 2009) warrants their inclusion in Phase I, because these cognitions (e.g. believing that one's offending has no impact on others, or that one has no choice about offending) undermine recognition that change is both desirable and achievable. At the end of Phase I, a prosocial and therapeutic group process is beginning to develop, and individual group members have identified some treatment goals.

Phase II focuses on skill acquisition. Specifically, offenders learn skills that can enhance the quality of prosocial lifestyle (e.g. problem-solving, communication, assertiveness, conflict resolution and perspective-taking skills) and improve coping with difficult emotions and impulses, reduce substance abuse and support rejection of antisocial peer influences.

The final phase of the programme focuses strongly on the future. Offenders develop personalised safety plans, based on their most common high-risk situations, and identify the resources and practise the specific strategies that will counteract them. Reintegration plans are also completed during this phase (see below).

Adjunct interventions

As far as possible, formal treatment occurs during group sessions, maximising cohesiveness of learning and making use of group interpersonal processes. Time-limited individual psychological treatment is provided for those who may have problems that interfere with full participation in group (e.g. social anxiety and extreme mistrust). For Maori, external therapists appointed through the Psychological Services' bicultural therapy model may provide additional individual interventions focusing on specialised cultural needs (e.g. building whanau/family support, developing prosocial cultural knowledge and identity).

Preparation for release into the community (reintegration) is also integrated into the treatment model. Offenders are encouraged to develop – and begin enacting within the unit – positive plans for a more fulfilling life. The unit's limited resources prioritise arrangements that will help the prisoner survive the first few months of parole, including developing positive social support, accommodation and opportunities for employment.

Prisoners' current reintegration needs and strengths are assessed on arrival in the unit. The process of reintegration and of developing a release plan continues throughout the stay, and beyond. Residents develop their own plans, but staff identify and connect them to key community resources, and organise meetings that facilitate the development or enhancement of relationships between residents and their families and other supports, while also informing supports about the treatment process, and the offender's progress, needs and strengths. Employment-related reintegration often starts with prisoners undertaking employment skills training and employment while in the unit. Later they may undertake 'release to work' (i.e. daily parole to employment in the community). Reintegration planning complements safety planning: an ideal reintegration plan will enable the offender to set up a lifestyle in which exposure to acute risk factors (e.g. drugs, antisocial peers and interpersonal conflict) is minimised, and there are good personal and interpersonal resources to draw on if they are encountered.

Data on programme participants

The information in this section is based on data collected on the 264 prisoners who entered one of the four units between 2008 and mid-2011. On average they were 34.2 years old (SD = 8.3), most were New Zealand Maori (64%), 25% were European New Zealanders and a further 9% were from Pacific Island nations. Other descriptive variables are presented in Table 1. Almost all (97%) had previous convictions for violence, and 44% were members, associates or 'prospects' (i.e. working to earn entry) of criminal gangs. Their estimated likelihood of reconviction within 5 years of release was 97% (SD = 4%), and of returning to prison within 5 years of release was 73% (SD = 13%). Taken together these variables confirm the high-risk nature of the sample. The most serious current offence was a violent one for most of the sample: serious assault/kidnapping (21%), robbery (21%), homicide or attempted murder (17%) or sexual offending against an adult victim (5%). The remainder were serving sentences primarily for property offending (25%), drug offences (5%) or some other type of offence (e.g. breach of parole and obstruction of justice). Sixteen per cent were serving sentences of indeterminate length. For the remainder, the mean sentence length was 4.47 years (SD = 3.17).

Participants' scores on the Wechsler Abbreviated Scale of Intelligence (WASI; Wechsler, 1999: a four-subtest version of the WAIS-III), completed prior to programme commencement, show that their verbal IQs were typically in the low-average range.

Of those entering the unit, two-thirds (66%) completed the full core treatment programme, and 95% completed at least part of the programme. Non-completers most often left voluntarily (46%), citing personal reasons such as wanting to be closer to family. However, anecdotally, some of these individuals left for security reasons that they were unwilling to disclose (e.g. running up gambling debts and conflict with gang members). Evictions for misconducts accounted for 31%, 15% were removed because of poor responsivity and 8% were transferred for known security reasons (e.g. personal safety). The mean stay in the unit was 310 days (SD = 1510): including 42 days (SD = 33) in starters' group, and 200 days (SD = 71) in the core programme.

Table 1. Sample demographic and criminal history characteristics.

Variable	Mean (SD)	Variable	Mean (SD)
Years schooling	9.4 (1.3)	Number of previous convictions	64.4 (49.7)
Age first conviction	17.5 (2.1)	Number of previous violent convictions	6.5 (5.2)
Age first violent conviction	19.5 (4.3)	Years in prison before unit entry	3.9 (4.6)
WASI verbal IQ	86.4 (15.3)	WASI performance IQ	99.0 (14.0)

Non-completers' mean unit stay was still 176 days (SD = 105), including 113 days in the main treatment programme (SD = 73).

The VRS (Wong & Gordon, 2006) is completed before and after the core programme. Programme participants also completed Spielberger's State-Trait Anger Expression Inventory (STAXI-II; Spielberger, 1999). These data are used below to further describe the sample by comparing completers and non-completers, and describing change in completers.

Completers differed from non-completers on very few pre-treatment indices. In addition to the mainly non-significant results shown in Table 2, there also were no significant differences on current age, age of first conviction and age of first violent conviction. However, non-completers were significantly angrier pre-programme, and although they had the same number of pre-treatment needs, overall they had a lower stage of change scores for those needs on the VRS than those who stayed in the programme through to completion. These scores suggest that before treatment commenced, non-completers were almost always in the pre-contemplation or contemplation stage, while completers were significantly more likely to be making preliminary changes on some factors.

Post-programme, programme completers showed, as expected, no change on static risk factors but changed significantly on dynamic factors (mean reduction = 4.8, SD = 4.3). A fifth of the sample changed seven or more points; the equivalent of progressing to the next stage of change on 14 treatment targets, while 13% made no change or deteriorated slightly, and 8% changed one stage on 33 treatment targets or fewer.

Wong and Gordon (2006) categorised VRS total scores into three risk-bands: low (0–35), medium (36–50) and high (51 and above). Using these categories prior to treatment, 3% of this sample scored in the low range on the VRS, 20% in the medium range and the remaining 77% in the high range. At the end of treatment 58% remained in the high range, with 37% in the medium range and 5% in the low range.

Table 3 also shows that pre-programme, for most participants most VRS dynamic items are worthwhile treatment targets (i.e. on average men scored 2 or more on almost 80% of dynamic items). However, the mean stage of change data show that most participants either do not acknowledge the relevance of these areas as personal treatment goals, or are in contemplation about whether they should be changed. Further analysis of the individual dynamic items (not presented here) shows that

Table 2. Comparisons of completers and non-completers' risk and needs prior to treatment.

	Completers	Non-completers	Cohen's *d* [95% CI]
VRS total score	55.8 (8.8)	58.1 (7.0)	0.28 [−1.6, 1.4]
VRS static score	12.7 (2.9)	13.3 (2.4)	−0.22 [−0.66, 0.35]
VRS dynamic score	43.1 (7.6)	44.7 (5.9)	−0.23 [−1.4, 1.2]
RoC × RoI	0.73 (0.13)	0.75 (0.12)	−0.16 [−0.18, −0.13]
Mean no. treatment needs	15.7 (3.1)	16.1 (2.3)	−0.14 [−0.61, 0.34]
Mean stage of change*[a]	1.24 (0.40)	1.05 (0.56)	0.42 [0.36, 0.56]
STAXI anger index**	33.6 (14.1)	38.6 (15.1)	−0.35 [−2.85, 3.72]

[a]1 = Pre-contemplation/contemplation; 2 = preparation; 3 = action; 4 = maintenance.
*$p = 0.002$.
**$p = 0.04$.

Table 3. Completers' pre- and post-programme VRS and STAXI scores.

$n = 164$	Pre	Post	M_{diff} [95% CI]
VRS total score	55.9 (8.6)	51.1 (9.1)*	4.9 [4.2, 5.5]
VRS static score	12.7 (2.9)	12.7 (2.8)	0.04 [−0.02, 0.10]
VRS dynamic score	43.5 (7.5)	38.4 (7.8)*	4.8 [4.3, 5.6]
No. of treatment needs	15.7 (3.2)	12.2 (4.3)*	3.5 [3.0, 3.9]
Mean stage of change	1.28 (0.34)	1.86 (0.49)*	−0.62 [−0.68, −0.55]
STAXI-II anger index	33.6 (14.1)	25.8 (14.1)*	7.8 [4.8, 10.9]

*$p = 0.001$.

almost all participants have as treatment goals violent lifestyle, criminal attitudes, emotional control, violence cycle, impulsivity and cognitive distortions and that each VRS dynamic item, except mental disorder, is a potential treatment goal for more than half of the sample.

Post-programme stage of change data show that on average treated men's progress has brought them close to the preparation stage on VRS dynamic items. Preparation is the first stage in which change can be observed: it indicates that observers have seen a mix of new more prosocial or positive behaviour, and instances of old behaviours. These figures indicate that although participants make important progress, many of those changes are still very preliminary and not reliable.

At this time an evaluation of programme effectiveness is in progress: case-matched treated men and untreated controls are being compared both on post-programme prison-based disciplinary infractions, and for those who have been released, community recidivism rates.

Conclusions and future directions

HRSTUs provide intensive residential rehabilitative treatment to prisoners at high to very high risk of further imprisonment and, as the VRS data show, most also are at moderate to high risk of future violence and have myriad potential treatment needs. Although these men have often spent some years in prison prior to transfer, they arrive in the unit with low levels of problem recognition and prior engagement in change. They also often have ingrained skills for surviving in mainstream prison culture, skills that may serve them poorly on parole. They are a challenging population to treat and likely to require intensive and extended assistance, both in the unit and well beyond. Both the relatively high rates of treatment completion (see Wormith & Olver, 2002) and the similarity between completers and non-completers replicate earlier findings with the TWM (Rimutaka; Polaschek, 2010) and suggest that these programmes are responding well to, and retaining, many of the clients who most need treatment (Wormith & Olver, 2002).

Faced with such high levels of need and low levels of potential responsivity, programme designers may be tempted to 'throw everything' at the treatment endeavour, resulting in overly complex treatment curricula that swamp participants' cognitive and learning abilities so that they retain little of what they have been taught, and learn to use even less of it. Such approaches can become elaborately cognitive in focus, inadvertently de-emphasising a more direct focus on demonstrable behavioural change. The hybrid treatment model described here is an alternative approach that instead (1) combines formal treatment sessions and community processes to emphasise the generalisation of learning and develops a limited range of core skills fitted to each offender's most important needs and (2) intensifies the treatment experience not by increasing the formal content, but instead by increasing the opportunities and supports for addressing those needs in new, prosocial ways within and following the treatment environment. Within limited resources, the HRSTU project shows New Zealand's progress in operationalizing the RNR model with high-risk prisoners, many with high levels of PCL-psychopathic characteristics, and various other types of disordered personality traits and habits. It demonstrates the importance of working to ameliorate men's criminogenic needs – not by focusing excessively, and of course ineffectively – on a list of behaviours people should stop doing (Ward, Melser, & Yates, 2007) but by helping them to construct and practice new, more effective and rewarding ways of thinking, behaving and relating to others (Polaschek, 2012).

Since TWM (Rimutaka) was joined by the three newer HRSTUs in 2007 and 2008, there have been gradual improvements in the implementation of treatment that are consistent with this alternative approach. Most notable is the recent progress made in the expansion of treatment into the residential environment, and the gradual induction and integration of custodial staff into treatment processes. If the model is to continue to evolve in the direction of a high-level comprehensive forensic therapy programme (Polaschek, 2011b), then further developments are needed. Areas that require attention include (1) the criteria for retaining only those participants who are engaging in change; (2) the alignment of assessment and reassessment methods and measures with programme goals and objectives; in particular, few self-report psychometric tools are currently in use and the contribution they make to assessment and treatment is not clear; (3) the style of programme manualisation; treatment delivery needs to be able to be tailored more towards achieving individual therapy goals rather than being a 'one size fits all' experience and (4) the development of therapy staff skills to facilitate the provision of a tailored approach of this type.

The VRS data also raise several important issues for future attention. The first is the provision of support services and placements following treatment completion. In some cases graduates are able to stay in the units through to parole. However, many others are moved into other units for a variety of purposes. Most graduates are likely still to have significant dynamic risk factors unchanged and other factors in the early stages of change. A return to a mainstream environment lacking active support for the approach taken in treatment may challenge the maintenance and generalisation of graduates' changes. Furthermore, on release into the community, an important but not fully realised opportunity exists for ensuring that the gains made in treatment, and the 'next steps' for that offender, are passed on to the supervising probation officer and any others involved in the community support of the offender.

Another issue raised by the VRS concerns the extent to which of the myriad identified treatment needs actually *need* treatment, given the rehabilitative ideals of reducing reoffending and increasing community safety. Are they all functional variables related to change or, for that matter, equally important within the change process? How are they linked to each other? VRS data suggest that by the end of formal treatment, most men only make noticeable changes on a few needs, leaving a significant number unchanged. Does the ongoing presence of these needs maintain the likelihood of recidivism? How might the programme achieve more change? Should it aim to?

Relatedly, must a need be addressed directly in treatment to change, or does spontaneous change occur on some needs in response to targeting others? A good example – the VRS item 'criminal personality' – suggests that direct targeting may not be necessary. About half of programme graduates were judged to have reduced the extent to which their criminal personality was evident in their behaviour around the unit. Yet, the HRSTU programme does not directly seek to effect change on this item, suggesting complex relationships between needs and change. Understanding how to identify whether there are particular dynamic risk factors that are a higher priority for change or that, if changed, have cascading effects on other factors, is an essential part of future etiological theory development that will better inform programme design, individual treatment planning, and evaluation of treatment progress with high-risk offenders (Polaschek, 2012). With a growing number of treatment graduates being released from prison there may be an opportunity to examine these questions in some greater detail by identifying the variables most consistently associated with reductions in offending.

Finally, this programme is increasingly working with older offenders. Although older men may be more ready to change, they also may be past the peak of their lifetime offending trajectory (e.g. Hughes, 2010). The HRSTUs have admirable completion rates for programmes with this population, but it is also the case that a majority of eligible prisoners do not attend HRSTU programmes. Understanding why many younger offenders are not attending is also an important part of developing programme provision for these high-risk prisoners. Adapting the programme to be more available and responsive to this younger offender population could yield increased benefits for both offenders and the community, by providing an opportunity to divert more men from an ongoing pattern of offending through their middle years.

Substantial progress has been made in a relatively short time with a challenging group, using a model that requires specialised therapy staff, but operates in a custodial environment rather than a 'hospital'-type setting. Although additional improvements can, and will, be made to the unit model, further gains may now be achieved by increasing the responsivity of the programme to younger offenders and attending to processes that help to stabilise or continue change beyond the end of the programme.

Acknowledgements

Our thanks to Bronwyn Rutherford, Lucy King and Paul Whitehead for providing current programme information, to Nikki Reynolds for supporting the research that generated these data, and to all the dedicated staff who assisted with data entry.

Notes

1. Now renamed Te Whare Manaakitanga (TWM). The other three units are: Karaka (Waikeria Prison); Puna Tatari (Springhill Prison) and Matapuna (Christchurch prison).
2. The programme manual had suffered ad hoc modifications, therapeutic integrity monitoring, and therapy staff training and supervision was inconsistent.
3. For Maori, the beginning of the New Year, in June.

References

Anderson, C. A., & Bushman, B. J. (2002). Human aggression. *Annual Review of Psychology, 53*, 27–51. doi:10.1146/annurev.psych.53.100901.135231

Andrews, D. A., & Bonta, J. (2010). *The psychology of criminal conduct* (5th ed.). Newark, NJ: Matthew Bender.

Aos, S., Miller, M., & Drake, E. (2006). *Evidence-based adult corrections programs: What works and what does not*. Olympia, WA: Washington State Institute for Public Policy.

Crick, N. R., & Dodge, K. A. (1996). Social information-processing mechanisms in reactive and proactive aggression. *Child Development, 67*, 993–1002. doi:10.2307/1131875

Day, A., & Doyle, P. (2010). Violent offender rehabilitation and the therapeutic community model of treatment: Towards integrated service provision? *Aggression and Violent Behavior, 15*, 380–387. doi:10.1016/j.avb.2010.06.006

Farrington, D. P. (2003). Developmental and life-course criminology: Key theoretical and empirical issues—The 2002 Sutherland award address. *Criminology, 41*, 221–255. doi:10.1111/j.1745-9125.2003.tb00987.x

Farrington, D. P. (2007). Origins of violent behavior over the life span. In D. J. Flannery, A. T. Vazsonyi, & I. D. Waldman (Eds.), *The Cambridge handbook of violent behavior and aggression* (pp. 19–48). Cambridge, UK: Cambridge University Press.

Farrington, D. P., Coid, J. W., Harnett, L., Jolliffe, D., Soteriou, N., Turner, R., & West, D. J. (2006). *Criminal careers up to the age of 50 and life success up to the age of 48: New findings from the Cambridge study in delinquent development*. London: Home Office.

Frost, A., & Connolly, M. (2004). Reflexivity, reflection, and the change process in offender work. *Sexual Abuse: A Journal of Research & Treatment, 2004*, 365–380. doi:10.1177/107906320401600408

Hudson, S. M., Wales, D. S., & Ward, T. (1998). Kia Marama: A treatment program for child molesters in New Zealand. In W. L. Marshall, Y. M. Fernandez, S. M. Hudson, & T. Ward (Eds.), *Sourcebook of treatment programs for sexual offenders* (pp. 17–28). New York: Plenum.

Huesmann, L. R. (1988). An information processing model for the development of aggression. *Aggressive Behavior, 14*, 13–24. doi:10.1002/1098-2337(1988)14:1<13::AID-AB2480140104>3.0.CO;2-J

Hughes, T (2010). *Offending patterns of the 1965 birth cohort* (Unpublished paper). Wellington: Department of Corrections.

King, L., Creamer, C., Tiller, N., & Williams, C. (2007). *Special treatment unit rehabilitation programme manual* (Unpublished report). Wellington: Department of Corrections.

Linehan, M. M. (1993). *Cognitive-behavioural treatment of borderline personality disorder.* New York: Guilford Press.

Lipton, D. S. (1998). Therapeutic community treatment programming in corrections. *Psychology, Crime & Law, 4*, 213–263. doi:10.1080/10683169808520010

Livesley, W. J. (2003). *Practical management of personality disorder.* New York: Guilford Press.

Lösel, F., & Schmucker, M. (2005). The effectiveness of treatment for sexual offenders: A comprehensive meta-analysis. *Journal of Experimental Criminology, 1*, 117–146. doi:10.1007/s11292-004-6466-7

Marshall, W. L., Marshall, L. E., Serran, G. A., & O'Brien, M. D. (2011). *Rehabilitating sexual offenders: A strength-based approach.* Washington D.C: American Psychological Association.

Marshall, W. L., Serran, G. A., Fernandez, Y. M., Mulloy, R., Mann, R. E., & Thornton, D. (2003). Therapist characteristics in the treatment of sexual offenders: Tentative data on their relationship with indices of behaviour change. *Journal of Sexual Aggression, 9*, 25–30.

McMurran. M. (Ed.) (2002). *Motivating offenders to change: A guide to enhancing engagement in therapy.* Chichester: Wiley.

Miller, W. R., & Rollnick, S. (2002). *Motivational interviewing: Preparing people to change* (2nd ed.). New York: Guilford.

Moffitt, T. E. (1993). Adolescence-limited and life course persistent antisocial behavior: A developmental taxonomy. *Psychological Review, 100*, 674–701. doi:10.1037/0033-295X.100.4.674

Nadesu, A. (2009). *Reconviction patterns of released prisoners: A 60-month follow-up analysis.* Retrieved from http://www.corrections.govt.nz/research/reconviction-patterns-of-released-prisoners-a-60-months-follow-up-analysis2.html

Padesky, C. A., & Mooney, K. A. (2006, March). *Cognitive therapy for persistent problems: A new paradigm.* Workshop presented at the meeting of New Zealand College of Clinical Psychologists, Wellington.

Polaschek, D. L. L. (2010). Treatment non-completion in high-risk violent offenders: Looking beyond criminal risk and criminogenic needs. *Psychology, Crime, & Law, 16*, 525–540. doi:10.1080/10683160902971048

Polaschek, D. L. L. (2011a). High-intensity rehabilitation for violent offenders in New Zealand: Reconviction outcomes for high- and medium-risk prisoners. *Journal of Interpersonal Violence, 26*, 664–682. doi:10.1177/0886260510365854

Polaschek, D. L. L. (2011b). Many sizes fit all: A preliminary framework for conceptualizing the development and provision of cognitive-behavioral rehabilitation programs for offenders. *Aggression and Violent Behavior, 16*, 20–35. doi:10.1016/j.avb.2010.10.002

Polaschek, D. L. L. (2012). An appraisal of the risk-need-responsivity model of offender rehabilitation and its application in correctional treatment. *Legal and Criminological Psychology, 17*, 1–17. doi:101111/j.2044-8333.2011.02038x

Polaschek, D. L. L., Calvert, S. W., & Gannon, T. A. (2009). Linking violent thinking: Implicit theory-based research with violent offenders. *Journal of Interpersonal Violence, 24*, 75–96. doi:10.1177/0886260508315781

Polaschek, D. L. L., & Dixon, B. G. (2001). The Violence Prevention Project: The development and evaluation of a treatment programme for violent offenders. *Psychology, Crime & Law, 7*, 1–23. doi:10.1080/10683160108401779

Polaschek, D. L. L., & Ross, E. C. (2010). Do early therapeutic alliance, motivation, and change readiness predict therapy outcomes for high risk violent prisoners? *Criminal Behaviour and Mental Health, 20*, 100–111. doi:10.1002/cbm.759 Wiley.Interscience.wiley.com

Polaschek, D. L. L., Wilson, N. J., Townsend, M., & Daly, L. (2005). Cognitive-behavioral rehabilitation for high-risk violent offenders: An outcome evaluation of the Violence Prevention Unit. *Journal of Interpersonal Violence, 20*, 1611–1627. doi:10.1177/0886260505280507

Prison facts and statistics (2010, March). Retrieved from http://www.corrections.govt.nz/aboutus/facts_and_statistics/prisons/march_2010.html#rate

Raine, A., Moffitt, T. E., Caspi, A., Loeber, R., Stouthamer-Loeber, M., & Lynam, D. (2005). Neurocognitive impairments in boys on the life-course persistent antisocial path. *Journal of Abnormal Psychology, 114*, 38–49. doi:10.1037/0021-843X.114.1.38

Rawlings, B. (1999). Therapeutic communities in prisons: A research review. *Therapeutic Communities, 20*(3), 177–193.

Safran, J. D. (1998). *Widening the scope of cognitive therapy: The therapeutic relationship, emotion, and the process of change.* Northvale, NJ: Jason Aronson.

Skeem, J. L., Polaschek, D. L. L., Patrick, C. J., & Lilienfeld, S. O. (2011). Psychopathic personality: Bridging the gap between scientific evidence and public policy. *Psychological Science in the Public Interest, 12*, 95–162. doi:10.1177/1529100611426706

Spielberger, C. D. (1999). *State Trait Anger Expression Inventory-2: Professional manual.* Odessa, FL: Psychological Assessment Resources.

Uggen, C., & Piliavin, I. (1998). Asymmetrical causation and criminal desistance. *Journal of Criminal Law and Criminology, 88*, 1399–1422. doi:10.2307/1144260

Van Rensburg, J., Berry, S., Rutherford, B., Williams, K., Whitehead, P., & van Rensburg, P. (2009). *Special treatment unit operations manual* (Unpublished report). Wellington: Department of Corrections.

Walmsley, R. (2009). *World prison population list* (8th edn). London, UK: International Centre for Prison Studies, King's College London.

Ward, T., Melser, J., & Yates, P. M. (2007). Reconstructing the risk, need, responsivity model: A theoretical elaboration and evaluation. *Aggression and Violent Behavior, 12*, 208–228. doi:10.1016/j.avb.2006.07.001

Ware, J., Frost, A., & Hoy, A. (2010). A review of the use of therapeutic communities with sexual offenders. *International Journal of Offender Therapy and Comparative Criminology, 54*, 721–742. doi:10.1177/0306624X09343169

Wechsler, D. (1999). *Wechsler abbreviated scale of intelligence.* New York, NY: The Psychological Corporation: Harcourt Brace & Company.

Wilson, N. J. (2004). *New Zealand high-risk offenders: Who are they and what are the issues in their management and treatment?* Retrieved from http://www.corrections.govt.nz/research/high-risk-offenders.html

Wong, S., & Gordon, A. (2000). *The violence risk scale.* Canada: University of Saskatchewan.

Wong, S. C. P., & Gordon, A. (2006). The validity and reliability of the Violence Risk Scale: A treatment-friendly violence risk assessment tool. *Psychology, Public Policy, and Law, 12*, 279–309. doi:10.1037/1076-8971.12.3.279

Wormith, J. S., & Olver, M. E. (2002). Offender treatment attrition and its relationship with risk, responsivity, and recidivism. *Criminal Justice and Behavior, 29*, 447–471. doi:10.1177/0093854802029004006

Yalom, I. D. (2005). *The theory and practice of group psychotherapy* (5th ed.). New York: Basic Books.

Young, J. E., Klosko, J. S., & Weishaar, M. E. (2003). *Schema therapy: A practitioner's guide.* New York: Guilford.

Treating high-risk rapists in a New Zealand intensive prison programme

Nick J. Wilson[a], Glen Kilgour[a] and Devon L.L. Polaschek[b]

[a]*Department of Corrections, Psychological Services, Rehabilitation and Reintegration Services, Hamilton, New Zealand;* [b]*School of Psychology, Victoria University of Wellington, Wellington, New Zealand*

The focus of this article is on the pilot development and implementation of a prison-based intensive treatment programme for high-risk adult-victim rape offenders in New Zealand. Advances in actuarial risk assessment enabled the identification of a group of high-risk adult sex offenders for whom no dedicated treatment programme existed. Based on a review of the treatment literature for rapists, a pilot programme was developed called the Adult Sex Offender Treatment Programme (ASOTP). The programme, based on the risk–need–responsivity and cognitive behavioural therapy principles, also used an adaptation of Young's schema therapy to address personality responsivity issues and specific idiosyncratic schema associated with participant offence pathways identified by the Massachusetts Treatment Centre classification (Version 3 for rapists). Measures of responsivity and dynamic risk administered in the ASOTP indicated some success in addressing treatment needs for the pilot participants ($n = 10$). The programme has subsequently been expanded across prison specialist treatment unit sites and delivered to a further 52 participants. Although intermediate measures continue to indicate change in dynamic risk, recidivism outcome evaluations have not yet been possible, due to low numbers of paroled participants.

As with other international jurisdictions, in New Zealand the offence of rape – defined here as a sexually penetrative assault against an adult – is recognised as a serious crime resulting in significant victim impacts, social costs and long periods of imprisonment (Gannon, Collie, Ward, & Thakker, 2008). However, in New Zealand, early research estimated that rapists had relatively lower base rates (BRs) of reoffending than child sex offenders (McLean & Rush, 1990). This conclusion led, in part, to a lack of specialist rehabilitative programming for these offenders. During the 1980s and 1990s most rapists were treated individually by correctional psychologists, or with occasional *ad hoc* group-based treatment efforts: typically low-intensity interventions adapted directly from more established programmes for sexual offenders with child victims (Wilson, 2005).

The only extant New Zealand evaluation of a group treatment initiative for rapists was for a 1986 prison-based programme (Huddleston, Vaughan, & Beale,

1992). They used a quasi-experimental design with intervention and control groups that were similar on age, ethnicity and risk of sexual offending (Automated Sexual Recidivism Scale score, see below). After an average 45 months of follow-up, 8% of the treatment group were reconvicted for sexual offending compared to 30% of the control group, and 16% of the treatment group were reconvicted for violence compared to 70% of the control group. When sexual and violent failures were combined, the difference was statistically significant ($p = 0.02$).

The development of reliable and valid measures of actuarial offence risk over the last decade (Hanson & Thornton, 1999; 2000) facilitated the design and allocation of treatment services according to risk. More recently, New Zealand developed and validated the Automated Sexual Recidivism Scale (ASRS; Skelton, Riley, Wales, & Vess, 2006). The ASRS estimates the probability of sexual recidivism using electronically accessible static factors: enabling the identification of a subgroup with a significantly higher-than-average sexual recidivism rate. In May 2005, a preliminary investigation found 182 prisoners with medium-high or high ASRS scores. Those with medium-high ASRS scores in the validation sample for this measure had a 24% sexual recidivism rate and those in the high-risk category a 50% sexual reoffending rate over a 10-year period post release. The recidivism rate for all rape offenders released in the same period was 14.8%, indicating that the medium-high and high-risk groups combined were almost three times as likely to reoffend as the sample in total (Wilson, 2005). The resulting ability to identify high-risk rapists among those in prison for rape offences led to increased interest in prioritising them for treatment and devising better specialist treatment options for such offenders. The Adult Sex Offender Treatment Programme (ASOTP) was subsequently developed to enable treatment of this high-risk subgroup (Wilson, 2005).

Programme development

Theoretical and empirical bases

Treatment efficacy with rapists has yet to be firmly established. Relatively few rapists complete sex offender treatment, and even fewer programmes are exclusively designed for or delivered to rapists (Lalumière, Harris, Quinsey, & Rice, 2005; Polaschek & King, 2002). In many jurisdictions, rapists and child-sex offenders undergo group treatment together. Often such programmes are heavily dominated by child-sex offenders, and their efficacy with rapists cannot be discerned because reoffending outcomes are not reported specifically for rapists (Polaschek & King, 2002). Consequently, both Furby, Weinrott, and Blackshaw (1989) and later, Polaschek and King (2002) reported little or no direct evidence of programme effectiveness with rapists, due to a lack of methodologically adequate relevant research. A rare exception is the evaluation data from the Clearwater programme in Canada (see Olver & Wong, 2013). Nicholaichuk, Gordon, Gu, and Wong (2000) compared a matched sample treated in this programme with comparison untreated prisoners. They initially reported that just 14% of the treated group were reconvicted sexually compared to 42% of the matched untreated group. However, a methodological problem with the criminal history records of the comparison group (inclusion of older records with disproportionate numbers of recidivists) is thought to have biased the results in favour of treatment. The programme effect for the final 10 years in the sample was re-estimated to be positive and significant (treated recidivism = 13.1%, untreated recidivism = 24.3%, odds ratio = 0.47, confidence interval [CI] = 0.29–0.76), but smaller than the original study results (treated recidivism = 14.5%, untreated recidivism = 33.2%, odds ratio = 0.34, CI = 0.23–0.51; Hanson & Nicholaichuk, 2000).

Based on overall research findings on effective offender treatment, rapists, in common with other sex offenders, should be treated using behavioural and cognitive-behavioural treatment approaches, and by adhering to the risk–need–responsivity (RNR) model (Hanson, Bourgon, Helmus, & Hodgson, 2009). The specific programme models for rapists are often those used with child-sex offenders (Gannon et al., 2008): relapse prevention with a focus on an offence chain, behavioural techniques to modify deviant sexual arousal (e.g., covert sensitisation, masturbatory reconditioning), social competence, and other putative offence-related components (e.g., anger management, sex education, victim empathy; Gannon et al., 2008; Marshall, Marshall, Serran, & O'Brien, 2011). However, rapists are heterogeneous, often have a much higher risk of non-sexual violence than child-sex offenders (Polaschek & King, 2002), and may also diverge from child-sex offenders on some dynamic risk factors for sexual offending (e.g., sexual deviance; Hanson & Morton-Bourgon, 2005). Therefore, there may be some justification for developing specialist rapist programmes, rather than simply adopting or adapting existing programmes.

Effective assessment and treatment of rape offenders demand an understanding of the aetiology of rape, not only the origins and persistence of rape proclivity, but also the conditions under which men act on these interests (Blackburn, 1993). Although a number of general theoretical approaches explain rape behaviour, it is the focus on individual characteristics from both 'nature' and 'nurture' explanations that holds the most potential for effective psychological treatment (Gannon et al., 2008). This use of individual differences is logical if one considers that transient and immediate circumstances do not provide a complete understanding of rape (Lalumière et al., 2005). As with other offenders, the personality styles and antisocial belief systems of rapists are some of the strongest predictors of further reoffending (Hanson & Morton-Bourgon, 2005), making these factors important treatment targets.

High-risk rapists are characterised by diverse offence-related motivations. The most well-known system for classifying heterogeneity in rapists is the Massachusetts Treatment Centre: Revision 3 (MTC: R3) system developed by Prentky and Knight (1991). In this classification five sexual pathways for rapists have been identified, formed around two motivational types: sexual and anger motivation. The MTC: R3 subclassifications for the sexual motivation type included the *opportunistic rapist* where the offender has pervasive antisocial beliefs, including beliefs about sexual violence, and the *non-sadistic sexual rapist* with a high level of sexual fantasy and offence specific planning prior to their offending. These fantasies are linked to sexual arousal and reflect distorted beliefs about women and sex, and often include deviant sexual acts. Typically, sexually motivated offence types involve a lower level of violence with an instrumental focus on compliance from the victim (e.g., acquaintance and date rape). In contrast, the final sexual motivation subtype, the *sadistic sexual rapist*, has a higher level of violence that is the result of a fusion of sexual and aggression motivations: anger has become eroticised (Prentky & Knight, 1991).

There are two types of anger-motivated rape pathways in the MTC: R3 classification system. The *vindictive rapist's* offences express misogynistic anger focussed solely on the humiliation, degradation, and harm to women. The *pervasively angry rapist* is motivated by undifferentiated reactive anger towards males and females, with pain and injury the primary focus.

Such different offence pathways provide an opportunity to improve the 'fit' of the treatment programme to the offender, by tailoring treatment needs to motivational subtypes, rather than following a 'one size fits all' approach (Polaschek, 2011; Reid, Wilson, & Boer, 2010). This argument was partially supported in an analysis of HMP sex offender treatment programmes (UK SOTP) using the MTC: R3 pathways. Treatment effectiveness differed across subgroups with no change for the grievance-motivated (vindictive and pervasively angry) subtypes but positive change for the sexually motivated (sadist and non-sadistic) subtypes (Beech, Oliver, Fisher, & Beckett, 2005).

High-risk rapists also appear to have high rates of personality disorder. For example, psychopathy is more prominent in high-risk rapists (Vess, Murphy, & Arkowitz, 2004), as are other complex forms of personality psychopathology. Particular forms of personality disorder may link to particular patterns of offence characteristics, and certainly pose problems for treatability. If so, treatment impact may be increased by tailoring treatment not just to offending-related characteristics (e.g., MTC:R3 subtype; sexual vs. angry motivation) but to the associated dysfunctional personality characteristics as well. The findings of Beech et al. (2005) support this contention, based on data from the Millon Clinical Multiaxial Inventory-III (MCMI-III; Millon, Millon, & Davis, 1997). The MCMI-III is a client self-report measure of personality and severe clinical psychopathology. A cluster analysis of MCMI-III scores of MTC:R3-typed rapists and sexual murderers attending the UK SOTPs found that grievance-motivated offenders had an avoidant, negativistic, self-defeating and dependent personality style (cluster 3, MCMI-III) with opportunistic, sexual non-sadistic offenders having MCMI-III cluster 1 and 2 profiles. Cluster 1 profile offenders presented themselves in a defensively positive light. Cluster 2 profile offenders presented as depressive and self-defeating, but with less denial of problems. Beech et al. found that the cluster 3 group showed less change on most research measures pre- to post-treatment, with greater post-treatment acknowledgement of sexual preoccupation.

Cognitive-behavioural interventions for the treatment of personality disorder have increased in sophistication and impact over the last decade (Livesley, 2008). Schema-based therapies hold promise with offenders (Bernstein, Arntz, & de Vos, 2007; Lobbestael, Arntz, & Sieswerda, 2005; Richardson, 2005; Tarrier et al., 2010), because of their potential to alter deeply entrenched belief systems that underpin both personality disorder and offending, thus bringing together in treatment the key risk factors identified by Hanson and Morton-Bourgon (2005). Beech and colleagues' research suggested a model for using Young's schema-focussed therapy (Young, Klosko, & Weishaar, 2003) to tailor treatment to distinct forms of offence motivation based on the MTC:R3 categories, associated personality disorder and entrenched offending-related cognitions in high-risk rapists (Fisher & Beech, 2007). Because the ASOTP intended to target repetitive rape offenders, a focus on conditional maladaptive schemas that serve to maintain a particular offence pattern was regarded as a promising direction for programme development.

Practical considerations

The pilot ASOTP had two practical aims – safety and effectiveness – in relation to establishing whether there should be an ongoing treatment programme for adult sex offenders. The pervasive antisociality, instrumental violence, sexual preoccupation and personality pathology of high-risk rapists pose significant safety risks for other therapy participants and therapists, especially female therapists (Beech et al., 2005). In addition to physical safety, facilitators may become the target of obsessional and distorted thinking by participants. For example, 70% of the female staff from HMP involved in treating rape offenders in England and Wales reported being subject to offenders' hostility or sexual remarks (Beech et al., 2005). Such issues can be particularly challenging to manage in group sessions which were to be a major component of the ASOTP.

The second aim of the pilot related to the lack of robust evidence of treatment effectiveness with rapists, and, in this case, the development of a somewhat novel programme approach. At a minimum, if the pilot was to be extended, it needed to show preliminary evidence of changes for participants on measures of responsivity and readiness to change, as well as offence-related proximal dynamic needs (Jung & Gulayets, 2011).

Programme design

The design of the ASOTP was consistent with the RNR model (Andrews & Bonta, 2003) and the principles of cognitive behavioural therapy (CBT) which underpinned New Zealand and international research on effective correctional therapy initiatives for sex offenders (Anstiss, 2003). The target population was anticipated to have extensive personality pathology and pervasive histories of interpersonal violence, and would already have served a long period in prison, often on indeterminate sentences. Therefore, the first phase of therapy focussed on engagement, safety and emotional management (Livesley, 2008) to facilitate the development of therapeutic and constructive group alliances, before moving on to the challenging area of offence disclosures. The programme was not designed to directly address personality pathology, but to do so indirectly by improving emotion regulation, increasing disclosure, strengthening healthy personal boundaries, and challenging distorted beliefs. Participants were also taught about schema formation and the link between these metacognitive processes and their interpersonal behaviour.

The middle phase of treatment focussed on each individual's offending: targeting both general (Hanson, 2006) and specific dynamic risk factors associated with sexual offending: the latter based on the MTC:R3 results. Schema therapy was used to address the maladaptive coping styles and responses identified through analysis of participants' personal histories, personality pathology and particular unconditional and conditional schemas (Young et al., 2003) associated with each man's MTC: R3 offence pathway. Therapists initially identified links between each participant's early maladaptive schema (conditional) and any dysfunctional emotional management (personality pathology). Next, they linked conditional schema to conditional idiosyncratic schemas (Mumma, 2004) identified in their MTC: R3 pathway during the offence disclosure at the end of the middle phase of the ASOTP.

The knowledge and skills developed in the first and middle phases of the ASOTP were then integrated, in the final phase of therapy, into a reintegration plan that supported desistance through the management of risk and the creation of protective assets (Serin & Lloyd, 2009). This final phase was influenced by the literature on applying the good lives model (GLM; Ward & Brown, 2004) with sex offenders, by focussing therapists and offenders on potential prosocial rewards consequent on engaging in change and maintaining hopefulness (Whitehead, Ward, & Collie, 2007). Offenders were encouraged to begin a 'new life' that met their values and goals while remaining safe in the community (see Table 1).

Many New Zealand high-risk prisoners are indigenous Maori. Adapting cognitive-behavioural programming for their particular needs – especially with regard to responsivity – is an important aspect of programme design and delivery (Larsen, Robertson, Hillman, & Hudson, 1998). For the pilot programme, efforts were made to consult with Maori stakeholders to ensure that the programme had addressed cultural issues and did not miss important information sources. The consultation process identified the need to have a cultural consultant who worked within the programme and in a parallel process with the non-Maori facilitators. This involvement was additional to the provision of both group cultural supervision and individual supervision for programme therapists. It was also considered that pre- and post-programme cultural assessments would assist each participant to identify any individualised cultural needs and would support the gathering of research data in a culturally sensitive manner (Nathan, Wilson, & Hillman, 2003).

Table 1. Detailed description of ASOTP session content by programme phase.

		ASOTP session overview
Phase	Sessions	Content
One	1–20	Build environment of support, rapport, comfort and trust and group cohesion. Improve self-awareness, discussion of programme and rape using participant presentation of media reports of their crimes. How beliefs are formed (maladaptive schema, 'life traps') and affect life decisions and emotion identification and management. Life maps developed and presented.
Two	21–52	Focus on offending, identification of situational and environmental factors, masculine identity, attitudes women, sex and rape, sexual interest and deviancy, power and control, distorted beliefs (idiosyncratic schema), motivations for rape using MTC-3, functional analysis of behaviour, cognitive restructuring, preparation of offence narrative, disclosure of participants offence narratives with group and facilitator review and feedback.
Three	53–74	Introduction to life values, related goals and barriers (Life Compass), mindfulness skills, new me focus (GLM), view of new life a work in progress, social skills training (problem solving, communication, conflict management, relationship skills, relapse prevention), protective asset formation, put together and presented by participants to group/facilitators for review and feedback. Note during the final phase facilitators also met with key family supports on role in risk management and desistance process. Graduation with key family and prison staff present.

Note: A complete session guide is available from the first author.

Description of the pilot ASOTP implementation

In recognition of the multiple needs and interpersonal pathology of high-risk rape offenders, two experienced clinical psychologists, a man and a woman, were selected to co-facilitate group therapy sessions for pilot-ASOTP participants. Along with the first author, they also provided weekly individual treatment sessions. This experience and level of facilitator involvement allowed greater flexibility in addressing treatment needs (individually or in group), provided participants with more choice of therapist, and spread the workload for therapists.

Specialist cultural assistance was provided by a Maori cultural advisor. Reviews of session videotapes, session observations and regular clinical supervision of programme facilitators noted the presence of a high level of effective therapist variables (Marshall, 2005). Facilitation was characterised by warmth and empathy, impartiality, flexibility of style, questioning skills, maintenance of boundaries, participation and open coping style, and openness to feedback.

Selection of programme participants

Auckland prison was chosen as the pilot site, with the therapy delivered in a medium security segregation unit. All prisoners in this or nearby prisons who had the following characteristics were identified: serving five years or more for an index offence of serious sexual assault against a victim over 16 years of age, and medium-high or greater ASRS score (risk of sexual recidivism; see below). File reviews were conducted for eligible prisoners and suitable candidates were then approached and invited to participate. Ten men subsequently volunteered to take part.

Overall, participants were older than other imprisoned rape offenders (range: 31–49 years, $m = 38.5$), primarily due to the lengthy sentences of imprisonment being served. The majority were of European descent with 40% identifying as Maori. All participants had previous periods of imprisonment, with five committing their index rape offence while on parole from a previous sentence. The majority were not in a relationship at the time of their last sexual offence and had not engaged in a prosocial lifestyle after previous periods of imprisonment for sexual offending.

Although nine participants indicated being under the influence of drugs or alcohol during the index offence, only one reported difficulty recalling offence details due to intoxication. Sixty percent of index victims were unknown to them: either strangers or prostitutes. Only one participant had raped a former intimate partner as their index offence.

Assessment process and measures

All ASOTP pilot participants completed a period of assessment during the first two weeks that included a clinical interview on relevant psychosocial and sexual history information, motivation to change and past treatment engagement. In addition to interview, participants completed measures of personality psychopathology, risk and dynamic sex offender risk factors. The information from this period of assessment was used to create a working formulation around their rape offending. This included an MTC: R3 classification to identify individual responsivity issues, along with therapy goals that would be best addressed in individual therapy sessions.

*Risk of reConviction*Risk of reImprisonment*

The Risk of reConviction*Risk of reImprisonment (RoC*RoI) (Bakker, O'Malley, & Riley, 1998) is the New Zealand Department of Corrections' tool for actuarial risk assessment, developed and cross-validated on two samples, each of 24,000 offenders. Expressed as a probability, the RoC*RoI is an offender's estimated risk of reconviction leading to re-imprisonment over the following five years. Therefore, RoC*RoI scores can range from 0 to 1 and provide an estimate of *serious* reconviction risk. The RoC*RoI score is static and generated by computer algorithm based largely on criminal history variables. It requires no clinical judgement or manual calculation. During development, the RoC*RoI demonstrated high predictive validity – an area under the curve (AUC) of 0.76 (Bakker et al., 1998) – and later analyses confirmed its predictive validity over three years post-release (Nadesu, 2007).

Automated Static Risk Scale

In common with the RoC*RoI, ASRS scores – which are static-factor-based risk estimates for sexual recidivism – are computer generated using an algorithm based on seven routinely available dichotomous conviction history variables (Skelton et al., 2006). The ASRS has good predictive validity for sexual recidivism alone, and in combination with violent recidivism over 15 years of follow-up (Skelton et al., 2006; Vess & Skelton, 2010). The ASRS accurately classifies sex offenders into three or four risk categories, from low- to high risk of sexual recidivism (AUC = 0.78 for five-year follow-up). Static-99 scores were also calculated manually to facilitate comparisons with international research.

The Multiphasic Sex Inventory II

Nichols and Molinder's (2002) 560-item self-report questionnaire assesses sex offenders' psychosexual characteristics to assist clinicians in their evaluation and treatment. There are 40 subscales and indices covering sexual offending motivation, sexual socialisation, deviant arousal, universal sex offender behaviour (planning, pre-assault behaviours), individual sexual behaviour (i.e., pornography, paraphilias) and self-report validity (i.e., social sexual desirability, assessment of sex obsessions, and lying). The results for the pilot participants were interpreted in terms of each participant's baseline pre-treatment scores rather than in comparison to others (i.e., an idiographic rather than nomothetic approach).

Violence Risk Scale: Sex Offender Version

The Violence Risk Scale: Sex Offender Version (VRS-SO) (Wong, Olver, Nicholaichuk, & Gordon, 2000) was developed and validated on a sample of 321 sex offenders admitted to the Clearwater Sex Offender Program in Canada. Three factors have been derived from analyses of the dynamic items: sexual deviance, criminality and treatment responsivity (Olver, Wong, Nicholaichuk, & Gordon,

2007). The VRS: SO assesses risk, and treatment-related change in risk, using 10 static and 16 dynamic items,[1] each rated on a four-point scale (0, 1, 2 and 3).

Dynamic items are regarded as changeable, and the VRS-SO uses the stages of change model developed by Prochaska and DiClemente (1994) to indicate quantitatively behavioural, attitudinal and affective changes as the result of treatment. Pre-treatment, each dynamic item is rated both for current risk level and current stage of change. Using this method, treatment change represents the difference between participants' pre-treatment and post-treatment stage of change rating. The VRS: SO has demonstrated good inter-rater, concurrent and predictive validity with a sample of 321 sex offenders, including 169 rapists (Olver et al., 2007; see also Olver & Wong, 2011; Olver, Wong, & Nicholaichuk, 2009). The 2004 version also has been validated in New Zealand, although only with sexual offenders against children (Beggs & Grace, 2010).

Other measures chosen for the pilot programme included the *Treatment Readiness, Responsivity, and Gain Scale: Short Version* (*TRRG:SV;* Serin, Kennedy, & Mailloux, 2005); *The Psychopathy Checklist: Screening Version* (*PCL:SV*; Hart, Cox, & Hare, 1995) to enable comparison with a New Zealand validation sample for the PCL:SV (Wilson, 2003); and the MCMI-III: a self-report inventory designed to assist with identifying prominent problematic personality traits to be addressed in therapy.

Programme delivery

The programme lasted a total of eight months including pre- and post-programme assessment phases, each of two weeks, respectively. Participants attended three 2½-hour group sessions each week and 1 hour of individual treatment. Following treatment completion they were reassessed by therapy staff using session case notes, offender and custodial staff interview, and re-administration of the MCMI-III, multiphasic sex inventory II (MSI-II), TRRG:SV and VRS-SO. Breaks between the three phases of treatment (two and three weeks, respectively) included debrief sessions with therapy staff on how successful the ASOTP had been in addressing the phase goals (see Table 1). Where the debrief identified participants having difficulties with the goals of particular sessions, 'spare' sessions in the next phases were used to revisit these sessions. If the lack of progress was limited to one participant, then his later individual sessions were used to address this issue.

Pilot participants' characteristics and outcomes

Prior to treatment, the selected participants were generally at high risk for all types of offending (see Table 2). Analysis of the MCMI-III personality profiles[2] focussed on the severe personality pathology triad: paranoid personality disorder (PPD), borderline personality disorder (BPD) and schizotypal personality disorder. Five had BR scores deemed likely to meet Diagnostic and Statistical Manual – Version Four (DSM-IV) (American Psychiatric Association, 1994) diagnostic criteria for personality disorder; two met PPD and three BPD criteria. An additional two had significant subclinical BR scores on one of these three.

Although some offenders had several functional explanations for their sexual assaults, it was possible in all cases to identify a primary motivation for their rapes

Table 2. Distribution of scores on risk measures for pilot programme participants.

Risk measure	Mean	Range	Risk category
RoC*RoI	0.71	0.28–0.90	High
ASRS	4	2–6	Medium-high
Static-99	7	4–10	High
PCL:SV	17	10–21	High

using the MTC:R3. Four were vindictive, three were non-sadistic sexual and two were opportunistic subtypes; these two had the highest scores on static risk scales. Finally, one offender had a pervasively angry rape classification pathway.

Nine of the original 10 participants completed the pilot programme. All of those completing treatment evinced increases in readiness and responsivity (TRRG:SV), although some showed limited change due to high scores before treatment. Post-treatment MCMI-III BR scores indicated clinically significant reductions for six of the seven participants with significant personality pathology.

MSI-II results indicated a decrease in participants blaming others for their rape offending with the mean scores for the *Denial* subscale significantly reduced from 12.3 ($SD = 1.27$) to 7.0 ($SD = 0.094$); $t(8) = 7.4$; $p < 0.001$. There was also a significant reduction in justifications for sexual assault on the *Justification* subscale ($M = 3.7$, $SD = 2.3$) to 2.4 ($SD = 2.9$); $t\ (8) = 2.6$, $p = 0.034$. There was a large decrease in the *Cognitive Distortions Immaturity* subscale ($M = 7.2$, $SD = 3.7$) to 5.1 ($SD = 3.6$); $t\ (8) = 4.3$, $p = 0.003$, small decreases in emotional neediness (n.s) and a small increase in insight into social sexual inadequacy (n.s). There was little change in planning (*Scheming* subscale) and excitement/pleasure (*Superoptimism* subscale) in regards to rape offending.

Table 3 shows the pre- and post-VRS-SO scores both for the 16 dynamic variables, as well as for the total score which includes the 10 static risk variables. All participants reduced their dynamic risk scores over the course of treatment (mean reduction = 5.5).

Table 3. VRS-SO pre- and post-programme dynamic and total risk scores for the nine pilot participants who completed treatment.

	Pre-treatment		Post-treatment		
Participant	Dynamic	Total[a]	Dynamic	Total[a]	Change
1	34	43	30	39	4
2	38	47	30.5	39.5	7.5
3	29	35	25	31	4
4	29	33	23.5	27.5	5.5
5	36	42	32.5	38.5	3.5
6	37	43	30	36	6
7	28	33	21	26	7
8	22	27	16.5	21.5	5.5
9	38	48	31.5	41.5	6.5
Mean	32.33	39	26.72	33.39	5.5

[a]Total risk score for the VRS-SO is the sum of the dynamic and static items.

Discussion of pilot programme implementation

The aims of the pilot treatment programme were to establish if it was possible within a New Zealand prison setting to deliver therapy safely to a group of high-risk rape offenders, and to determine if this particular intervention was effective in changing dynamic sexual risk needs.

The pilot programme finished with no violent or sexual prison misconducts incurred during the therapy period. As expected, significant barriers to engagement were evident; most offenders showed personality pathology that resulted in hostility and poor interpersonal boundaries. These barriers were successfully addressed for all but one participant. His treatment was terminated after his romantic fixation on his female therapist was not able to be managed therapeutically. Overall, the programme was able to be implemented safely.

The programme's effectiveness in creating therapeutic conditions conducive to change was evident in the change scores on the TRRG:SV and the MCMI-III. As a result it was possible to work on specific dynamic needs relating to risk of sexual offending (MSI-II, VRS-SO changes). The average 17% reduction in dynamic risk on the VRS:SO is evidence that the programme was achieving a degree of effectiveness.

The three-phase design piloted in this study was effective in addressing responsivity challenges and in unpacking each individual's offence pathways and reintegrative needs. The final phase – combining risk management with a positive future focus – was viewed by participants as the best part of the programme.

Although complex personality pathology was anticipated, the degree of its complexity and severity was still greater than expected, with 70% reporting the presence or prominence of personality pathology (significant difficulties in social functioning; Millon et al., 1997). It is possible that the selection criteria and location of the pilot resulted in a greater concentration of personality dysfunction among participants than in the following programmes.

Repeat sexual offending usually indicates chronic difficulties with emotional or interpersonal functioning or the presence of a pattern of deviant sexual behaviour: all factors associated with personality disorder. The implications of this level of personality pathology for successful treatment are likely to be lower readiness for treatment and responsivity to change. Personality difficulties may also require a higher level of reintegrative planning (more structured and externally managed) to manage risk and promote a valued prosocial life, whether the man is released into the community or into a mainstream prison placement.

The pilot found high levels of hostility in most of the men, with more than half having rape pathways in which anger was either pervasive, or directed at a particular individual. A review of responsivity issues confirmed that, for rape offenders, a hostile interpersonal style is common (Looman, Dickie, & Abracen, 2005). Yet, research into addressing the relationship between personality pathology and the treatment of rape offenders is often limited to consideration of psychopathic personality within the treatment environment (Olver & Wong, 2009). Some efforts to match the delivery of treatment to more varied patient personality profiles has been shown to improve therapy outcomes (Livesley, 2008), and the observations from the ASOTP pilot reinforce this approach.

In terms of therapeutic engagement, the variety of dysfunctional interpersonal styles required clinical staff facilitating the programme to understand personality disorder and the transference and counter-transference this pathology elicits within treatment interactions. The programme also had to be flexible to deal with process issues when they occurred, for example, to counter the rise in hostility or treatment distress that could undermine participants' engagement and learning. The need for flexibility supported the decision to provide simultaneous group and individual therapy, as well as optional cultural therapy for the men and clinician supervision from Maori practitioners.

As expected, a number of transference issues arose during the delivery of the pilot programme. Although most took the usual forms (*Invalidation, Flattery, Similarity* and *Intimidation;* Allen & Brekke, 1996), there was also a degree of transference of both negative (hostility) and positive feelings (infatuation) towards the sole female therapist during treatment. This was expected and was able to be addressed within supervision and programme delivery. However, it is also noted that these treatment issues would not have been able to be addressed as effectively if the programme had been facilitated only by male clinicians.

No irresolvable counter transference issues were identified, although the facilitators found the ASOTP group extremely challenging on occasion. The availability of a clinical supervisor who had experience both with sex offender treatment and with severe personality pathology was seen as an important management factor (O'Connell, Leberg, & Donaldson, 1990).

The ASOTP pilot was the first New Zealand psychological programme to provide parallel group and individual therapy throughout the course of treatment. Individual sessions were highly valued by participants. They were viewed as 'safer' than group interactions, permitting therapeutic work on personal issues that participants were unwilling to disclose within the wider group.

The classification of ASOTP participants using the MTC: R3 system was very useful in therapy when considering individual offence characteristics and in understanding the role that risk variables (from the VRS-SO) played in maintaining risk. It drew attention to factors of relevance that were not necessarily identified by other measures such as the MSI-II: confirming the importance of examining assessment information as a whole, rather than relying on one or two sources.

The delivery of therapy in a standard prison unit, along with the relatively short time of observation during the ASOTP, meant that although clinically significant change was documented using the VRS-SO, all participants had areas that they needed to continue to work on after the completion of the programme. Post-programme feedback to participants based on VRS-SO changes reinforced for them that completion of the ASOTP did not end their need to focus on effective management or reduction of their risk for further sexual reoffending.

The transition from pilot to routine provision in high-risk special treatment units

Following the successful completion of the pilot programme in 2006, the ASOTP programme was allocated for delivery in three of New Zealand's four prison-based high-risk special treatment units (HRSTUs). Since these units opened in 2007–2008, the ASOTP has been offered on five occasions to closed groups of 10 prisoners. In contrast to the pilot, each man in the treatment cohort is therefore part of the HRSTU therapeutic community, alongside 20–30 other high-risk, physically violent offenders who are attending the main HRSTU programme (see Polaschek & Kilgour, 2013, for more information about the HRSTUs).

Participant selection and implementation issues in the HRSTUs

Consistent with the RNR model and principles, selection into the ASOTP has continued to focus on individuals with existing sexually violent offending and at a medium-high or high risk for further sexual reoffending based on actuarial measures (in particular the ASRS). Given the complexity of the population (e.g., personality pathology and treatment needs), co-facilitation has continued as the model of treatment delivery, albeit with a psychologist/programme facilitator pair rather than two psychologists. Other aspects of delivery remain fundamentally the same (e.g., assessment measures, treatment content, individual/group therapy mix, supervision), although there is less on-site cultural support available in the HRSTUs than in the pilot, unstructured rather than structured debriefs about the progress of participants, and less focus on MTC:R3 pathways in identifying participants' treatment needs.

To date, there have been few practical difficulties with conducting the ASOTP within the broader HRSTU environment. The therapeutic community aspects of these units is expected to further enhance participants' ability to practice new interpersonal skills within a supportive regime. An outcome evaluation of the ASOTP is currently underway although it is hampered by the very small number of custodial releases of ASOTP graduate prisoners: many on indefinite sentences for sexual offending. Intermediate change data from that evaluation are presented next.

Assessment processes and measures

The assessment process remains similar to that of the pilot, except that the MTC:R3 is no longer used routinely to formulate responsivity issues. In addition to demographic and criminal history variables, data presented here were collected during assessment, and re-assessment post-programme, on those attending the five ASOTP intakes since routine implementation within the HRSTUs. Specifically assessment used measures of static and dynamic risk detailed in the description of the pilot programme above (RoC*RoI, ASRS, VRS-SO, MSI-II, Static-99), excepting the PCL-SV.

HRSTU-based ASOTP participant characteristics and outcomes

Since transfer from the pilot phase to the routine STU environment, the ASOTP has accepted 52 prisoners for treatment, of whom 79% completed the programme. At programme entry, the mean age in years was 47.4 ($SD = 9.2$). Ethnically, 63% described themselves as Maori and 25% as European. The remainder identified with Pacific Island nations (Fiji, Tonga, Samoa). Seventy-three percent had no school qualification. Criminal gang membership was reported by 40% of the men.

Table 4 shows various other sample characteristics. For most men (83%) their most serious current offence was a serious sexual assault against an adult, but for 11% it was murder, and for 5%, another form of serious violent offence. Almost half (45%) were on indefinite sentences, and of the remainder, the mean sentence length was 7.4 years ($SD = 4.0$). On average, those on indefinite sentences had spent

Table 4. Sample demographic and criminal history characteristics for HRSTU-ASOTP.

Variable	Mean (SD)	Variable	Mean (SD)
Years schooling	9.7 (1.8)	No. previous Convictions	47.0 (41.0)
Age at first conviction	18.5 (4.2)	No. previous violent convictions	6.3 (7.6)
Age at first violent conviction	21.0 (5.7)	Years in prison before unit entry	10.3 (7.2)
Age at first sex conviction	24.6 (7.1)	No. sexual convictions	4.4 (2.8)

significantly longer in prison before coming to treatment (12.04 years, $SD = 6.7$) than those on determinate sentences (7.1 years, $SD = 6.3$; $t[44] = 2.6$, $p = 0.013$).

Table 4 risk indices suggest that the sample is high on general criminal propensity: early-starting, prolific and versatile (i.e., with convictions for sexual, violent and other offending). The mean Roc*RoI of 0.50 ($SD = 0.23$) indicates an estimated 50% likelihood, if released at programme entry, of returning to prison within five years of release. ASRS scores ranged from 1 to 7 with a mean of 3.5 ($SD = 1.3$). Using Vess and Skelton's (2010) criteria, 56% were at medium risk, and the other 44% at high risk of sexual offending. Table 5 shows that Static-99 scores had a mean of 6.0 ($SD = 1.6$), which is in the high-risk range. The table reports mean VRS-SO dynamic scores based on 16 items. VRS-SO dynamic item scores were also converted to a 17-item-based score[3] to enable comparison later with the findings of Olver et al. (2007). After conversion the VRS-SO mean dynamic item score was 37.3 ($SD = 6.3$).

Treatment completion

Of the 11 prisoners who left treatment prematurely, 3 did so for undisclosed personal reasons, 4 were evicted because of serious misconduct and a further 4 because of poor treatment responses. On average, non-completer men spent 107 days in the programme (which is approximately 250 days in length). They had higher scores than completers on a number of criminal indices, including measures of static sexual and general criminal risk. Significant differences were found for total convictions: $m_{\text{completers(c)}} = 38$, $m_{\text{noncompleters (nc)}} = 80$; $t(52) = 3.2$, $p = 0.002$, for age at first adult violent conviction: $m_c = 21.7$, $m_{nc} = 18.7$; $t(52) = 2.5$, $p = 0.016$, risk of reimprisonment (RoC*RoI): $m_c = 0.47$, $m_{nc} = 0.63$ $t(52) = 2.2$, $p = 0.036$, and risk of further sexual

Table 5. VRS-SO pre-programme scores: HRSTU-ASOTP ($n = 45$ programme starters).[a]

Variable	Mean (SD)	Variable	Mean (SD)
Static total (Static-99)[b]	6.0 (1.6)	Factor 1 Sexual deviance[c]	11.7 (3.2)
Dynamic total (16 items)	35.1 (5.9)	Factor 2 Criminality[d]	12.7 (2.9)
VRS-SO total	41.1 (6.8)	Factor 3 Treatment responsivity[e]	8.2 (1.9)
Mean stage of change[f]	1.2 (0.2)		

[a]There were no significant differences between programme completers and non-completers on pre-programme VRS-SO variables.
[b]Included here because the early version of the VRS-SO used here based its static scale on the Static-99. This is no longer the case.
[c]Five items.
[d]Six items.
[e]Four items.
[f]Scoring: 1 = pre-contemplation/contemplation, 2 = preparation, 3 = action, 4 = maintenance.

offending (ASRS): $m_c = 3.2$, $m_{nc} = 4.5$; $t(52) = 2.8$, $p = 0.006$. The estimated sexual recidivism rates – correcting for age, based on age at treatment entry (see Wollert, Cramer, Waggoner, Skelton, & Vess, 2010) – were marginally significantly different: 18.25% ($SD = 2.9$) for non-completers and for completers: 12.9% ($SD = 7.9$); $t(49) = 1.9$, $p = 0.06$. VRS-SO data were only available for four non-completers, making further quantitative analyses impracticable.

Of the 52 men who commenced the main treatment programme, 40 attended the unit's weekly starters' group (see Polaschek & Kilgour, 2013), with a mean stay of 39 days before commencing the main programme. There was no significant difference between non-completers and completers in respect of time in starters' group. However, a significantly higher proportion of non-completers did not attend starters' group at all (55% vs. 15% of programme completers); $X^2(1) = 7.9$, $p = 0.005$.

Treatment change

When programme completers' ($n = 41$) VRS-SO post-programme and treatment change scores were analysed, all change variables were significantly improved post-treatment with large effect sizes, except for Factor 1 (sexual deviance) which showed a medium effect size. The mean change for sexual deviance was significantly less than for treatment responsivity: $t(80) = 2.1$, $p = 0.04$, and non-significantly less than for criminality: $t(80) = 1.7$, $p = 0.10$. Also, noteworthy is that, on average, graduates' stage of change for identified treatment needs moved from pre-contemplation/contemplation to just short of preparation: reflecting early signs of change in relevant behaviour. This result represents clinically important progress in a challenging-to-treat group. However, it also suggests that graduates would benefit from further treatment prior to being considered for parole (Table 6).

Table 6. VRS-SO pre- and post-programme and treatment change scores: HRSTU-ASOTP ($n = 41$ programme completers).[a]

Variable	Pre-mean (SD)	Post-mean (SD)	t^b	Mean change pre-post	95% CI mean change	Cohen's *d* (pre–post change)
Dynamic total (16 items)	35.0 (6.0)	31.3 (6.0)	8.7	3.8	3.0, 4.7	1.35
Mean stage of change	1.2 (0.23)	1.8 (0.41)	4.1	−0.59	−0.70, −0.46	1.72
Factor 1 Sexual deviance	11.7 (3.2)	10.9 (3.0)	8.1	0.83	0.42, 1.2	.65
Factor 2 Criminality	12.7 (3.0)	11.4 (2.9)	9.5	1.3	0.95, 1.6	1.27
Factor 3 Treatment responsivity	8.2 (2.0)	6.9 (1.9)	10.1	1.4	1.1, 1.6	1.49

[a]Scoring: 1 = pre-contemplation/contemplation, 2 = preparation, 3 = action, 4 = maintenance.
[b]For all t-tests, df = 40, $p < 0.001$.

Overall discussion and conclusions

The ASOTP pilot demonstrated that it is possible to deliver a high-intensity, long-duration group programme to high-risk rapists in a mainstream New Zealand prison unit. The pilot showed very good retention of participants, improvements in personality functioning and treatment responsivity, a clinically meaningful amount of risk-related change, and the ability to manage the safety of therapists. On this basis it was concluded that the ASOTP offered a viable and promising rehabilitation option for sexual offenders with adult victims.

Following the pilot, a decision to deliver this programme on a regular basis at multiple sites led to its co-location within the new HRSTUs, a preferred therapy-focussed option (see Polaschek & Kilgour, 2013). Offering the ASOTP in 3 separate HRSTUs has meant that up to 30 treatment places are available per year.

High-risk rapists are now treated in their own self-contained group, while residing in a specialist therapeutic community with other violent offenders. In contrast to some overseas jurisdictions, there have been few difficulties with having this combination reside together, perhaps because as Table 4 shows, these rapist prisoners may be more similar than different to the other residents. They would be considered high-risk violent offenders in their own right, were they not also repetitive sexual offenders.

The results to date from the prisoners who have participated in treatment in the HRSTUs' ASOTP indicate that the programme is continuing to treat high-risk sexual offenders. Mean VRS-SO dynamic item totals, which have been found to predict sexual but not other offending, are almost two standard deviations higher than those reported by Olver et al. (2007) for graduates of Canada's Clearwater high-intensity programme for high-risk sex offenders (see Olver & Wong, 2013). The mean factor scores were less than one standard deviation higher for criminality and treatment responsivity but almost three times – almost two standard deviations – higher than the Clearwater mean for the sexual deviance factor. Interestingly, the main static-factor-based measure of risk (the ASRS), when corrected for age, predicts quite low rates of sexual recidivism, reflecting the long periods of imprisonment for ASOTP participants. The discrepancy between the age-adjusted ASRS (static) scores and the VRS-SO dynamic scores suggests that the VRS-SO may be particularly useful in identifying whether risk of sexual recidivism remains high in older men still in custody.

Compared to a sample from one of New Zealand's high-intensity treatment programmes for prisoners who have sexual offences against children (Kia Marama), the present sample has strikingly higher risk, with mean Static-99 scores almost two standard deviations higher, and mean VRS-SO dynamic scores more than two standard deviations higher. Interestingly, when the factor scores were compared, those in the ASOTP sample were only slightly higher on sexual deviance, but criminality was almost three times greater and (lack of) treatment responsivity scores were double those of the Kia Marama sample (Beggs & Grace, 2010).

In comparison to the pilot, the HRSTU ASOTP sample had a lower overall risk of reimprisonment (RoC*RoI) and slightly lower static risk estimates for sexual reoffending (ASRS). In contrast, mean dynamic risk scores (VRS-SO) are higher than in the pilot. Implementation of the ASOTP has continued to achieve high rates of treatment completion.

Arguably, we might expect larger treatment effects in the HRSTU than were seen in the pilot, both from a statistical perspective – pre-programme scores on dynamic risk measures are higher – but also clinically, as a result of embedding the programme in the therapeutic community environment of the HRSTU (Polaschek, 2011). Yet the mean level of change as indexed by the VRS-SO is somewhat lower than in the pilot (3.8 vs. 5.5). Possible sources of reduced treatment effect could lie in the reduced availability of parallel culturally specific support and treatment, less focus on individual participant needs identified using the MTC:R3 classification system, and less therapist skill as a result of using combined psychologist and programme facilitator therapy teams instead of three senior clinical psychologists.

The larger HRSTU sample has enabled preliminary examination of the characteristics of treatment non-completers. As is often the case, they are clearly higher-risk cases on static risk indicators (Olver, Stockdale, & Wormith, 2011). But why were non-completers less likely to attend starters' group? One possibility is that the starters' group creates greater readiness for treatment; however, comparison of the mean stage of change scores at the start of the main programme for those who did vs. did not attend starters' group shows that they were statistically equivalent. Maybe participation in a starters' group promotes engagement by forming relationships with treatment providers and other participants, independent of 'treatment readiness' or 'motivational' variables assessed by existing measures. However, another possibility is that – in common with non-completers – those who do not attend starters' group have other – as yet unmeasured – characteristics that predict greater risk of treatment failure. For example, perhaps they make more impulsive decisions about attending treatment, resulting in them arriving at the unit 'at the last minute', and thus rendering them ineligible for starters' group. Given the high-risk nature of non-completers, it would be beneficial to consider making attendance at starters' group mandatory if they consent to treatment (i.e., transfer them into the unit earlier) in order to evaluate whether starters' group might be particularly helpful for this subgroup.

Reassuringly for the continuation of the ASOTP, there have been limited practical and operational issues associated with transitioning the programme into the HRSTUs. New ASOTP groups are running regularly and successfully using existing experienced therapy staff.

However, on average, treatment completers' risk-related treatment needs remain at a level typified by a mix of improved behaviour and unchanged behaviour. This early and inconsistent progress may explain why few of these men have yet been paroled, making it impossible to establish whether the programme has an overall effect on recidivism. Therefore, graduates experience extended periods of imprisonment following ASOTP completion, during which they make a transition back into mainstream units where insufficient specialist follow-up assistance may be available to maintain gains. This practice may lead to difficulties in creating continuity between treatment and reintegration planning, which is unlikely to be beneficial in reducing risk (Beech & Hamilton-Giachritsis, 2005). It is possible that graduates need further psychological treatment if they are to meet requirements for parole, but it would also be worthwhile establishing whether needs that have not yet changed sufficiently are prevented from doing so by a lack of opportunities in prison to demonstrate such change. These concerns represent the next priorities to address in the ongoing implementation of New Zealand's ASOTP.

Notes

1. The version used in the ASOTP was an earlier iteration than the current 2004 version which has different static variables and 17 rather than 16 dynamic variables.
2. MCMI-III, TRRG:SV and MSI-II data are not presented here due to space constraints. Details are available from the first author.
3. See Note 1, above.

References

Allen, B., & Brekke, K. E. (1996). Transference and counter-transference in treating incarcerated sex offenders. *Journal of Offender Rehabilitation, 23*, 99–109. doi:10.1300/J076v23n01_10

American Psychiatric Association. (1994). *Diagnostic and statistical manual of mental disorders* (4th ed.). Washington, DC: Author.

Andrews, D. A., & Bonta, J. (2003). *The psychology of criminal conduct* (3rd ed.). Cincinnati, OH: Anderson.

Anstiss, B. (2003). Just how effective is correctional treatment in reducing re-offending? *New Zealand Journal of Psychology, 32*, 84–91.

Bakker, L., O'Malley, J., & Riley, D. (1998). *Storm warning: Statistical models for predicting violence.* Christchurch: Department of Corrections, Psychological Service.

Beech, A., Oliver, C., Fisher, D., & Beckett, R. C. (2005). *STEP 4: An evaluation of the relevance of the core sex offender treatment programme for rapists and sexual murderers.* A report to the British Home Office by the STEP team.

Beech, A. R., & Hamilton-Giachritsis, C. E. (2005). Relationship between therapeutic climate and treatment outcome in group-based sexual offender treatment programs. *Sexual Abuse Journal of Research & Treatment, 17*, 127–140. doi:10.1177/107906320501700204

Beggs, S. M., & Grace, R. C. (2010). Assessment of dynamic risk factors: An independent validation study of the Violence Risk Scale: Sexual Offender Version. *Sexual Abuse Journal of Research & Treatment, 22*, 234–251. doi:10.1177/1079063210369014

Bernstein, D. P., Arntz, A., & de Vos, M. (2007). Schema focused therapy in forensic settings: Theoretical model and recommendations for best clinical practice. *International Journal of Forensic Mental Health, 6*, 169–183. doi:10.1080/14999013.2007.10471261

Blackburn, R. (1993). *The psychology of criminal conduct: Theory, research and practice.* New York, NY: Wiley.

Fisher, D., & Beech, A. R. (2007). The implicit theories of rapists and sexual murderers. In T. A. Gannon, T. Ward, A. R. Beech, & D. Fisher (Eds.), *Aggressive offenders' cognition: Theory, research, and practice* (pp. 31–52). Chichester: Wiley.

Furby, L., Weinrott, M. R., & Blackshaw, L. (1989). Sex offender recidivism: A review. *Psychological Bulletin, 105*, 3–30. doi:10.1037/0033-2909.105.1.3

Gannon, T. A., Collie, R. M., Ward, T., & Thakker, J. (2008). Rape: Psychopathology, theory and treatment. *Clinical Psychology Review, 28*, 982–1008. doi:10.1016/j.cpr.2008.02.005

Hanson, R. K. (2006). Stability and change: Dynamic risk factors for sexual offenders. In K. R. Hanson (Ed.), *Sexual offender treatment: Controversial issues* (pp. 17–31). New York, NY: John Wiley & Sons.

Hanson, R. K., Bourgon, G., Helmus, L., & Hodgson, S. (2009). The principles of effective correctional treatment also apply to sexual offenders: A meta-analysis. *Criminal Justice and Behavior, 36*, 865–891. doi:10.1177/0093854809338545

Hanson, R. K., & Morton-Bourgon, K. (2005). The characteristics of persistent sexual offenders: A meta-analysis of recidivism studies. *Journal of Consulting and Clinical Psychology, 73*, 1154–1163. doi:10.1037/0022-006X.73.6.1154

Hanson, R. K., & Nicholaichuk, T. (2000). A cautionary note regarding Nicholaichuk et al. (2000). *Sexual Abuse Journal of Research & Treatment, 12*, 289–293. doi:10.1177/107906320001200405

Hanson, R. K., & Thornton, D. (1999). *Static-99: Improving actuarial risk assessments for sex offenders* (User Report No. 1999–02). Ottawa: Department of the Solicitor General of Canada.

Hanson, R. K., & Thornton, D. (2000). Improving risk assessments for sex offenders: A comparison of three actuarial scales. *Law and Human Behavior, 24*, 119–136. doi:10.1023/A:1005482921333

Hart, S. D., Cox, D. N., & Hare, R. D. (1995). *The Hare Psychopathy Checklist: Screening Version*. Toronto, Ontario: Multi-Health Systems.

Huddleston, A., Vaughan, G. M., & Beale, I. (1992). *Evaluation of a group program for prison inmates convicted of rape*. Paper presented at the annual conference of the New Zealand Psychological Society, Dunedin, New Zealand, August 1992.

Jung, S., & Gulayets, M. (2011). Using clinical variables to evaluate treatment effectiveness in programmes for sexual offenders. *Journal of Sexual Aggression, 17*, 166–180. doi:10.1080/13552601003802238

Lalumière, M. L., Harris, G. T., Quinsey, V. L., & Rice, M. E. (2005). *The causes of rape: Understanding individual differences in male propensity for sexual aggression*. Washington, DC: American Psychological Association.

Larsen, J., Robertson, P., Hillman, D., & Hudson, S. M. (1998). Te Piriti: A bicultural model for treating child molesters in Aotearoa/New Zealand. In W. L. Marshall, Y. M. Fernandez, S. M. Hudson, & T. Ward (Eds.), *Sourcebook of treatment programs for sexual offenders* (pp. 385–398). New York, NY: Plenum.

Livesley, J. (2008). Integrated therapy for complex cases of personality disorder. *Journal of Clinical Psychology, 64*, 207–221. doi:10.1002/jclp.20453

Lobbestael, J., Arntz, A., & Sieswerda, S. (2005). Schema modes and childhood abuse in borderline and antisocial personality disorders. *Journal of Behavior Therapy and Experimental Psychiatry, 36*, 240–253. doi:10.1016/j.jbtep.2005.05.006

Looman, J., Dickie, I., & Abracen, J. (2005). Responsivity issues in the treatment of sexual offenders. *Trauma, Violence, & Abuse, 6*, 330–353. doi:10.1177/1524838005280857

Marshall, W. L. (2005). Therapist style in sexual offender treatment: Influence on indices of change. *Sexual Abuse A Journal of Research & Treatment, 17*, 109–116. doi:10.1177/107906320501700202

Marshall, W. L., Marshall, L. E., Serran, G. A., & O'Brien, M. D. (2011). *Rehabilitating sexual offenders: A strength-based approach*. Washington, DC: American Psychological Association.

McLean, A. P., & Rush, C. A. (1990). *Base rates and characteristics of convicted sexual offenders: A New Zealand study*. Wellington: Department of Justice.

Millon, T. D., Millon, C., & Davis, R. (1997). *Millon Clinical Multiaxial Inventory-III 3rd Edition*. Minneapolis, MN: National Computer Systems.

Mumma, G. H. (2004). Validation of idiosyncratic cognitive schema in cognitive case formulations: An intra individual idiographic approach. *Psychological Assessment, 16*, 211–230. doi:10.1037/1040-3590.16.3.211

Nadesu, A. (2007). *Reconviction patterns of released prisoners: A 36-months follow-up analysis*. Report from Policy Development. Wellington: Department of Corrections. Retrieved from http://www.corrections.govt.nz/research/reconviction-patterns-of-released-prisoners-a-36-month

Nathan, L., Wilson, N. J., & Hillman, D. (2003). *Te Whakakotahitanga: An evaluation of the Te Piriti special treatment programme for child sex offenders in New Zealand*. Wellington: Department of Corrections, Psychological Service.

Nicholaichuk, T., Gordon, A., Gu, D., & Wong, S. (2000). Outcome of an institutional sexual offender treatment programme: A comparison between treated and matched untreated offenders. *Sexual Abuse A Journal of Research & Treatment, 12*, 139–153. doi:1177/107906320001200205

Nichols, H. R., & Molinder, M. A. (2002). *Manual for the Multiphasic Sex Inventory II (MSI-II)*. Published by test authors.

O'Connell, M. A., Leberg, E., & Donaldson, C. R. (1990). *Working with sex offenders: Guidelines for therapist selection*. London: Sage.

Olver, M. E., Stockdale, K. C., & Wormith, J. S. (2011). A meta-analysis of predictors of offender treatment attrition and its relationship to recidivism. *Journal of Consulting and Clinical Psychology, 79*, 6–21. doi:10.1037/a0022200

Olver, M. E., & Wong, S. C. P. (2009). Therapeutic responses of psychopathic sexual offenders: Treatment attrition, therapeutic change, and long-term recidivism. *Journal of Consulting and Clinical Psychology, 2*, 328–336. doi:10.1037/a0015001

Olver, M. E., & Wong, S. (2011). A comparison of static and dynamic assessment of sexual offender risk and need in a treatment context. *Criminal Justice and Behavior, 38*, 113–126. doi:10.1177/0093854810389534

Olver, M. E., & Wong, S. (2013). A description and research review of the Clearwater Sex Offender Treatment Programme. *Psychology, Crime & Law, 19*(3), 271–286.

Olver, M. E., Wong, S. C. P., & Nicholaichuk, T. (2009). Outcome evaluation of a high intensity sex offender treatment program. *Journal of Interpersonal Violence, 24*, 522–536. doi:10.1177/0886260508317196

Olver, M. E., Wong, S. C. P., Nicholaichuk, T., & Gordon, A. (2007). The validity and reliability of the Violence Risk Scale—Sexual Offender Version: Assessing sex offender risk and evaluating therapeutic change. *Psychological Assessment, 19*, 318–329. doi:10.1037/1040-3590.19.3.318

Polaschek, D. L. L., & King, L. L. (2002). Rehabilitating rapists: Reconsidering the issues. *Australian Psychologist, 37*, 215–221. doi:10.1080/00050060210001706896

Polaschek, D. L. L. (2011). Many sizes fit all: A preliminary framework for conceptualizing the development and provision of cognitive-behavioral rehabilitation programs for offenders. *Aggression and Violent Behavior, 16*, 20–35. doi:10.1016/j.avb.2010.10.002

Polaschek, D. L. L., & Kilgour, G. T. (2013). New Zealand's special treatment units: The development and implementation of intensive treatment for high-risk male prisoners. *Psychology Crime & Law, 19*(3), 305–320.

Prentky, R. A., & Knight, R. A. (1991). Identifying critical dimensions for discriminating among rapists. *Journal of Consulting and Clinical Psychology, 59*, 643–661. doi:10.1037/0022-006X.59.5.643

Prochaska, J. O., & DiClemente, C. C. (1994). *The transtheoretical approach: Crossing traditional boundaries of therapy.* Malabar, FL: Krieger Publishing.

Reid, S. L., Wilson, N. J., & Boer, D. P. (2010). Application of the Massachusetts Treatment Centre-Revised rapist typology to New Zealand high-risk rapists: A pilot study. *Sexual Abuse in Australia & New Zealand, 2*, 77–84.

Richardson, G. (2005). Early maladaptive schema in a sample of British adolescent sexual abusers; implications for therapy. *Journal of Sexual Aggression, 11*, 259–276. doi:10.1080/13552600500402419

Serin, R., & Lloyd, C. (2009). Examining the process of offender change: The transition to crime desistance. *Psychology, Crime & Law, 15*, 347–364. doi:10.1080/10683160802261078

Serin, R. C., Kennedy, S., & Mailloux, D. L. (2005). *Manual for the Treatment Readiness, Responsivity and Gain scale Short Version (TRRG:SV)*. Unpublished report, Carleton University, Ottawa, Ontario, Canada.

Skelton, A., Riley, D., Wales, D., & Vess, J. (2006). Assessing risk for sexual offenders in New Zealand: Development and validation of a computer-scored risk measure. *Journal of Sexual Aggression, 12*, 277–286. doi:10.1080/13552600601100326

Tarrier, N., Dolan, M., Doyle, M., Dunn, G., Shaw, J., & Blackburn, R. (2010). *Exploratory randomised control trial of schema modal therapy in the personality disorder service at Ashworth Hospital.* Retrieved from http://www.justice.gov.uk/publications/research.htm

Vess, J., Murphy, C., & Arkowitz, S. (2004). Clinical and demographic differences between sexually violent predators and other commitment types in a state forensic hospital. *Journal of Forensic Psychiatry & Psychology, 15*, 669–682. doi:10.1080/14789940410001731795

Vess, J., & Skelton, A. (2010). Sexual and violent recidivism by offender type and actuarial risk: Reoffending rates for rapists, child-molesters and mixed-victim offenders. *Psychology, Crime & Law, 16*(7), 541–554. doi:10.1080/10683160802612908

Ward, T., & Brown, M. (2004). The good lives model and conceptual issues in offender rehabilitation. *Psychology, Crime & Law, 10*, 243–257. doi:10.1080/10683160410001662744

Whitehead, P. R., Ward, T., & Collie, R. M. (2007). Time for a change: Applying the good lives model of rehabilitation to a high-risk violent offender. *International Journal of Offender Therapy and Comparative Criminology, 51*, 578–598. doi:10.1177/0306624X06296236

Wilson, N. J. (2003). *The utility of the Psychopathy Checklist-Screening Version for predicting serious violent recidivism in a New Zealand offender sample* (unpublished doctoral thesis). Waikato University, Hamilton, New Zealand.

Wilson, N. J. (2005). *Review of the treatment of high-risk rape offenders* (Unpublished report). Department of Corrections, Wellington, New Zealand.

Wollert, R., Cramer, E., Waggoner, J., Skelton, A., & Vess, J. (2010). Recent research (N = 9,305) underscores the importance of using age-stratified actuarial tables in sex offender risk assessments. *Sexual Abuse Journal of Research & Treatment*, *22*, 471–490. doi:10.1177/1079063210384633

Wong, S., Olver, M., Nicholaichuk, T., & Gordon, A. (2000). *The Violence Risk Scale: Sexual Offender version (VRS-SO)*. Regional Psychiatric Centre and University of Saskatchewan, Saskatoon, Saskatchewan, Canada.

Young, J. E., Klosko, J. S., & Weishaar, M. E. (2003). *Schema therapy: A practitioner's guide.* New York, NY: Guilford.

Index

FSC
www.fsc.org
MIX
Papier | Fördert
gute Waldnutzung
FSC® C083411

Kolibri 360 GmbH
Ferdinand-Jühlke-Straße 7
99095 Erfurt, Deutschland
produktsicherheit@kolibri360.de